Philosopher's Quest

BOOKS BY IRWIN EDMAN

Human Traits and Their Social Significance

Poems

Richard Kane Looks at Life

Adam, the Baby and the Man from Mars

The Contemporary and His Soul

The Mind of Paul

Four Ways of Philosophy

Philosopher's Holiday

Arts and the Man

Candle in the Dark

Fountainheads of Freedom (In collaboration with H. W. Schneider)

Philosopher's Quest

IRWIN EDMAN

NEW YORK
The Viking Press
MCMXLVII

Published by The Viking Press in February 1947
Published on the same day in the Dominion of Canada
by The Macmillan Company of Canada Limited

Manufactured in U. S. A.
by H. Wolff Book Manufacturing Company

To

B. W. Huebsch

Contents

Philosopher's Quest

ONE

In Explanation of a Noble and Misunderstood Profession

I HAVE often envied friends of mine in other professions—doctors and lawyers and engineers. When anyone asks them what they do, they can answer in a sentence, "I am a doctor; I am a lawyer; I am an engineer." But if anyone asks me what I do, and I recklessly answer, "I am a philosopher," or, less arrogantly, "I am a professor of philosophy," I notice that instead of having answered one question, I have provoked many. And I never know what to say next. Am I to explain that I lecture on first and last things Monday, Wednesday, and Friday at ten? Or, perhaps, that I brood professionally all summer long? Nor do I get much help from my colleagues. For it is notorious in my profession that each man thinks what he does is philosophy. And he has no exact enough term of opprobrium or abuse to describe what it is his colleagues do.

For many years now I have been placed in the embarrassing position of trying to answer the apparently simple question of literate friends as to what philosophy is. I have, in the course of being so badgered, gradually come to realize that I myself, in the midst of trying to teach the "subject," have been trying to define to myself what it is I am teaching. I think at long last, if I have not come any nearer defining it, I have come a little closer to discerning what it is, or, as we say, what it is about. I have found this out, not from the books of the learned, or at least not simply and exclusively from those. For the written words of the great dead yet lack the voice of the vivid and perplexed living. I have come, I think, to realize what philosophy is from conversations in which men and women, sometimes unwillingly, often unwittingly, reveal their ultimate views on life and nature and destiny.

So this book will consist largely of conversations, some remembered and some, frankly, contrived (as in the case of colloquies with the dead that at certain dreamful moments will find their way into these pages). And I have good precedent for this. It was Plato himself who said in a famous epistle, held to be genuine, "There does not exist, and there never shall, any treatise by myself on the matter." For philosophy is a conversation in which the soul catches fire.

Now, often in conversation one tells a story to illustrate a point. So there will be stories, perhaps philosophical stories or philosophical parables, in this book, intended to illustrate philosophical points. The reader will have remarked that often in conversation, when the spirit moves him, he will, transcending the bounds of strict courtesy, indulge in soliloquy. So I must warn him that there are likely to be soliloquies in these pages, and naturally some of them will be by the author.

TWO

First Lesson

EVERY autumn in normal times I walk, with rather deliberate briskness, into a classroom in which are gathered about forty young men who have voluntarily enrolled themselves in a course entitled "Introduction to Philosophy." They have come to this class not as they come to similar enterprises in physics, chemistry, or history. They come to those subjects expecting to find out more about what they already know something about. They come to this class hoping to find out by the end of the year what it is that they are studying. And, as I am a disciple of Socrates, I do not propose to tell them. I propose, by asking the proper questions, to have them tell me, and to assist them in the discovery that they have in essence always known what philosophy is.

I look around and light on the most likely looking candidate. I find a young man whom I know by sight, Alfred Jeremy, hitherto undebauched by philosophy.

"Mr. Jeremy," I say without preamble, "I suppose you believe you exist?"

Young Jeremy looks at me quizzically. I feel he is wondering if this is what professors of philosophy are paid to do.

"Of course I exist," he says, and I detect the slightest tone of impatience in his courteous and somewhat surprised tone.

"What makes you so sure?" I ask.

The large football player in the second row shifts his bulk impatiently in the seat too small for him, as if suddenly wondering what is going on here.

"Well," says Jeremy, "it's me. I mean I. I brought myself in here." The class smiles a little at that.

"How do you know it's you?" I say.

"I can pinch myself," he says. The football player does that very thing. Then he pinches his neighbor. I tap warningly on the table with a piece of chalk.

"I can feel my hands if I press them hard, and I have a pain in the crick of my neck."

"You mean you have sensations," I say. "But how do you know they're yours?"

"Well, whose else would they be?" asks Jeremy in great surprise.

"But who are you?" I insist. "Simply this cluster of sensations at the present moment?"

"Oh, no," says Jeremy. "I'm the guy, excuse me, the fellow, who went through the Horace Mann School, and who entered Columbia College last year as a freshman. I left the dormitory this morning and had breakfast at the Sandwich Shop, no, it was in the Lion's Den, and I had a class in advanced French, and I talked to a couple of guys, I mean fellows, and now I'm here."

"But all that was up to the present moment; it was all in the past, wasn't it?"

"Yes, sir," says Jeremy.

"It was pure memory," I say. "Might it not be false memory, pure fiction? You know how difficult it is to get a reliable witness of what has happened in the past. You can't be sure, can you, that it *was* you, can you now?"

"Who else could it be?" asks Jeremy.

"It might be a dream that you in the present are having of what you call the immediate past, mightn't it?"

During this colloquy some members of the class are sitting in absorbed attention. There is a bright-looking, very young man who can scarcely wait until I ask him a question. His hand is already up. The football player is not exactly absorbed, but he looks a little as if he would like really very much now to know what is going on here. The nice-looking boy in the third row seems vaguely troubled. Several look as if they think I am trying to play some trick on them.

The very young-looking boy can wait no longer.

"Well?" I say. (I recognize him, too. He had come to interview me yesterday for the college paper.) "Mr. Gottesman, what do *you* think?"

"Well, I not only remember, but I expect," he says. "I know for pretty certain that I'm going to be around tomorrow, having breakfast and lunch and coming to classes."

"But that," I say, "is mere expectation, is it not? It's an act of faith. You can't really believe you exist on the ground that somebody to whom unhappened things have not yet happened is going to be there to have them happen to him. And is that the ground for your believing that you now exist—because somebody not in existence is going to exist? That future 'you' does not yet exist, does he?"

"No," says young Gottesman ruefully, "I suppose he doesn't."

There is a hand raised in the back now. I look at the pleasant blue-eyed Irish face behind it.

"Your name, please."

"Farrell, John."

"Well, Mr. Farrell, what do you think? Why do *you* think you exist?"

"Because I can't think of myself not existing while I'm sitting here talking—or thinking," he adds after a moment's thought. "Who else is doing it?"

"Have you ever read Descartes?" I ask.

"Never heard of him," he says, almost in a tone of disclaiming unsavory acquaintance.

"Well, he is a famous French philosopher of three centuries ago. He would be inclined to agree with you."

"He would?" asks Farrell.

"Well, let's see where we are," I say. "The past is an illusion, the future a gamble. We have only ourselves of the moment—feeling, thinking, sensing—to be sure of. But surely, Mr. Farrell, you wouldn't call that enough to call 'Mr. Farrell,' would you? The John Farrell your parents know has a past and a future, hasn't he?"

"I sure hope so," says Mr. Farrell. "So do my parents, especially about the future."

"Well," I say, "let's take a vote for a moment. How many are willing to assume they exist?"

The class is unanimous in favor of their own existence.

"But it's only an assumption, mind," I say. "We haven't proved it yet. Now how about other people?"

John Farrell looks appraisingly at his neighbor to the left and then to the right. Many members of the class do the same. The football player looks appraisingly at me.

"How do we know other people exist?"

"How do we know other people exist?" Farrell repeats.

Jeremy raises his hand. I nod.

"Well, I hear them, I see them. Seeing is believing, as they say."

"Yes, but gentlemen, we are obviously often deceived. There are mirages in the desert; we think we see things that turn out to be not there, or to be something else. The man you see is not the one you thought you saw, but his brother. The stick looks broken in water, but it is the shadow, not the stick, that you see. Perhaps it is a devil who has masked as your friend and classmate. Perhaps it is a dream, or a nightmare."

The bright youngster in the front row looks at me as if he wondered if I were more than half joking.

"And how about *things,* this blackboard, this desk?" I ask, turning to Farrell, whose blue eyes seem to be speculating curiously on this panorama of illusion I have opened before him.

"Me?" he says, his attention recalled. "Well, the same thing as other people. I see it, I can touch it. The blackboard has a sort of odor, too."

I take the class on a little imaginary tour through the history of thought. I remind them how uneasy Plato was about the senses; how Berkeley whisked the world away into a semblance constituted by our ideas; how Schopenhauer emphasizes the dreamlike quality of existence, despite the regularity and order of the dream.

"But things," persists the bright young boy, "are there in space, and that blackboard will be there tomorrow when we come back. Or," he added, "if we don't."

I had been rather waiting for this opening.

"What," I say, turning to Smith, having found his name next to his seat number, "what, Mr. Smith, is *space*?"

Mr. Smith considers a moment. He waves his hand comprehensively in the air. "Space is what everything else is in," he says.

The football player leans forward. "Yeah, like a box," he bursts out.

"But what," I say, "is space in?" Some of the boys look faintly disgusted, some perplexed.

"Yes, sir," says the football player slowly and ruefully, "what *is* it in?"

For the next fifteen minutes or so, without knowing the words, the young men, aided and abetted by myself, explore, in elementary form, some of the mysteries and paradoxes that Immanuel Kant turned up. We come out at about the same place he did. Perhaps space is just a way our mind has of arranging our sensations. Experience, we determine tentatively, is impossible without space, and yet it is impossible to find space in experience.

"Is it the same about time?" says a rather blasé youth in the third row who has not up to that point taken any part in the discussion.

"Well, surely the present is here," says Mr. Gottesman.

"And the past *has* been here," says the football player.

"And the future is surely going to be here," says Mr. Jeremy.

"You are going too fast for me, gentlemen," I interrupt. "Why are you so sure, Mr. Jeremy, that the past *was* here? Is it not, like yourself of yesterday, a memory? You cannot see the past clearly, can you? Or hear it? It's gone forever.

"And as for the future, you can bet, if you care to, that it is going to take place, but surely at the present moment it does not exist. If it did, it would be the present, wouldn't it? There's just this moment, isn't there? All the rest is memory or imagination."

"It doesn't leave us very much," says Mr. Smith.

There are several students who have not entered into the discussion at all. But I suspect I know what is going on in their heads. Some of them look bored, and I am not sure they will not change their registration after all. Some of them are pleasantly bewildered, some embarrassed by their bewilderment. The football player finally says, "But that's all very well, maybe, for philosophers. But for plain ordinary people, time and space and other people and themselves do exist, don't they now, professor? Right here now, aren't we in this actual room, talking to each other, today, Monday?"

For the next ten minutes we have quite a heated controversy. There are those who side with the football player, who take the side of common-sense men in all ages, who will have no traffic with such nonsense. In a class every sort of temperament in the history of mankind is likely to reveal itself. Young Gottesman is a kind of poet, and I can see already that he is impressed by the poetry and suasion of the idea that all that we see and hear is a dream.

I intend myself before the term is over to try to show these young men that it would be silly to pretend that they need seriously doubt their own existence, that of the world, of time and space and other people and things. My purpose this morning has been to get them to look at these things with a difference. If only one can get them to be critical of their most usual preconceptions, one is on the road. A little later we'll see what we can do about good and evil, right and wrong, justice and injustice. These students are very young, but they are already full of age-old prejudices. At least an Introduction to Philosophy may start them on the quest for more rational standards of life, of knowledge, of action, of society.

The bell is ringing, announcing the end of the hour. Young Farrell leans forward. "But *do* we exist?" he says.

"Here endeth the first lesson," I say.

THREE

The Philosophic Neurosis:

OR, THE PSYCHIATRIST'S STORY

I BELONG to a kind of club or association, consisting, for the most part, of men more or less eminent in the various arts or professions. It was founded nearly a hundred years ago, so the club-book tells us, by "a hundred gentlemen of New York engaged or interested in the arts and sciences." There is a long table at which one is placed by the waiter if one comes in alone for lunch or dinner. These chance meetings with people one does not know—for the club has grown to considerably more than the original hundred—are fine for everybody. General conversation at the long table, or, for that matter, casual encounters with fellow literates in the lounge, afford an agreeable opportunity for a salutary exchange of ideas, or at least for exercise in audible grammatical soliloquy—or, more often, discipline in the art of patient listening! At various times I have learned a good deal at this club, if sometimes not much more than the personal exploits of fishing or golf or textual criticism of some of my fellow members. And I have learned how various representatives of medicine, the arts, and the law regard my own métier.

I have noticed that the lawyers rather fancy themselves as controversialists, that the artists are partly frightened and partly contemptuous of general ideas. But it is the doctors whose views on philosophy have usually interested me most. Most of them have a very strong interest in questions concerning first and last things. I do not presume to say just where this concern of theirs comes from, though I should judge it is not unconnected with their rather special opportunity to behold what human beings think and feel at moments of intense or final crisis. And in their witnessing of the final crisis itself, in their presence when death comes, often despite their most ingenious and informed and devoted efforts, it is not unnatural for them to reflect on the meaning of the life of the patient they have lost, or of the lives they themselves are spending to save other people, or on life and death in themselves.

I am reminded that Socrates in one of Plato's dialogues says that the pilot does not in stormy weather ask whether his passengers are worth saving, nor a physician in healing the sick whether it is worth curing his patients. The doctor has taken the Hippocratic oath, and it is not in his capacity as a physician to ask questions as to the preciousness of the life he is trying to rescue from extinction. But the doctor is a man, sometimes a cultivated and reflective one, so that it is natural for him to ask such a question—and others, too. Some of my medical friends here at the club and elsewhere (I gather from the things they sometimes say quite incidentally) have felt more and more (also like Socrates) how close the body is to the spirit. Is it not Socrates who says to the youthful Charmides, when he complains of a headache and asks for a cure, that he, Socrates, cannot cure the ills of the body without first curing the soul? Nor have my intelligent friends of the healing arts failed to observe how many human illnesses are the consequences of human folly on the part of individuals or how many are the results of stupidities in the body politic; the rich gorge themselves, and our society permits malnutrition. These things may account for the recurrence of the occasions on which some doctor at the club has insisted on talking shop—my shop, philosophy.

This particular evening I was sitting after dinner in the library with an eminent psychiatrist. I had always liked Jamieson. He had a shrewd Scottish common sense that saved him from some of the more fanciful flights of some of his fellow practitioners. Nor did he confine his psychiatry to the fashionable rich whom not leisure or boredom, as is sometimes charged, but deeper causes, including a vague sense of social guilt, had led to the brink of insanity or suicide, or at any rate to the psychiatrist's office: he gave of his time generously —and fruitfully—to clinical practice among the quite poor. Moreover, his knowledge of books was not confined to the perhaps necessary barbarities of the newer psychiatric rhetoric. He was a fine old-fashioned humanist, and like all such he was not unversed in philosophy. He was, and felt himself to be, well enough versed to twit a professional, and I was by this time used to his good-natured taunts. "We *progress* in medicine," he had said to me once when I had told him that the Greeks had really said almost everything there was to say in philosophy.

This evening at dinner when he had sat down beside me, we had talked about various matters, but neither philosophy nor psychiatry had been specifically mentioned. That was, I think, partly because an elderly Englishman, a visitor at the club who was sitting opposite us, had launched into a long discussion of salmon fishing in Canada. As neither of us knew much or anything about the subject, we had both lapsed into listening. But now, as we settled into our comfortable chairs, Jamieson took a Corona-Corona cigar out of his pocket—I used to twit him on the luxuries he could afford in his profession—and carefully cut off its top. "I've been thinking of you these last few days," he said, "and about both your work and mine, and their curious resemblances. I've been particularly reflecting that the typical classical symptoms of psychiatric disorders and the typical notions of the classic philosophies are almost identical."

"Oh?" I said, and my voice, I think, betrayed just a touch of scornful indignation.

"Don't take it personally," said the psychiatrist, who had a quick ear for nuances in mood. "But there are definite resemblances, truly. The delusions of grandeur, the hysterias, the sense of dawning Reality or sudden supercharged Being, the fevered assertion of the will, the overwhelming sense of futility—you can find them all among the patients who come to my office or my clinic, or among the philosophers. As a matter of fact, I've been thinking of asking you to collaborate with me on a history of the Philosophic Neurosis, although that's too summary a name of a neurosis that is peculiarly varied and complex."

"The philosophic neurosis?" I queried. "What on earth is that?"

The psychiatrist smiled. "Like most neurotics, of course, philosophers don't know they're neurotic, and feel a little uneasy when they are labeled so. It's curious how people still flinch at the word. After all, nobody is ashamed of having a bad cold, though he has caught it by doing as silly a thing as standing in a draft after a hot bath. Well, as to the philosophic neurosis—let me see how we might define it. As a matter of fact, as you once said to me about philosophy, it seems perfectly easy to recognize what it is, but it is one of the hardest things in the world to define. Instead of giving you a definition of the philosophic neurosis, suppose I give you a case history of it? We psychiatrists, especially those of us who practice, more or less, psychoanalysis, are really novelists thinly disguised. We piece together the fragments, pell-mell and dissociated, of our patient's autobiographical confessions as he lies on the couch talking in free associations about his past. We assemble these odds and ends and call it the life or the psychological organization of our patient, and we recount it in a book with interpretative commentary and present it to you as a 'case history.' It is a *story*, really, and usually, I think, an essentially true one. But it is a fiction put together by the psychiatrist who, like other authors, may be a more or less competent artist. So, with your permission, I'd like to tell you the tale of Edward Brodvue, a case history—a peculiarly clear one, I think—of the philosophic neurosis.

"Edward Brodvue did not become my patient until he was nearly thirty-nine years old. Up to the age of thirty-five there is no evidence, I think, that he had ever had the mildest symptoms of the philosophic neurosis, whose character will become evident as the story goes on. He had not the slightest trace of *Weltschmerz* or *Weltanschauung*. He had gone all through college without asking one basic question, making one critical judgment, or questioning one of the mores of the middle-class culture pattern, as they call it now, in which he had been brought up. You would recognize the type; you have dozens of them in your classes, though the perfect flowers of it are to be found, possibly, in the New England country colleges. He was well mannered and well trained enough, as well as intelligent enough, to get into college. When I say he asked no basic questions and did not wake to any critical judgments, I do not mean that he got nothing at all out of his college course. He got a good deal, even scholastically. He learned to read the poets with taste and perception, developed a sincere though genteel interest in music, and got A's in nearly everything, including philosophy. But by the time of his graduation he had not really been punctured out of the usual assumptions of his family (Westchester) and his class (upper middle). He knew about other kinds of worlds, and he knew, intellectually, the limitations and faults of his own, but it never occurred to him not to conform or to inquire too closely or to be made at all uneasy by the stupidities or even the mere sillinesses of the world into which he had been born, the society in which he wished, like other personable and intelligent youths of his social stratum and his period, to be a success.

"I say he was highly intelligent, and he was. And he showed it by becoming editor of the *Law Review* of the first-rate university law school he attended—a distinction attained, as you know, only by the top man in his class. As such gifted young law students do, he at once found a job, with Caldwell and Fitzsimmons, one of the leading law firms in the country. Within the field of the practice of the law, especially the practice of corporation law, his mind worked—what is the overworked phrase?—like a steel trap. He had such faith, justifiable faith, in his own competence that he took the daring step—it was the first daring one he had ever taken—of striking out for himself at the age of thirty. By the age of thirty-five (when the relevant part of this story really begins) he had for some years been practicing law with distinction and with considerable profit to himself. But all this time it had never occurred to him, for example, to question the meaning of property, which he was dealing with daily, or its uses for his clients' happiness —or even for his own.

"Then, one morning, just as he had come into his office and was about to merge two corporations, he put his hand to his head and found himself asking himself what he was doing and why. Now, this had never happened before. The question and the pain he had been feeling in his head both persisted. He set it down to too many cocktails at the party he had attended too long the evening before, as he suddenly felt he had been too long attending such affairs altogether. But the symptoms persisted and assailed him at the most unexpected times all day long, and not that day only. He would find himself asking himself the same question as to what he was doing while he was carefully going over income taxes with a very wealthy old lady whose life seemed a nuisance to herself and had certainly become one to everyone else, including her patient nurse and her conscientious lawyer. He found it occurring to him in the midst of a large formal dinner he was attending. He paused suddenly one day in court in the midst of making a very cogent argument, stopped for a full minute until the judge said sharply, 'Will counsel for the defense please proceed?' His wife repeatedly noticed his apparent abstractedness at dinner, both when they were home alone and when guests were present. In the first instance she was annoyed; in the second, embarrassed. Usually she could set it down to preoccupation with an important or difficult case, but for the next few months these symptoms appeared so often that she was in various ways disquieted. There had been only one occasion in their married life when it had been a question of another woman, and somehow she felt that what was bothering or absorbing her husband this time was something different.

"Once she went so far as to ask him. 'I am afraid you wouldn't understand, dear,' he said. 'No, I don't mean that,' he added as she flushed a little, for ever since the days when they had met at Junior Proms he knew that she had observed how he regarded her as something less than his mental equal. 'No, I don't mean that. But you'd think I was a little crazy. And perhaps you'd be right.'

"She began to notice strange books lying about in their living room: *The Meaning of God in Human Experience, Physics and Philosophy, The Nature of Thought, The Two Sources of Morality and Religion.* She now, for the first time, had no difficulty in getting him to let *her* read first the novels that came from the Book-of-the-Month Club.

"His colleagues (he had by this time three partners) began to notice his long absences from the office during parts of their busy season. He used to tell them that he was going to the Bar Association Library and that he did not wish to be disturbed. But it was to the university library he went, the philosophical division of it. He became a familiar sight afternoons to the graduate students working or talking there. Occasionally he would engage some of them in conversation, but they seemed lost in issues that seemed to him not quite the major ones with which he was now concerned. Some of them seemed to him almost as legalistic as his colleagues in the law, and not as sharp or as logical.

"What had happened to my friend was that he had developed what we psychiatrists call a 'compulsion.' Just as some patients we see feel it absolutely necessary to wash their hands fifty or sixty times a day, so Edward began with absolute urgency to feel it necessary to have a clear and comprehensive view of the world. And it will not surprise you, either, that he went to look for it among the philosophers, and that he failed to find it there. The compulsion became so acute that it assailed him at all hours of the day and even at night. Lying beside his wife, he would wake up at three in the morning and wonder not only what he was doing in the world, but what *anyone* was doing, and what coherence, if any, all the hurried and miscellaneous lives of men and women could be said to make—or the life, for that matter, of the universe itself. The thing became so obsessive that in some dim way he recognized that he had a neurosis and decided to work it out for himself, by himself, and alone.

"Luckily his wife had an income of her own, there were no children, and he had an income, by this time, of his own. So he left his wife to her income and to her interests, which, when he explained his to her, were, she admitted, quite clearly different. She had never been at all curious as to his law practice, but at least she had shared his leisure. She had no wish to share his new preoccupation, and she told him so. 'A whole and consistent view of the world,' she said, looking at him blankly. 'But, dear, what do you need or want that for? No one we *know* has one!' She thought it really rather a good idea when he said he wanted to go off alone to a spot he knew in Southern California, a headland above the Pacific which, when they had once passed it on a motor trip, he had thought might make an ideal spot if he ever wanted to write a book on corporation law. She went as far as Reno with him, where she left him for good and all. Before leaving New York, Edward had packed into his trunk three hundred works of philosophy, classic and contemporary.

"On the lovely headland overlooking the bland blue monotony of the Pacific, he had built for himself (it was easy in prewar days) a modernistic, quite functional little house, mostly steel and glass, with a wonderful broad uninterrupted view of the western sea. There he proceeded, as I said, to try to find somewhere in these three hundred works of philosophy a clear and consistent view of the world. And, as I said, you will not be surprised to hear that he did not find it. There was, of course, always something left out, something that did not fit in. And what did not fit in, as doubtless you've guessed, were the brutal miscellaneous facts of the world. It was during the depression and millions were starving. But coffee crops were being destroyed in Brazil and wheat crops in Kansas. There was meeting after meeting of diplomats in Europe, allegedly intent on making war illegal or impossible. But there were increasing and increasingly credible rumors of war. Like many another philosopher, Edward had a basic way of dealing with recalcitrant facts. He ignored them, and even arranged to keep himself systematically ignorant of them. In his case it was simple. He simply stopped reading the newspapers, except local ones which carried very few facts anyway.

"Then," the psychiatrist continued, "he began to develop what we philosophers call a phantasy. Now I know the word 'fantasy' spelt with an 'f' suggests something altogether light-hearted and free. But a phantasy as psychiatrists use it means something different. It is a systematic delusion by which neurotics, often for a long period, manage to live. It is an *imaginary* pattern of order. Well, Edward half found, half created, a phantasy, a dream world in which everything added up to Beauty, Goodness, and Truth. You, as a professional philosopher, know where he found his materials. At least you can guess. For Edward had found that though the great systems always left something out, with a little rearrangement they could be made to include even recalcitrant facts, even all those oddities (and worse) in the scheme of things that can be summed up under the name of evil. He borrowed a little (don't we all?) from Plato, from Plotinus, from Spinoza, and from some of the German idealists, particularly Hegel, whom, all the better for his purposes, he did not understand too well. Within three or four months he had arrived at an equilibrium in his own mind in which, he believed, he did now clearly see that everything added up to Goodness, Beauty, and Truth. It was a phantasy, of course. The world in which he had stopped reading the newspapers still went on, disturbed and chaotic as ever. He had, as we sometimes put it, *escaped* into phantasy. But if one has an independent income and a bland blue unobstructed view of the Pacific, one can live by a phantasy indefinitely. Edward, save for the accidental and well-intentioned kindness of one of his friends, might have done so to this day.

"Edward had continued to correspond with his friends in the East. It saved him from the unmitigated emptiness of reverie. He saw almost no one among his local neighbors, most of them retired bankers from the East and retired farmers from Iowa. His long vigils with philosophical works might have led him to the almost mad loneliness that assails serious seekers after their own salvation, or serious seekers after the secret of the universe *in order* to find salvation. But letters from and to old friends in the East, chiefly college friends, gave him that near-substitute for society that the postman brings to the solitary. He found, for one thing, that with several old friends he became really more intimate at a distance than he was when they had met each other often, face to face. For one thing, friends in New York seldom see each other alone; they see each other surrounded by their respective families and in the midst of their respective professional preoccupations and at large crush cocktail parties. But now, when friends wrote to him, out here alone in the West, of their deeper hopes and fears, and he read their letters in his steel-and-glass cottage facing the Pacific, he, too, felt the need to draw near to someone by mail. There were a few friends, including a few classmates teaching philosophy or English at eastern universities, who seemed glad of a chance to talk over philosophical issues with one who, as one of them put it, had really given his life over, entire and undivided, to the quest for the Holy Grail.

"One of these friends, fearing, with a certain justice, that the fresher intellectual currents took rather a long while to get to California, sent him a new volume on the reigning new intellectual enthusiasm, semantics. From that tome, a sort of summary index written by a young economist who had just discovered the subject, Edward learned something that seemed to reduce to absurdity the phantasy of Goodness, Beauty, and Truth that he had built himself out of cards drawn from the decks of various philosophers, different decks differently constituted. From this then-current gospel, which was to be found on all the more literate suburban living-room tables, Edward learned a few things that wrecked his little system and his careful happiness. He learned that everyone, but particularly philosophers, misused words. Philosophers never could say exactly what they meant, and if they succeeded in doing so, which was very rare, there was never any great probability that anyone else would exactly understand. Moreover, people took words not as signs of actualities in the world, of indubitable objects, events, and situations; they took them rather for their values as weapons or as flatteries or as self-flatteries. Men misled themselves and others systematically by the words they used, words which often meant nothing whatever outside the neat little verbal games or systems in which they appeared.

"Philosophers peculiarly well exemplified these traits. Their whole systems were nothing but tautologies, the long-winded development of a few unverified assumptions. The history of thought was simply the gray tale of vicious abstractionism, and philosophers were nothing but adroit talkers about a few terms, vast, vague, and undefined, relevant to nothing at all. These were their whole capital to begin with, and, after all their elaborate dialectical developments, to end with. 'All flubjubs are dingbats,' cited I. A. Richards. 'This is a flubjub, therefore it is a dingbat.' This, he pointed out, was blank and empty reasoning, and a perfect paradigm of what most systematic philosophers did most of the time. The only words that really do mean anything, the semanticists pointed out, are those that point to things, persons, and events; words that can be 'cashed in' in actual experience. Now how could one point to Beauty, Goodness, and Truth? Edward reflected on the so-called great systems of thought he had been wading through. How beautifully articulated they were in their development of premises themselves fantastic. 'Dialectic' it was called, the systematic self-deception of the mind where there were no facts at hand to begin with. Edward saw what had been seducing him in these systems, and in his own. It was the clarity and cogency with which any thinker, or he himself, could build up a watertight world. He saw he had been deceived. One day he took his own notes on his own little world system and threw them into the sea.

"There was just a little of other people's philosophies that he kept. David Hume's *Treatise on Human Nature,* for one thing, and his *Dialogues Concerning Natural Religion.* For David Hume was obviously a sensible man who seldom talked nonsense, who kept his eye on actual human nature and its unmistakable experience. He used an ax skillfully to destroy human pretense and illusions, and had himself no ax to grind. Edward reluctantly did *not* keep Plato. For all the beauty of his art, Plato did use terms very loosely indeed, terms like Beauty and Goodness and Truth, and he bandied terms about and developed their internal relations to each other without much concern for what the original terms referred to. Edward threw out also all of medieval philosophy as a monk's abstracted and abstractionist reverie. He kept some of John Stuart Mill and a little of Auguste Comte, who had had at least a glimpse of what a truly positivistic method might mean. He allowed himself a few indulgences, about which he felt, it must be admitted, a sense of guilt. One was Immanuel Kant's *Critique of Pure Reason.* The whole thing was a gigantic piece of verbalism, there were ingenious solutions of gratuitously created problems, and connections established between the parts of an elaborate intellectual fairy tale. But the architectonic was fascinating, like the structure of a musical composition. And this was still more true of Bradley's *Appearance and Reality,* which developed almost like a Bach fugue.

"But the thought of a Bach fugue itself made him uneasy. Like Othello, he found his occupation gone, but now that it was, he could not turn gladly, as a relief from the strain of his philosophic studies, to the freshening resource he had once had in music. His occupation was gone, and his recreation, too. Music had been for him a great and soothing easement from the ardors and endurances of intellectual labor. Music was a release from the sharp brittlenesses of words, from the confinements and constraints of practical affairs. The sounds in music were not tied to the hard specificity of words. The structure of music was not the strict necessity of verbal logic, but the free movement, or so it seemed, of spontaneous song. In music, the logical and the lyrical became one.

"Moreover, for a lonely soul (lonelier than he had ever cared or dared to admit to himself) music provided objects on which emotion could be expended and by which it could be absorbed. He saw no one, loved no one, but love had not died in him. He had given up conventional ambition, but a sense of frustration and defeat was vaguely present to him, a sense of helplessness in not finding any stable coherence by which he might live and to which he might commit himself wholeheartedly. Grief and hope, sorrow and gaiety, daily played their changes of mood upon his solitude, despite his dedication—high, intellectual, and austere. And in listening to works of the great composers on the excellent phonograph he had purchased, he could find the fulfillment of all these vague emotions, heart-warming harmonies by which their floating residue could be absorbed. Many persons passing his small house at night would hear the strains of Schubert or Beethoven and remark on his apparently great love for music. Perhaps they were right. But the sounds floating on the clear, still night air were testimony, rather, to his having found a vent for romantic love and less mentionable emotions that had no other outlet. Even his passion for logic, never quite fulfilled by the systems of philosophy, found a wordless fulfillment in the structure of a fugue, the development of a classical sonata.

"But he found now he could not permit himself to lose himself in the half-emotional, half-intellectual orgy of music. How could an adult mind allow itself to listen to sounds that had, by definition, no meaning, that said nothing precise, clear, or particular, that were simply a debauch of amorphously touching, illicitly moving notes? No, music was out of bounds, and he stored all his records, and his machine as well, in the cellar, which he locked. Lest he be tempted to unlock it, he threw the key into the sea.

"He had also fallen into the way of reading poetry late at night before he went to sleep. Poetry played the same part in his life that it had played once in the life of John Stuart Mill. When abstractions suddenly made life seem thin and empty and bleak and gray, Wordsworth restored to life its quality and its color. Life became vivid and satisfying again when poets lighted upon the bright right words, and translated experience into radiance once more. So he had thought, and in some of the darkest days of his confusion and his depression he had turned to the poets, to 'that inward eye which is the bliss of solitude.' And his heart had danced with Wordsworth's daffodils.

"That was all over and impossible now. It was bad enough that philosophers used words loosely because they couldn't help themselves. At least some philosophers, according to their lights and after their fashion, struggled to be quite clear and specific about what they meant, even if what they meant meant nothing, ultimately, at all. But poets seemed deliberately to exploit the ambiguities, the double or triple resonances of meaning, in words. Poetry was a little better than the murmurous music which it closely resembled. But it was also more deceptive, because it pretended to be saying something. It used words that responsible and practical men used in the affairs of life, but used them for the delights of tintinnabulation, for the vague dreaming associations of syllables, for the adolescent luxury of soft unprecise reverie, of indolent recollection and wistfulness. Poetry was not emotion recollected in tranquillity, but emotion deliberately befuddling and nourishing itself with metaphor and melody. No, poetry, too, had to be erased from his life.

"And there was no possible return to any sound philosophy. For now there was clearly no sound philosophy to return to. Philosophy in itself was not even as reasonable as it seemed by its own definitions. Philosophers either used terms loosely or defined them willfully, and once they had defined terms in their own willful way, they went through the motions of developing from their absurd premises their necessary but trivial conclusions. You came out of the most subtle development of a logical system with nothing more than you brought into it; and in the case of most philosophies, practically all, you came in at the beginning with nothing at all. Nature, God, the One, the Absolute, Matter, Spirit—so much abracadabra. No, it was no use turning to the classic tradition, the sanctified verbologies of the past, for wisdom.

"One could really turn nowhere. Edward found himself going one step beyond the semanticists; he could trust no external reports and certainly nobody else's language. And he was not, in the last analysis, more certain that he could trust his own. Where to turn now? Well—" The psychiatrist paused for the first time in quite a long period. "I gathered from him later," he said, "when he had become my patient, that he decided to turn inward, to retire to the indubitable certainties of his soul."

"Oh," I said, "like Descartes, you mean; he was going to rely on clear and distinct ideas."

"Clear and distinct ideas were the last thing Edward wanted now," said the psychiatrist. "He had been deceived by ideas. One can be clear and distinct about nothing at all. That's what the semanticists had taught him. No, he took a different line. He wanted to retire from the superficial level of logic to the very center of his own soul. If one cannot trust external reports or formal language, he thought, perhaps it is possible, by penetrating to the very living center of one's own being, to become one with the One, to be alone with the Alone. I've had patients like that," said the psychiatrist. "They come in and say they've heard a bell sound; they've plumbed to the very center of all-being; they're in tune with the infinite. Or, when they have delusions of grandeur, they think that they *are* the infinite. And you've read similar asseverations, I know, in the mystics: in the Greek Plotinus, in the Arab Al-Ghazali, in the Spaniard St. John of the Cross. The language is often very beautiful, and in the hands of the Hindus or of the Platonists very convincing. But it does not make the experience or the wish that prompted it any the less abnormal!

"It's a curious thing about the mystics. They talk a great deal about the concentrated brevity of their rapture. They tell us time and again that their experience is a point of flame, a rapt instant of ecstasy. Some of them say that the intensity sustained a moment or two longer would be unbearable. They are quite right. But they don't know the reason. A moment of rapture continued a little bit too long would be just as monotonous and maddening as a pain or a headache that persisted too long. It would be a very ecstasy of boredom. Then the mystics like to tell you that what they saw is indescribable. There's nothing they can say about it, and no wonder. Have you ever tried to describe pure emptiness? The mystics exclude everything specific. They tell us what they were at one with *was* the One, not just *this* or *that;* not this beauty, nor that beauty, but *all* Beauty; not this or that at all, but the Absolute Thatness. Now it is very difficult to distinguish the ineffable from the inane.

"That's what Edward found out. He thought that if only he ever came to the pure interior being of himself, he would be one with all things, with the rich plenitude of all-being. He had followed the mystic path as he remembered it. He had stopped thinking, he had quit outside distractions. He was utterly alone, without desire, without conflict or torment of desire. And one night he did have a vision. He felt all things melting into oneness. He felt himself becoming one with all unity, and he felt very intensely how blank and empty and foolish that unity was. He was walking alone by the sea at sunset. There was not a breath stirring. The sky was a perfect California blue. He was alone. He felt millions, not thousands, of miles from his friends.

"He felt cut off by his intellectual doubts and scruples from all reality. As you know, that's a familiar psychoneurotic symptom—that is, a sense of the unreality of everything—everything being far, far removed. Then, suddenly, Edward felt the blue grow intenser, the silence itself more acute. He felt all things merge into oneness, and he himself merging into that unity. There was nothing but the hum of awareness, and that seemed to be the very hum of silence, of being itself. All was light, and he was one now with that light. All was radiance, and he was at the very core of the radiance, of that flame of love all at the center of himself.

"It lasted but an instant, or rather the happiness did. For then he seemed to be experiencing a curious variation of the mystical rapture. The oneness continued, the sense of merging with the undifferentiated continuum of being. But it seemed a mere dull and dead blankness now He seemed at the center of the vast All-ness, and it was all irretrievably empty and colorless and valueless and dead. It was as if he were a dead soul inhabiting a dead planet. All conflict, it is true, had vanished, but all color, all intensity, all variety, all richness, too. There was nothing in him, and only nothingness everywhere. And he came back to the world, to his house of steel and glass, dispirited, disquieted, disillusioned. He had retired, as the mystics had suggested, to the very core of his own being, and, worst revelation of all, he had found, save for a brief and perhaps illusory flash of time, nothing but nothingness there. The one rock bottom of believable reality, the pulse of his own being, opened to him nothing but endless and infinite stretches of gray monotony. Not the radiance of a sunlit world, but the dull perpetual half-dawn of eternal ennui was what he had found by retreating into his soul. He had apparently arrived not at the rich plenitude of all-being, but at the horrid and foolish inane."

The psychiatrist paused. "Have you ever felt your life to be filled, if I may put it so, with emptiness? Sans everything, as Shakespeare puts it?"

"Oh, once in a while," I said, "but only when I am dead tired."

"Well, Edward felt it all the time. He had gone inward as far as he could, and he was nowhere. The world had failed him, other men's systems had failed him, and in his own inner consciousness he had found nothing but the blankest, most meaningless darkness. He sat staring at the blue monotony of the Pacific and it seemed more blank than ever. No music, no poetry, no philosophy, no world, nothing in the world, nothing in the self! He felt, as you may imagine, in as deep an abyss as Tolstoi records in *A Confession.*

"For weeks he hardly ate, for he could not bring himself to sit down to his own solitude. And he did not read, and he began to go a little mad whenever he began to think. It gradually dawned on him that he was *quite* neurotic, and like a good many neurotics he thought he'd cure himself. It can't be done; a neurotic needs professional aid. He saw nowhere to go. The outer world offered but disillusion, the inner world worse still: emptiness absolute. It was bad enough to find confusion and delusion, futility and phantasmagoria in the world outside himself. But worst of all—he shuddered as he thought of it—in the inner core of his own being he found an utter vacuum, an ultimate vacuity. Where to now? He could imagine that these morbid little items one reads in the papers of suicides who left no notes had had this discovery of zero and absolute emptiness as their cause. It would require a whole volume, not a note, to explain how one had arrived at such terrifying nullity. No Western philosopher, except perhaps Schopenhauer, had dared to write such a volume, and even Schopenhauer had pretended Nirvana was a goal. *Nothingness* was just that, nothingness, and perhaps suicide was indicated. But suicide might not, as Hamlet saw, be the end; and an eternal nothingness—why plunge one's self deliberately into that ambiguity? Death in any case was an evasion, not a solution, of life.

"He decided now that he could see clearly what was wrong with him. He had been upsetting himself with these vast unsettling theories. None of them had done anything but lead him down blind alleys or open vistas which dissolved into ironic disappointments, like the mystical rapture. He had seen it happen to his friends, this search for the ultimate in happiness, in wisdom and truth. He had seen some of them fool themselves or drug themselves with systems. Goethe was right: '*Grau ist alle Theorie*'—gray is all theory. He must experience the bright colors of life again, the actualities of practical compulsion, the dear brightnesses and vividnesses of human beings with actual faces and hands.

"For two years or more he had been living quite alone. He had made it a point not even to know his neighbors, and he had been set down as a curious sort of hermit—possibly a member of one of those Oriental cults that flourish in Southern California. He was rumored to have become an adept at Yoga. But he bothered no one and no one bothered about him, though his handsome, slightly troubled, slightly spiritualized face had been remarked upon admiringly by some of the dowager ladies whom he greeted courteously when he met them on their morning walks.

"'Perhaps,' he thought, 'I should go back to the practice of the law.' But the thought of the abstractions he should get into there frightened him even more than he had been frightened away from philosophy by semantics. No, he would begin his return to the actual world by cultivating his neighbors. Luckily, though he had kept his distance, he had never been rude to them. And so quiet was this little village of retired rentiers that any chance of company was treasured, and many of his neighbors had been waiting for a chance to show him some hospitality. Mrs. Elder, who had long thought he looked like a poet (because he was tall and thin and had fair hair and seemed vaguely troubled), after he had, with pointed amiability, stopped to talk with her one morning when they were both on a walk, said, 'Mr. Brodvue, won't you come to dinner next Tuesday?'

"'Madam,' he said, '*just what* do you mean by *Tuesday*?' She looked at him in alarm and fled.

"But he did get himself invited to dinner and to several parties, and he found that it was not quite as easy to resume the normal world as he had supposed. People would talk of politics and economics, of war and peace, of art and science, or capital and labor, and the comments of the semantic critics would stick obdurately in his mind. The conversation seemed compounded of foolish tautologies and meaningless ejaculations. He had all he could do not to interrupt at every word the absurd confusions with which everyone blandly studded his conversation. He could not even bother to judge among the types of nonsense. It all seemed to him equally foolish and he felt very remote from it all. He showed it in what was generally interpreted to be a snobbish smile. One evening, when somebody had said, 'Is not Communism nonsense?', he had said, 'Is not *everything,* except the absolute—if there *is* an absolute?' He himself distrusted the relative so much that he would not believe the timetable and missed the bus three times running from Los Angeles.

"He decided to give up the West, and self-cure. He turned East, hoping vaguely that the familiar associations there would restore him to normalcy. But New York seemed no less absurd and unreal than Southern California, and the pursuits of his friends rather sillier even than they had come to seem before he left. And these grown-up children took their illusions with such seriousness. 'Perhaps,' he thought, 'the surest sign that I am ill is that I can't take anything as real or serious.' He tried to persuade himself that the reason the preoccupations of his friends seemed so remote and trivial was that they actually were so artificial, so timid, so second-hand, and so dishonest or so pretentious. These people went through the motions of formal dinner parties, talking to people they did not care about concerning things that did not interest them. They read books they did not wish to read, attended concerts that bored them. And for all the fret and fever of their lives, they had not the courage to follow their actual impulses; despite their gray paganism, they had not even the conviction or the virility of the senses. Though they affected to satirize gentility, they continued to follow all the regular, now slightly modified, tabus. They used first names more promiscuously than their parents would have done at formal dinners; they wore black ties instead of white ones, or sometimes dared to come in business clothes. But they went to the same dinners, and, though they changed wives somewhat casually, they were all involved in the routines of domesticity.

"Edward plunged, without much success, into a life he had always wished to try. He went to Havana, where Cuban acquaintances from the days of his legal practice helped him find his way to sophisticated dissipation. For a little while he thought he had arrived at a lasting absorption in guiltless, idea-less sensuality. Wine and sex and sunlight seemed to be one answer, or one escape from seeking one. But he suddenly found it absurd to be toasting in the sun or guzzling at night—he found liquor no longer really agreed with or delighted him—and, though he hated to admit it to himself, for he was only middle-aged, sex turned out to be both tiresome and tiring, and in the arms of some dark carefree girl he felt the psychical distances that separated them and discovered sex was no solvent of his miseries. At the very height of a night's rapture the awful sense of the eternal blankness returned. One of the girls to whom he had become much attached finally found him too mysteriously preoccupied. And he was too melancholy quite to mind her leaving him for good.

"He finally decided to seek psychiatric aid, and came to me. He was introduced by another lawyer, whom I had managed to cure of delusions of grandeur."

The psychiatrist paused. "Remarkable case," he said, "and remarkable cure."

"Oh," I said, "he *was* cured then?"—wondering what it was, to be cured of philosophy.

"Oh, yes," he said, "he was cured all right, but it was a long, slow business. We psychiatrists are said to be overpaid, but we have to put up with a painful lot of boredom. You know, I suppose, of our free association technique. What we do (for all of us now in one form or another are practicing psychoanalysis) is to let the patient talk spontaneously and sufficiently for his blocks and forgotten fears to come into the light. We hope that if he talks long enough the pattern of his disorder will become clear and, becoming clear, will be got rid of. It's almost like having the patient talk the devil out of himself. And when he has his complexes exteriorized, he will see clearly what has been bothering him. Seeing it clearly, it should become possible for him to live at one with himself and with the order of things in which and with which he must, as an adult, live."

"It takes a long time, doesn't it?" I asked.

"A very long time, often a very boring one for the doctor. Take Edward Brodvue. For the first year he said nothing at all. He came to my office every day for an hour (and you remember our charges are—and have to be—high) and kept perfectly mum. He would pucker his lips as if he were about to say something, and nothing would come. It was against my principles to try to help him. The associations must be free. You can imagine, meanwhile, that it ceased to be a pleasure, even a scientific one, to sit there hour after hour listening to a patient say nothing at all. And the high fee I was getting made it no more agreeable, really.

"It was not until a year later that I learned what the trouble was. I sometimes scolded myself for not having guessed it sooner. Edward had been quite sure that he could not say exactly what he intended, or that if he did, I would understand it, or not misunderstand it. The second year was much better."

"The *second year*!" I exclaimed. "How long did it go on?"

"It's going on right now, into the third year, though Edward comes only every other day now. In the second year, worse boredom for me; the first eight or nine months were much the worst. What came out in the free associations was a quite amateurish history of Eastern and Western thought, all mixed up together, with some childhood memories and some very odd sexual imagery indeed. But toward the end of the year, I began to see light, and so did he. He had been brought up by a very devoted mother, an overdevoted one, and a highly disorganized one. She could never talk coherently about the same subject for more than two minutes at a time at most. His father was a practical man who was always contemptuous of people with intellectual interests.

"Edward had been brought up in New York, where nobody belongs clearly to any one fixed pattern of culture or ideas. Once, when he was a little boy, an older boy who was playing with him on his birthday threw down a castle which he had built out of blocks and said, 'This playing with blocks just doesn't make any sense!' It became clear to Edward without my pointing it out (which is best) that this desire for a clear and consistent view of the world was a childish hangover from the ruined castle of blocks, over which he had wept bitterly. As for the passion for theoretical consistency, and for saying nothing that was incoherent, that was clearly a kind of perfectionism which, now that he saw its origin, he must and would get over. It was a rebellion against his father's practicality and his mother's vagueness.

"As a matter of fact, he's getting on fine now. He's not practicing law, of course, but he goes out into ordinary middle-class society, uses words as loosely as anyone else, and doesn't mind it in the least. He listens to the confused and inchoate nonsense that passes for intelligent conversation among the literate bourgeoisie, and it doesn't bother him a bit. He's a well-adjusted, normal, middle-class American citizen again."

"No relapses?" I asked.

"No," said the doctor, "not a single burst of poetic meditation, no asking of basic questions, no raising of fundamental criticism. He's perfectly normal, or pretty near."

"Doctor," I said, "do you suppose you could cure me?"

"I've been thinking about you," he said. "You do think about these things a good deal. But after all, you get paid for it, it's part of your job, and you take ideas with a sense of proportion. Still, I *have* been wondering about you."

FOUR

The Private Thinker and the Public World:

OR, A SHORT HISTORY OF A DIFFIDENT PHILOSOPHER

ONCE upon a time, not very long ago, there was a philosopher. He laid the flattering unction on his soul that he wrote not only about, but for, eternity. Ideally, he thought, he was not concerned with a public at all. He was the meditative monk, he told himself, the discarnate intelligence thinking in self-sufficient silence on first and last things. He told himself that he did not care what was the incidence of his conclusions on other minds. He said to himself that his writings were simply the notebooks of his spirit, the journal of his private intellect. They were reminders to him of what he once said, or what he once meant to say. He wrote at all only to help clarify himself to himself. His books were the log of his "voyagings through strange seas of thought, alone," the strict account of the storms and fogs and occasional calms through which he had passed in his intellectual wanderings toward ports he himself had scarcely found on a map. He thought if his memory were better he would not write at all, not even for himself. He remembered Plato's *Phaedrus* and knew that the word living in the mind can be dead on the page.

In common with many others in his profession, he was aware that philosophy is a soliloquy, and has to be, when it is serious and sincere. It is a thinking in silence and solitude; it is analysis that begins and ends in personal awareness. It is meditation spoken aloud by the unwary thinker and sometimes overheard by others. He rather particularly cherished those works in philosophy that are first and last personal meditations: Marcus Aurelius earnestly addressing himself, St. Augustine doing likewise in his *Confessions,* even though his book was addressed not to himself but to God; for though St. Augustine was addressing God, he was speaking really to his own soul. Our philosopher also loved to browse in those solitary and retired thinkers whose writings are interior monologues and whom one seems simply to be overhearing. Pascal and his *Pensées*, Amiel and his *Journal,* the reflections of Nietzsche, lyric and savage; in our own day the soliloquies of Santayana. It was touching and instructive to see how other minds had tried to settle their accounts with the universe, even when they had added up their accounts wrong, as our philosopher thought.

But he began to discover that the soliloquy is never quite as private as it looks. Memories came into his head of the old-fashioned state convention, of an actor speaking to himself though in the presence of a thousand spectators. Soliloquy, too, is a kind of stage convention in philosophy. He doubted whether the most solitary thinker was ever speaking, or even quite thought he was speaking, wholly to himself. He was addressing a not impossible friend, perhaps across the centuries, or a not impossible god. It had long amused and edified our philosopher to catch the soliloquizing character, on the other hand, in a system of thought that paraded its objectivity and declaimed that it constituted the lineaments of the universe, whereas what the reader really comes upon is the lineaments of the thinker's own temperament or the outlines of the culture in which he lives. The sober, provincial piety of an eighteenth-century German Protestant shone through the analyses of Immanuel Kant; the decent, civic-minded Englishman through Mill's cool and apparently detached analyses of liberty. And he had not failed to note, in what were apparently the most soliloquizing of thinkers, that the soliloquy is of a very special sort: the philosopher, no mere poet, speaking a first fine careless rapture. It is, if it is entitled to be called philosophy at all, an act of thinking. Thinking accomplished is a smooth junction of related thoughts, but thinking in act is confused and tentative. Soliloquy is an exploration, audacious and problematic. Its paths are filled with blocks. It is tempted off to side paths of irrelevance. It goes back in its own track, or starts over. The soliloquy that goes on in the mind and the one that may eventually get down on paper are totally different things. It is only on paper, and not in his secret heart, that the philosopher arrives smoothly at conclusions.

Our philosopher knew he was never quite talking to himself, and he had tried these many years to figure out to whom he could properly address himself. Well, it is very hard to say. He suspected from reading the journals of philosophy and many treatises on the subject that the philosophers write for one another; and that even if a philosopher intended writing for a larger public, it is doubtful indeed whether the apparatus of philosophical thinking is available, even for the educated. There are works in philosophy written in a language hardly to be distinguished from a special esoteric jargon, and philosophers are often condemned for so writing. As he read the works of some of them, our thinker wondered whether it was really necessary to use so formidable a vocabulary to say the simplest truths, or even the simplest untruths. But the layman who condemns the philosophers ought, he thought, to try some day to state quite accurately what is in his head on some basic theme. He pointed out to his lay friends who complained about philosophical jargon how hard it is to say what one intends; that even to convey the simplest sensation, Proust was driven to involved sentences pages long, and Joyce to breaking up English syntax altogether. The philosopher is trying to say either immediate things or ultimate ones, and neither is easy. The very words used in common discourse have their edges rubbed off, their contours too undefined. After he had wandered a while among the loose meanderings of Amiel or Kierkegaard, it was a real pleasure and relief to turn to thinkers who struggled to say precisely what they meant and who traced the implications of what they said. If philosophers wrote only for one another, our philosopher decided, it was because they would be speaking to dulled or deaf ears if they did not.

And yet he had observed among the professional philosophers he had known a great weariness of talking professionally only to one another. Our philosopher was in a position which is almost one of the occupational perils of his profession: he found himself on the horns of a dilemma. He turned the pages of the professional journals in a given year and the pages were filled with arguments and controversies about technical issues that had a life for a season only, distinctions that had a certain fashionableness in discussion. A few years later the distinctions, the discussions, had all disappeared. By middle life he found himself weary of the whole round of jargon and artificial questions.

The philosopher turned to speak to a larger public, for he had wearied of his colleagues who dealt with unreal issues in an artificial language. He wished to speak to a wider audience. But what was he to say to them, and in what tongue? He knew well enough that he could not employ the language of the schools, or discuss the problems that most philosophers continue to discuss. And yet he could not use the language of literature or of daily discourse. He must disinfect his speech of emotional overtone and of practical limitations.

Apart from language, he began to reflect on other difficulties. It suddenly dawned on him what occurs when a philosopher speaks to the multitude. Like many another thinker, he wondered what would happen to him if he dared to speak the truth. He thought of Socrates, condemned by the Athenian jury for corrupting youth and denying the gods. He thought of Bruno, burned at the stake; Spinoza, excommunicated; and philosophers everywhere, at best stupidly smiled at and quietly scorned, or silently ignored.

He thought how the patterns of ordinary life are really the deposit of philosophies centuries old. An appeal to reason, he realized, could not actually be an appeal to reason, for reason has to meet all the established stupidities which have passed as reasonable. In addition, he knew that the philosopher, in order to appeal to a general public, is in danger of perilously opposing its most cherished prejudices; or, what is worse, out of a human desire to please, he comes merely to express its own narrow views. At best, he can be merely a guide to the conventional, a prophet of the already established in life and thought. If he stands by his own insights, he is in danger of not being understood at all, or, if understood, hated. Spinoza was ignored except by the wise or the intellectually enlightened of his own day, and where known, often reviled. And he was not the only one.

Our philosopher was older now, and he knew that one could not come to grips with first and last things without revealing the absurdity of a great many intermediate things, like property and progress and a great many current fads and follies in religion and education. Humorists could hold these things up to ridicule, but a philosopher who pointed out the absurdities of current customs and beliefs could not expect to be well received. Observing some contemporary writers, our philosopher came to the conclusion that a popular philosopher is almost a contradiction in terms. The truth of things is never flattering to human vanities or even to the most generous human hopes and aspirations. If one is to speak the truth as one sees it, one is likely not to encourage human beings very much. There is much that will be distasteful to their dignity or to their desires. They will be quieted or saddened or discomposed by the picture, for instance, of what a tiny spot in the universe the human scene is, how unpremeditated, how transient, how precarious. The philosopher, if he persists in seeing clearly, will have to point out the insanity of many cherished human institutions and the silliness of the pet oracles of current human wisdom. Our philosopher knew that he might win a large public if he spoke a little more clearly than most what everyone already believed. He could win an audience by the device of losing his own soul and hiding his own vision. He could speak to others most successfully if he said lucidly what they already wanted to hear.

Our philosopher was puzzled and saddened by all this. But

he was an idealist and a simple man, for he had not moved much in the ways of the world. He confidently imagined that if men knew the truth, the truth would make them free. He was a naïve spirit and so the truth at first seemed clear to him, and he thought it would be clear and transparent to any candid and unbiased soul, of whom he supposed there were many.

But how is one to speak to a multitude, our philosopher wondered, in language whose refinements are known only to a few? Supposing, as is commonly assumed, that the truth would render men free? In what terms is the truth to be made viable, what words can be used to communicate it? The truth, as the philosopher knew from his complex studies, is never simple. It is crossed by a thousand complications. It is complicated by a thousand contradictions and, at its heart, is a mystery. There are the complexities of discourse itself. Our philosopher had, for one thing, studied many languages, and he knew how the very forms of grammar itself can transmute and distort the facts of existence, how the modulation of tone can change the force of the simplest word. He knew the tortuosities of thought, the plurality of paths open from the same hypotheses, the way in which one is trapped by the surface smoothness of a train of thought into thinking that surface smoothness follows the lines of reality or of truth. Every statement uttered is true only in part, for it is possible in human speech, even in the most artful human speech, ultimately to say only one thing at a time, and there are a thousand other aspects of the same fact that any one fragment of discourse can never even broach. Our thinker knew the philosopher's fallacy of being taken in by his own clarities, and the way in which an articulate system blinds the thinker himself to the morasses and obscurities of experience, and its ultimate central blindness or mystery or absurdity.

One could not even be clear without seeing clarity become an idol. It is easy enough, our philosopher thought, to get a reputation for clarity by avoiding or ignoring all the tangled jungles, by detouring round the blind alleys and dead ends of thought. The truth of anything, he more and more came to think, was not simple, nor was discourse adequate to the whole of truth.

Our philosopher knew that there were plenty of philosophers before him who had seen this. They were driven to arabesques of statement about moments of apocalyptic vision. To be understood even by all literate men in any generation is proof positive that one has uttered only the relatively intelligible half-truths.

Our philosopher realized, more than the ordinary man, how misleading clarities may be, how far from the turbid actuality of experience itself. But what course was he to use in his speech other than the lucidity which for so long he had made his ideal? He could resort, as had been done before, to gnomic utterance, to mystical aphorism. But he hesitated to do this. In the first place, how could one be sure that the flash of insight which welled up within one was not a phosphorescence seen in a fever, a glory wished for in a dream? How could one be sure that a difficult aphorism was not at its core merely a stupid failure in articulation? No, our philosopher could not follow these latter-day ecstatics who thought that the beginning of wisdom was to abandon even the attempt to make sense, to speak in ejaculations. He refused to believe that because one cannot tell the whole truth about anything, and because one cannot tell the whole truth about everything, one cannot tell partial truth about part of the whole of experience. To admit that there is a mystery about the heart of things does not mean that one cannot be clear and convincing about some phases of it, at least, and indeed, within limits, that one cannot make some part of the world or life or society perfectly intelligible. Particularly if one has had—or felt one has had—a flash of vast and cosmic luminosity, the rational mind hates to have its insight converted into a fanaticism of the vague and the vacuous.

Our philosopher felt better now. One could not say the whole truth about the whole universe, but one could say some wholesome and saving things about some of it. He would have rested at that point, content to say what saving and wholesome truths he could think of. But, unfortunately, he was living in the modern world. Like so many of his colleagues and so many of his friends, he had allowed himself to be bedazzled by the complexities of the contemporary scene. He wished rather that he had been born in Greece. It was not that he thought he knew everything, but he knew at least how much there was to be known and of the varieties of knowledge. He noted that there were sages in the modern world who were undismayed by the vast new areas of knowledge, who said that since logic was always the same, and had been so since Aristotle, they did not need to know the sordid irrelevant facts of transient contemporary existence. Our philosopher could not be so careless and innocent of the new avenues of knowledge. If he had been born in early Greece, he could have looked around the world and said that All is Water, or, like Parmenides, that the All is One. He could only be certain now, so subtle and new were the researches in logic, that even the standards of empirical science were uncertain. Physicists seemed to be doubting their tried formulas, and many scientists were saying that science itself could not tell the truth about reality. He himself had too wide an acquaintance with the literature and arts of the world not to know that there was much truth in them that was not dreamed of in any modern scientific philosophy he knew anything about.

Suppose for a moment he had the ear of the whole world, he said to himself, he could not but wish to make his revelation known to the vast listening human race. What was he to tell them? He suspected that not only he, but most others, except a few arrogant modern dialecticians, would be frightened nearly to death. He was not one of those who felt in himself the absolute truth, invented either by himself or borrowed from St. Thomas or Kierkegaard or some other among the illustrious dead. Our philosopher not only knew something about the vast accumulations of modern knowledge; he knew a good deal, too, that the early philosophers of Greece could not have known, about all views of the world current since their day. He was not only a philosopher, but, as the modern phrase runs, a gentleman and a scholar, and he had sufficient sympathy to realize that each of the great classic thinkers had a portion of the truth; that all, in their provincial accents, spoke something of the universal language of the spirit, and spoke fairly accurately about some aspect of experience or nature.

What, then, was he to tell the general public? For our philosopher was a kindly human being and a lonely one, and he could not bear to speak only to himself or to his fellow professionals. Could he go up on a mountain and speak to the multitude, simply to tell them all the doubts which he had arrived at instead of conclusions? That words are treacheries, even the firmest words? He could see the looks of disappointment on their faces turned upward for a revelation. That all philosophies have some truth in them, that each has some window for the soul? But from which window would one see the view that one had been seeking for—the wide and final vista of truth? That there is much at the heart of things that cannot be translated into discourse? But what was *that* to tell human beings already overburdened with the weight and importunity of things too confused, too heartbreaking, too brain-taxing, to be said? That no single philosophy is salvation and that perhaps there is no salvation at all? Nothing to go up on a mountain to announce, nothing to tell a multitude who in their unaided hearts already knew these things too well. Here was hardly anything calculated to instigate mankind to a new idealism. Yet, how could one go on feeding the public ideals that one knew in one's self to be illusions? To tell them all was vanity? They could get that from people other than philosophers. They need not turn to philosophers for that at all. They could borrow discouragements from the tired, the defeated, and the cynical, numerous enough in the world of ordinary men.

The trouble was (Plato saw it long ago) that it was no use to attempt to speak wisely until one, one's self, was wise. But who in the modern world could pretend to even the beginning of wisdom, unless it were the Socratic discovery that wisdom is not of man but of God, and man can only be a lover of wisdom?

Our philosopher was greatly distressed by all these doubts and diffidences about his own profession. He came very near deciding not to be a philosopher at all. If he had had manual gifts, he would have liked to be a craftsman of some sort, some honest workman making a clearly useful, a simply designed, cabinet or tool; he would have liked to be a gardener planting an ultimately visible garden. Or, since he was by nature an intellectual man, he wished he might go into some realm of knowledge where a man might know something precise and definite, and become a respectable authority in some unmistakable realm. A physicist or a chemist could find out things that could be known, and he knew what he knew and when he knew. Even historians, although they were, most of them, short on ideas, could at least claim, with respect to some small area of fact—say, a given county in New York State in the 1820's—to know whereof they spoke, and have documents to prove it. What could a philosopher claim to know? And if wisdom was his speciality, on what basis could he claim to be wise?

Our philosopher came very near abandoning his profession. But he had some acquaintances in other professions, too, and he came to realize that they were not in a much better case. Even the scientists were in an unhappy situation. They were frightened to death, and quite properly, at the consequences in human disaster of what they were finding out. And, since the dawn of the theory of relativity, the securities of the physical sciences, the old smug assumptions as to the nature of even space and time, were gone. Nor was it possible any longer to tell where one science, chemistry, ended and another, biology, began. It was even more impossible to tell how much of science there was, or ever could be, in the so-called social sciences. For these latter aped the methods and language of the physical sciences, but with less security and less success. They succeeded in not being literature without ever really becoming knowledge.

Nor was it any use deciding to be a practical man. Long professional preoccupation with theory had unfitted him for the life of action. And our philosopher had not been uncognizant of the fact that the practical men, above all, had brought the world into chaos; the short views had had the most fateful long-term consequences, the realistic diplomats had written the dossiers of disaster, and the practical men had not even arranged the world effectively for their own happiness. Philosophy might be in a parlous state, but it was clearly no worse off than that of any other human enterprise. Had business, government, or education been more successful?

As our philosopher saw the bad state in which most human activities found themselves, he became, if not arrogant, at least a little prouder of his own profession and a little less modest about its possibilities. He was wrong, he decided, nearly all modern philosophers were wrong, in being so bedazzled and confused by the modern world. The modern world was complicated enough, in all conscience, and so was the apparatus and the methodology of knowledge. But surely philosophy had become overscrupulous and overrefined and overfastidious. The eye was a complex enough organ, but it was simple for the undistracted and healthy eye to see. Had not thinkers a need to seek anew the indispensable innocence of mind and simplicity of heart? Not omniscience, but steadiness of vision, was required. It is possible to understand the whole without knowing everything in detail. A while ago, he knew, there was a movement called Critical Realism in philosophy. What philosophers needed now was a return to naïve realism. Philosophers live, after all, in the same world in which other people live. They might say, like Shylock, that they, too, bleed and suffer. They could at least report what the world seems like and feels like, how it impinges upon an absorbed intelligence unbribed by a desire to believe what it wishes, or to convert, or to bedazzle.

Simple men, despite the complexity of the world in which they lived, often have had a wonderfully steady sense of things, of the ways of the universe. But men did not stay simple long. They were distorted by the past they inherited, by their uneasiness, their practical necessities, and the urgencies of their passions. The philosopher could retain or recover the innocence of mind which men, unconfused, might all have. Just as a poet restored to us the direct colors of the world, it was the function of the philosopher to remind us of the basic simplicities of things which prejudice and verbalism often obscured. Our philosopher decided he would learn all he could from the scientists and the practical men of the world and from artists and from simple human beings in their daily doings. But he would keep his own counsel and speak his own mind and heart. And if he spoke with sufficient sincerity and followed the lead of knowledge, he would speak the heart and mind of all mankind.

The philosopher led from thenceforth a blameless and relatively happy life. He spoke of first and last things and his own mind was quieted and clarified—and, eventually, those of a few others, pupils and friends. There was a good deal he had to unlearn. What a sheaf of theories he had put between himself and the world! How much he had prevented himself from having any knowledge or increasing it, by cutting his fingers on the tools provided by the professional philosophers who proved that knowledge was impossible altogether. How much he had allowed himself to walk in daydream systems provided by the somnambulists who imposed their fantasies upon impressionable and wishful sages. He would have to become like a child again, to see with his own eyes, hear with his own ears, look at the world with his uncorrupted mind. He would have to learn, not to make his wishes identical with the geography of existence, or his hopes identical with the sometimes unpalatable truth, but to see where his ideas had their origin in life, and how they were verified in experience.

And, as for the language he would use to speak to others, ultimate things, both first and last things, were simple, and if he spoke clearly and simply as some of the greatest philosophers had spoken, he would not have to lapse into the jargon of the schools. He might even use the language of myth and poetry, because for some of the things he wished to say, particularly those concerning human values and human ideals, no literal language was adequate to express them. These ideals might *have* to be said in the vocabulary of drama and poetry.

The great world that came to read our philosopher was not sure, therefore, that he was a philosopher at all! "He is a poet," said some, and in their voices was a touch of scorn. "He is merely speaking common sense," said some, and turned away, for this was much too banal to be classed as philosophy. "He is perhaps on the road to wisdom," said some, "for, though he stammers a little, he is reading the script of nature, and one feels a kinship of feeling in listening to what he says. He is saying nothing new, nothing fantastic. He is saying what we all are trying to say, since we are born into the same world and live under the same sky. He says what we all should be saying if we had not been misled by whimsical thinkers who impose their private dreams on the public reality."

And by the time our philosopher's ideas were public property, they scarcely seemed to be philosophical ideas at all. They were everywhere regarded as the sanity of normal men awake in daily existence. Our philosopher was seen to be merely a mature human being speaking to other mature human beings. And as they understood him, they were all philosophers together.

FIVE

The Great Purgation:

A MORAL TALE PRESUMABLY WRITTEN IN 2060

NOBODY quite knew how it began, the movement that culminated some time about 1960, in the prohibition by Constitutional Amendment of the teaching or study, the writing or reading, of philosophy in the United States. For some time the feeling against philosophy had been growing in many parts of the country, and, for that matter, throughout the world. But, as in many things, such as the production of motorcars, movies, and atomic bombs, this country has always been notoriously in advance of the decadent and war-torn nations of Europe, and the movement gained most headway here. But the symptoms were world-wide, the causes universal, and it was soon suggested that while philosophy had not been abolished *legally* in France and England, at least some progress had been made in Russia, where only one philosophy, that according to Marx, was allowed to be taught. Though not actually forbidden in the Western democracies, what with the wear and tear of war and the fatigue of the general population, philosophical thought had languished. Where it survived at all, it existed only in the tepid controversies over purely technical questions discussed by tired elderly dons in the two old English universities, and in some of the Scottish and French ones. There were one or two highly literary causerie writers who used philosophical terms and had a vogue among the café cogitators in France. There were some importations of vague mysticisms from the East. But even without legal interdict, it was predicted that there would soon be as little philosophy taught and studied, written and read and even understood, as in the United States. In the latter country, as we shall see in the sequel, the forbidden interest somehow, despite all legal barriers, continued to exist.

It is quite easy now to understand, in the perspective of a hundred years later, why the prejudice against philosophy (an antipathy, as a matter of fact, as old as that against Socrates in Athens) came to full flower. It was pointed out at the time that the Second World War was a clash of ideologies. Obviously behind each culture and each nation there was a different philosophy. During the war it had seemed quite clear to many that the Nazi philosophy of brute strength and ruthless amorality and of the leviathan of the state had its origins in Hegel and perhaps in Nietzsche. Once the war was over, it was at once just as clearly seen that the true conflict lay not between Germany and the democracies, but between the Russian communist experiment and the liberal West. Philosophy, too, was clearly seen to be the cause of the conflict. If Lenin had not studied Marx, and if Marx had not studied Hegel and the philosophers of the French revolution, there would have been no revolutionary government with world-wide imperial ambitions, no suppression of individual liberties in the interests of a vast "classless" state. There would have been no dictatorship of the proletariat or of the bureaucracy that pretended to act for it. Meanwhile, in the United States especially, it was seen that a whole tradition of socialistic thinking (stemming partly from the Fabians in England and from Shaw's plays and his philosophic prefaces), threatened to impose a social regimentation on this country, too. Liberals and collectivists alike seriously argued that all the evils of business cycles and unemployment came from the dominance of concepts of free enterprise and laissez-faire that ultimately went back to the philosophy of John Locke. A large tome had recently appeared in which John Locke's theory of knowledge was held to be the cause of the failures of democracy in the United States.

Not only were the quarrels of various philosophies weakening to the sense of national unity: the percolation of philosophies into private lives and the consequences in personal malaise were becoming clear to the studious eye. Young men who came to the colleges full of rock-ribbed middle-class niceties of faith and respectabilities of morals returned home with all sorts of strange and upsetting notions. The philosophies of two foreigners, Freud and Jung, filled the air and young minds and hearts with all sorts of uneasiness about old scruples and new scruples about old established follies. The loyalties, the devotions, the quiet and sometimes complacent convictions which had built up America, were being called into question by self-conscious young intellectuals who, so far from having faith in their country, had no longer any faith even in themselves. There were still other currents. Bright young writers were importing strange doctrines from the East. It was pointed out that the United States had been built up by men of action, and as late as the Second World War, the miracle of production in the arsenal of democracy had shown what the breed of men of action could still accomplish. But now the sons of tycoons were falling delighted prey to the gospel of inaction, of leisure and of Buddhistic contemplation. With languid relish they ate only lotus leaves. Families whose enterprise and courage (and investments) had built up American civilization were bathing in the exotic waters of the mysticism of the Orient. Moreover, the logical tricks of the Occident also had their adherents. Western thought, too, was ruining the young. The colleges themselves had done so effective a job with philosophy that at graduation time the dullest student able to get his degree could recognize the failures in logic of the commencement orators, including some of the most eminent benefactors of the institution, and sometimes even the president of the university itself.

The evil, moreover, had begun to spread far beyond the colleges. Radio commentators and war correspondents based their comments concerning inflation, taxes, and procedures in government and business, on philosophies, some of them plainly half-baked, and some of them clearly outmoded. A new book on economics, of very considerable influence, presented, thinly disguised, the antique ideas of Ricardo, and Herbert Spencer. Or some fly-by-night notion of salvation by engineering would reappear, and time and again there would be some newfangled revival of Auguste Comte and Positivism.

There were those who argued that philosophy itself was not an evil, that it was simply the *wrong* philosophy that was the trouble. But the more there was inquiry as to which was the wrong, which the right, philosophy, the more unsettled everyone became. The quarrels that used to be confined to professional philosophers in seminars now divided whole families, and from Reno came word that divorces were being sought and granted where the husband was a pragmatist and the wife a convinced antipragmatist. What made it far worse was the wide diffusion of philosophical thought, or what at least had the earmarks of it. Philosophy was discussed over the radio, there were any number of cheap reprints of works on the most advanced philosophical thought. Finally the general public wearied of trying to decide which was the *right* philosophy, and at last there was an organized movement, known as the League for Common Sense, which began the campaign that finally resulted in the Federal prohibition of philosophy in America.

There was certainly plenty of material in opposition to philosophy that could be quoted from the most classic sources. It was pointed out what had happened to Athens, where philosophy had been current to an unparalleled degree, and how it had become necessary to execute Socrates (though a little late, for his execution made him a martyr and philosophy therefore a sacred cause). Greece began its decline just after the great flowering of Athenian speculative thought, and the slow disintegration of Rome might be said to have begun at precisely the moment when its higher classes, including at least one emperor, Marcus Aurelius, began to be addicted to philosophy. Progress stopped entirely during the Middle Ages, when practically anyone who could read and write argued metaphysical issues, and when adult and learned men would seriously debate all their lives whether universals were real or not—or, so it was said, how many angels could stand on the point of a pin. Francis Bacon, it was recalled, was arrested for bribery, and the public was reminded that in the First World War, Bertrand Russell, who at that time regarded any war as an unforgivable evil, was convicted of promoting disaffection among the troops and was therefore sent to jail. Coming to very recent times, the names of some eminent philosophers were attached to the most scurrilously radical petitions. Philosophers were the first to shout raucously for civil liberties, for the right of minorities (to which some of them belonged), for better distribution of wealth (which some of them badly needed). There was not a single movement for social reform that was not abetted by some contemporary thinker or other, and the sly scoundrels nearly always cited some philosopher of the past. Communism was to be found in the fourth book of Plato's *Republic,* now studied in every college in the country and even, three or four times a year, discussed on some so-called public service or educational radio program. Moreover, it had long been well known that a great many philosophers were agnostic or irreligious, or, if religious, that they espoused a religion so different from that generally recognized as religion in America, and so unintelligible and unattractive, that they might just as well have been atheists.

No, it was clear that philosophy must go. The support for the antiphilosophy program naturally came from an ill-assorted group. But some of the most ardent enthusiasts for its abolition might have been guessed in advance. The Deep South had a good many antiphilosophers, partly because, as southerners pointed out, philosophy had always flourished in the North, particularly in New England, and many unreconstructed rebels felt that philosophy might really have caused the Civil War. Isolationists from the Middle West had always felt a foreign influence in higher thinking, and most philosophers, from Grotius down, had been suggesting international leagues of peace and all such dangerous internationalist nonsense. The Catholic Church was rumored to be a solid block against philosophy, except that it regarded Thomistic philosophy as a special case, since it was the servant of religion, the true religion. The National Association of Manufacturers was against philosophy, on the ground that the most disturbing elements in the labor movement had come from crackpot theorists, many of them professors. Some of the more old-fashioned labor leaders joined, too, for they felt the labor movement itself was being riddled with disturbing, basic critical ideas.

The scholars and thinkers in the universities for a long time remained, as they had been before the Second World War, singularly unperturbed. It was a movement of fanatics, they said, a disease of the small-town mind. Philosophy had never been popular, they said, and the intellect itself had always been suspect in what was still in essence a pioneer country. Certainly in Faculty Clubs no one could take the movement against metaphysics seriously. The barbs thrown by historians and scientists against philosophy were regarded either as jokes or as the pinpricks of the ignorant.

The campaign finally reached the floor of Congress; all sorts of charges were hurled against philosophy: that it was too vague, that it was too precise, that it was too irrelevant, that it intruded too much into practical affairs. There was one member of the Cabinet who had once, the record showed, been a metaphysician. The familiar charges were leveled against philosophers themselves. Sometimes they were accused of being too starry-eyed and idealistic. The old saw was raked up about Thales, the first recorded philosopher in early Greece—that he had stepped into a well while looking at the stars. Recourse was had even to fictional peccadillos of alleged professional thinkers. The philosopher Square was dug out of *Tom Jones*—the passage where he is caught in a compromising situation and blandly points out that it has always been the special function of philosophers to distinguish between theory and practice. In general it was alleged that philosophers talked very grandiosely about moral ideals, but that in the ordinary relations of life they were as narrow, greedy, lustful, and mendacious as anybody else. The records of the divorce courts were cited in proof of the fact that philosophers did not respect the marriage tie, and studies were made of what happened to the children of philosophers brought up from their earliest influences under the sway, direct or indirect, of philosophy. Above all, the charge was made that philosophy was at best useless. It became the habit of the comic papers and of the conservative press to select passages from the *Journal of Philosophy* in which philosophers were shown to argue with each other interminably as to what was the meaning of any of the most ordinary words, or as to whether tables or chairs existed or not.

Psychiatrists pointed out how dangerous it was to confuse people on the most simple issues of life. They said that by the proper arguments you could make it impossible for people to move one step forward, for Zeno had shown they would have to move one-half that distance first and then one-half *that* distance first, and so on, ad infinitum. Young people fell, moreover, into the habit of imitating their teachers of philosophy. They would argue endlessly over the most inconsequential abstractions. Philosophical works (some quite recent ones, too) were cited to show that a steady diet of them would render their readers unfit to write or even to speak the English language. Furthermore, repetition of terms, so common in metaphysical treatises, and the play with the nonexistent, were verified as forms in which insanity began.

The antiphilosophy lobby had access to vast funds, and nobody quite knew where they came from. In accordance with the Hatch Act, the organizations which gave such monies had to be listed, but by some kind of political skulduggery the true donors were somehow hidden. It was said that various churches were giving money on the ground that philosophy was seducing the young from religion. Some young people had been known to absent themselves from Sunday services to attend Sunday seminars. The Republican party, then in power, said that there had been serious disaffection from its ranks among graduates of the more elite colleges. It was said also that there was one millionaire who, in his youth having fancied himself a philosopher, had not been able to buy himself either a position or a degree, even from a backwoods graduate school in a southern state known as the Cottonseed School of Philosophy. This frustrated would-be professor had long plotted his revenge. The Purgation was a wonderful chance to prevent *anyone* from being a philosopher.

The amendment was finally passed, though there was considerable difficulty in framing it. For it turned out that the boundaries of philosophy were very hard to draw. Where did it begin and where did it end? The committee enlisted the aid of a prominent advertising man who, seduced by a larger salary, had deserted the university in which he had been a teacher, and university life altogether. There were one or two professors long secretly disaffected and badly in need of money—for it was during an inflationary period and academic salaries no longer sufficed for their growing families. One of these professors had a theory that the population must increase. These men, for a large sum, helped the attorneys for the committee that framed the amendment.

It was easy enough to include in the abolition all the traditionally recognized parts of classic philosophy. These were forbidden to be taught, discussed, written about in books, or published. They included metaphysics, or the theory of being, itself (the newspapers had a hard time explaining *that* to the public), logic, the theory of knowledge, or epistemology, which always had had a vaguely obscene sound to the semi-informed; ethics, and aesthetics. The last-named, which had always been associated with Oscar Wilde, naturally was suspect to the moral leaders who supported the Purgation. It was decided, out of necessity, to leave unspecified the degree of philosophy which might be legally allowed to be present in other academic fields, such as economics, for instance, or the traces of logic or ethics or other similar abstractions in newspaper editorials or in radio commentaries. It was even suggested that an exact percentage of legitimate basic questions about first and last things could be determined. Some proposed three and a half per cent, reminding some of the older people of the kind of beer current in an earlier Prohibition period, during which more heady liquors than philosophy had been prohibited. It was made clear that no courses, specifically so labeled, in philosophy, no lecture or seminar or preceptorial group, could be given in any college or high school or prep school or kindergarten, in some of the more advanced of which last-mentioned the subject had, of late, been taught.

Professors of philosophy near the age of retirement were to be retired forthwith with an annuity paid by the government. All publishing of philosophical books was forbidden, and philosophical libraries, for possible later research into the diseases of the human spirit, were to be impounded.

Naturally, questions were raised as to freedom of speech and teaching, but it was at once pointed out by reputable organs of opinion that the democracies had *once,* during the

Second World War, imperiled their own future by allowing all sorts of poisons to be introduced into the body politic. After all, there were food and drug acts, and control of opiates and narcotics and stimulants. And was not a poison for the mind worse than one for the body? and a poison for the body politic worst of all?

Walter Lippmann, by this time the dean of all commentators, devoted a series of five articles to the subject. He pointed out with his usual cool clarity: "One must put first things first; the safety and vigor of the Republic is at stake; civilizations in the past, like those of Greece and Rome, were seriously weakened by philosophy, etc., etc." Nor did it detract from the force of his arguments that in his own youth he had, for three years, been assistant in philosophy to George Santayana at Harvard.

It was recognized on all sides that the move to abolish philosophy by Federal law was a very drastic procedure. There were warning voices raised, and from quite respectable quarters, too, that sumptuary legislation, even for *bodily* goods, had never been successful. There were vested interests, too, even in philosophy; the textbook publishers, for instance, and the writers of syndicated columns on "Moral Guidance" that had recently become popular. Even those most ardent supporters of the Purgation felt that something should be done for the older professors of the subject, who were clearly not convertible to other uses. These had, for the most part, nothing but the most general and often only the vaguest ideas, and it would be impossible to transfer them to teaching subjects where genuine information was required. As for practical pursuits, the senior professors were obviously quite hopeless at their age and with their training. It had to be admitted that they had pursued their profession in innocent good faith, most of them, quite unaware from the patent boredom of most of their students that they had been doing any effective corruption of their minds. And it was a notorious complaint in the philosophical profession at official meetings that philosophy played little or no role in the general course of American life. These men, many of them, had grown old and gray in academic service, and, what was more, they had contracts.

The government retirement allowances quieted the humane protest raised on behalf of the older professors; the textbook publishers received subsidies for ceasing the production of books on philosophy, which benefit reminded some of the older generation of the days when the Federal government had paid farmers money to plow under their crops, or to destroy them.

Younger instructors in philosophy were a special problem. They were youthful enough to be re-educated, but it was difficult to be certain that they were bona fide free of philosophical attachments. Some of their elders had, as a matter of fact, grown blasé, but these juniors, many of them quite ingenuous in their enthusiasm, had displayed fanatic devotion to philosophy and had been overheard telling their classes that it might save the world where religion had failed, or that, even if it could not save the world, it was at least the best thing possible to enjoy in a ruined or hopeless civilization. More than one of them quoted Milton's

> How charming is divine philosophy!
> Not harsh and crabbed, as dull fools suppose.

The citation did not endear them to the opposition.

It was predicted that within a few years philosophical ideas would be almost unknown in the United States. Undergraduate courses were out, and in four years, a college generation, philosophy would no longer be even a legend. And those breeding grounds of the poison, graduate schools, which had been the proud boast of more than one famous university—these, too, would shortly be a thing not even of memory.

The night before the Purgation, as it came to be called, was official, there were little orgies of last flings in many parts of the country. Into the amendment had been written the prohibition of meetings of more than four persons met expressly for the discussion of philosophical questions. On the eve of the Purgation there were many large philosophical parties given at which Plato's dialogues were read and passionately and intensely discussed, for it was (or it was predicted that it would be) the last time—certainly the last time openly—that such parties could be held. There were some really disgraceful debauches. At one famous graduate school of philosophy there was an intense discussion of epistemology, one of the most fiery anyone could remember, and by midnight, when such discussion became illegal, it had grown flagrantly philosophical. A policeman who had come in to warn that the Great Purgation had begun, was convinced from the perfect unintelligibility of what he heard that those present were in the very depths of the intellectual vice which was, from this point, no longer to flourish openly in the land. And such language as was being used—a jargon that clearly sounded blasphemous or obscene!

The first day of the Purgation the newspapers of the country said, as they always do say, the appropriate things. The *New York Times* observed that this was obviously the moment for Americans to realize that they were trying a new and noble experiment. They were going to live without the follies and dangers of profound and ultimate thought. America was going to be a model to the world of what democracy could accomplish if it made up not its mind but its will. The era of basic criticism, of fundamental querying analysis of all our institutions, the epoch of large and dreamy ideas, the years of reckless hypotheses, were over. Youth in the future in the colleges was going to be taught, as used to be the case in the storied old New England colleges, the fundamental virtues, the sturdy old moralities, of American practice and of Christian truth. Americans, it is true, were not accustomed to controls, but they had put up with rationing during the war, and this was a war also—a war against the depredations of intellectuals who with ready tongues and sly minds assaulted or undermined the solid and substantial sobrieties of the American tradition.

The Purgation had been scheduled to go into effect at the very beginning of the academic year in September, so as to make the transition standard and simple for all educational institutions. Various colleges reported that there had been no difficulties to speak of. Students who had registered the previous spring for courses in philosophy were easily diverted into other and more useful or innocent fields: cost accounting, banking procedure, the Bible. There were a few malcontents, and some of the more radical spirits at Harvard organized mass meetings, at one of which a volume of Spinoza was displayed against a black curtain of mourning.

It was surprising that even the liberal journals raised no protest. *The Nation–New Republic* (the two had been merged some years before) remarked editorially that liberals, too, must change with the times. Philosophy might have seemed a bulwark of liberties once; it had now become a dissolvent of the bonds of union among us. It was part of the outmoded individualism of the nineteenth century, and the sooner it was forgotten, the better. The day of the eccentric individual mind

—of mind itself—was over; now was the time for action, together. Shakespeare meant just that when he warned us against the pale cast of thought.

Very soon the direst predictions as to the working of the Purgation were proved to be not exaggerated. In the first place, it was early seen, as shrewd constitutional lawyers had predicted, that the amendment, necessarily vaguely drawn, could not possibly ensure the entire abolition of philosophy in the colleges and universities. The fact was that for the past generation or two philosophical ideas, philosophical points of view, had been seeping into other fields. There were courses in English literature hardly distinguishable from courses in ethics or aesthetics. The economists, unknown to themselves, had for years been doling out philosophies decked out or tricked out with statistics. There was even a general theory in economics as to why statistics were the only way to understand our economic system. And there were hypotheses, too, the business cycle theory, for instance, that could hardly be distinguished from what was taught by professors of political theory under the auspices of departments of philosophy.

As for the schools of education which trained the teachers who taught the children over the land, the legislators had quite forgotten them. They had not known that the whole apparatus of thinking and method in the teachers' colleges was sprinkled over or shot through with philosophical ideas. It is true that these had been thinned out very considerably, and sometimes were hardly recognizable. The great John Dewey once was asked whether he thought one of the big teachers' colleges was not giving a grotesque parody of his ideas. He is said to have replied: "I hope so."

There were still other sources of infection. The better law

schools were still giving, quite legally, courses that looked dangerously like philosophical consideration of the law and its meaning for civilization. Even the schools of business, which might be presumed to be safest from anything vague, ideological, and impractical, were teaching something called "the theory of business enterprise." Engineering institutes had long since introduced training in the theory of human relations, for they had discovered their graduates had to deal with men as well as with machines.

In the undergraduate colleges the new vogue of courses in the "great books" made a difficulty, too. It is true that most of the so-called humanities courses treated works of philosophy chiefly as works of literature. Plato, even though he was read in English, was read for his style. But obviously the philosophical classics, even though they were not allegedly read for intellectual purposes, ought not to be read at all. And all traces of the history of ideas and of current doctrines of life and nature had to be left out of the courses in Contemporary Civilization. So, as it turned out, though there was not a single course labeled philosophy in the curriculum of any university, though graduate seminars and undergraduate tutorials in the field had completely disappeared, it was perfectly clear to the knowing that philosophy could be and was studied in other ways and by other names and by other professors. And in many universities there was an unexpected access of students of the more intellectual sort to a particularly reflective anthropologist, to a professor of poetry who had ideas, sometimes even to some rare historian who had not forgotten the forest of general principles for the trees of fact.

Enforcement was more serious and more difficult still outside the universities. There were newspaper editorials that had more than a tincture of philosophical reflections, even when they were attacking philosophy. The great quarrel between those who favored national sovereignty and power politics as over against those who favored world government and world loyalty brought up issues deeply involved in the whole tradition of basic reflection on human destiny. The terrifying success of the atomic bomb constantly caused people to reflect on the wide gap between the technical mastery and the moral incompetence illustrated in what was commonly called human progress. Again, those who spoke with an easy glibness of the chasm, wide and uncrossable, between Russia and ourselves found themselves raising some of the most profound and ultimate of questions about the purposes of government, the rights of the individual, and the nature of human nature itself.

The century-old division between the East and West in feeling and in modes of thought had caused to seep into ordinary discussion questions of practicality versus detachment, intuition versus analysis, the material versus the spiritual, time versus eternity, the real versus the ideal.

Clergymen, in the days preceding the Purgation, if they were trained at orthodox theological seminaries, had been exposed in some degree to philosophy; and even if, attending more narrow biblical institutes, they had never heard of it, echoes of the great tradition found their way into their sermons and were implicit in the texts they quoted. Shrewd and informed observers knew, for instance, that it was impossible to quote the Gospel according to St. John without avowing the doctrines of Plato, or St. Paul without breathing at points the very temper and spirit of the old Greek and Roman Stoics. And Epicurus himself might have written the Book of Ecclesiastes. On the other hand, the most innocuous and banal commencement address by an eminently respectable Rotarian contained to the sophisticated ear more than a trace of what in an earlier day might have been called philosophy.

Government enforcement officers on the whole gave up trying to put too nice a point upon it, and as long as there was no explicit reference to specifically philosophical doctrines, they were satisfied. They kept a careful eye, however, on clergymen who had once been to a graduate school of philosophy, or who had taken a combined degree in philosophy and religion. And they watched, too, those physicians who, practicing what they called psychosomatic medicine, were often clearly known to be using philosophy as a form of therapy.

It was rather easier to control the distribution of books already printed and to prevent the publication of philosophical works, or even textbooks, in the field. The known stocks of all publishers of volumes of this kind were destroyed by government order, and the plates of all such works melted down. Some suspiciously reflective books of essays continued to be published, and there was always the enigma of the first page of *The New Yorker*. Many, including ex-professional philosophers, insisted that there was no question whatever that that famous page ought clearly to come under the ban. The Christmas commentaries of Mark Sullivan, Dorothy Thompson, and Anne O'Hare McCormick also came under suspicion, but were allowed as usual on the ground that they were not, for all the gravity of their tone, really dealing with philosophic fundamentals. And no one even noticed that children's books like *The Wind in the Willows* were filled with moral ideas, and that *Alice in Wonderland,* still very popular, was a whole course in logic.

The purgation of discussion groups and radio forums offered

a problem somewhat similar to those posed by publications, and the same delicate issues were raised. Such programs as "Invitation to Learning" were compelled to omit the classics of the history of philosophy, though there were those who thought that Montaigne and Erasmus, though not technically philosophers, were so close to wisdom that they really ought to have been forbidden. The University of Chicago "Round Table," debating usually the more practical political and social problems, and not really getting down to the root issues, was allowed to proceed. The government demanded scripts, however. One could never tell when quite out of the blue, and without having intended it, a member of the discussion panel might not blurt out some ideas, sovereign, fresh, comprehensive. It had happened twice in five years.

The hardest problem of control was, of course, private discussion. It was distinctly difficult to prove, when investigators raided a private home, that the theme there being discussed came under the ban. Sometimes a rather unlikely group of serious-looking scholars said that they had just finished a bridge game, and there was always a card table open and a few score pads to prove the point. But what the investigators had just been eavesdropping upon, something about mental substance and material qualities, did not sound exactly like bridge postmortems. Still, it was impossible to prove it. If the recording devices, sometimes previously installed in an apartment, showed that God, freedom, and immortality had been discussed, it was very hard indeed to demonstrate that that was philosophy rather than religion. It was only when some explicitly technical treatise was found on the premises, and when there was a stenographic report showing that the discussion was such as might once have taken place at meetings of the now-defunct

American Philosophical Association, that the government had a good case. What was more, the investigators knew by bitter experience that they *had* to have a very good case. For one thing, it was known that some of the Federal judges had in their youth been openly sympathetic to philosophy. One of them had been used in the old days to invite eminent philosophers to dine at his house for the express purpose of discussing the nature of things with them, "picking their brains," he called it. And his own decisions had often in the free past been used as happy illustrations in courses in logic and introduction to philosophy. This jurist had lately been known to laugh out loud and dismiss a case for lack of evidence, and to murmur contemptuously at some of the quotations brought in as evidence by the enforcement officers: "So that's what they think is philosophy nowadays!"

That there should have been bootlegging in the forbidden books goes without saying. It was rumored that a second-hand copy of one of Plato's *Dialogues* had brought five hundred dollars. There were bookshops dealing in *esoterica* that made small fortunes out of badly printed reprints of David Hume and John Stuart Mill. Even novels that some reviewer suggested contained general notions about life would zoom into popularity. Luckily such books seldom got into the movies, so there was one problem less for the harried government watchdogs. But the problem was serious enough, in all conscience. Loads of metaphysical works and works of moral philosophy were time and again highjacked on the way to New York from the caches on Long Island in which they were concealed. Everyone knew that some of those most virulent in their campaign against philosophy were secretly addicted to it and patronized the bootleggers. And the tourist trade to South America was augmented by those who went to Argentina and Colombia, where these ideas were said to flourish and to be available cheap and by the carload, and where every busboy could carry on a discussion with logic and precision on the deepest of moral themes, and waiters chatted amiably about Aristotle.

Meanwhile, it was pointed out that the Purgation had not improved the morals of our young people; it was shown that young men and women who used to discuss first and last things quietly and openly were now doing it furtively, in corners and in whispers. And young men who ordinarily might have discussed philosophy mildly and read it only occasionally, now talked about it intensely and read it nightly till dawn.

But the advocates of Purgation were, on the whole, satisfied. Philosophy, at least officially, was dead.

Within a decade, so the records show, there began to be a revulsion. It was noted that there was a great paucity of moral leadership and intellectual initiative in the country. One corporation executive complained that the young men who came to them from the colleges were earnest and polite and conscientious enough, but that they seemed to *want* someone else to do their thinking for them. He had not come across one young man with an idea in his head in a decade. On the other hand, congregations began to droop as they heard the old conventional platitudes doled out week after week. Even the big city churches whose prestige and salary could command the spiritual best the ministry had to offer, could find no one. The radio preachers on a national network, who had been the great middlemen of ideas, now had nothing whatever to say, and to save them embarrassment the radio companies reduced the "Church of the Air" from a half hour to fifteen minutes. In politics, the national leaders had degenerated so that to call them leaders at all was patently an abuse of the term. One began to hear repeated the quotation: "Where there is no vision the people perish," and since the quotation was from a religious source, no government agent objected. There was clearly no vision in business or education or art or science. Everyone felt that the country was going through a species of dog days, a perpetual hot and windless August without a breath of a new idea, without ever a west wind of the spirit. Ordinary conversation had become almost unbearably banal, minus any trace of initiative, of sharp and questioning query, of a flare of wit. Everyone seemed vaguely to feel that life had become a perpetual drowse of habit and stereotype.

Meanwhile, Americans coming back from abroad reported with enthusiasm the liveliness, the freshness, of other peoples all over the globe. They spoke of new concepts stirring, new modes in art and architecture, new experiments in social organization and adult education. Returning travelers made the eyes of stay-at-homes gleam longingly as they told of the excitement of conversation, books, concerts, and exhibitions in foreign cities. The utter emptiness of talk at cocktail parties and dinners at home had become notorious. One could pass the whole evening in the company of the most eminent and not hear from anyone present even the borrowed ghost of a notion.

Naturally, at the ports of entry the customs officers tried very hard, and with reasonable success, to prevent philosophical literature from entering the country. It was not as easy to prevent ideas from coming in (foreign ideologies, as they were called), because these came quietly inside people's heads. Even those notions were suspect that came from England, where all our own democratic axioms had been born. For a time it was proposed to have an oral interview given to each returning citizen, but the scheme was considered too elaborate. Moreover, not enough immigration officials could be found any more who had had enough training in philosophical ideas to identify one if they heard it.

What was true in politics and in society in general was true in all the arts. Not a single fertilizing notion had animated plays or novels in a generation, and the same was true of music and of painting.

Foreigners who had not been to the United States in many years could hardly believe their eyes. "Your country," they said, "was once the dynamic and inventive leader of the world. But even in mechanical invention every country in the world is now ahead of you." It was true. For the research departments of the great electrical and chemical companies had long since abandoned these divisions for fear the government would find out—which was true—that many of their most eminent scientists spent half their time on basic hypotheses in the physical sciences. Since basic research had been abandoned, inventions had gone with them.

In education, too, as the visiting foreigners pointed out, it was the same story. Teachers droned on in the traditional way, pupils went through the familiar motions, but the living and progressive temper that had animated education in this country for a generation had utterly gone. The colleges, too, had once been a ferment of experiment and change, and much of the dead wood of generations past had been swept away when educators began to ask themselves what were their ends and what were their means, and what were the relationships of these to one another. But the colleges now were like small, hidebound, inbred little cathedral towns in England. Few professors ever had a fresh idea, and deans and presidents never.

There were similar depressing phenomena in other fields. Everyone had remarked how, during the first decades of the twentieth century, in medicine, especially in the field of what was called psychosomatics—those diseases that lie somewhere between body and soul—there had been most fruitful healing developments, and that it was precisely men with leading ideas like Freud and Jung who were responsible. And in the subtle and complex realms of biophysics and biochemistry, it was the men of commanding concepts, of wide and dominant themes, who had opened up new vistas and made possible undreamed-of achievement. But for ten years now there had been a dead calm in medicine, in aviation, in engineering, in social reform and legislative procedure, in art, in politics, and human relations in general.

In the field of human relations, especially in the inter-relations of groups and classes, the absence of a general and generous flow of philosophic ideas came most egregiously to be felt. The student of American history knows how sharpened racial antagonisms had grown in the decades between the two world wars and in the decades immediately following. There were those who were wont to say that Hitler and his cronies had spread the virus of racial hate. But more careful observers knew that the germs of such destructive poisons—fatal to the soul of the haters as well as of the hated—had long been present in this country. Hatred of one minority or another had at one time or another flared up in American history: loathing of the Masons or the Catholics, foreigners in general, or, more generally and steadily, of the Negroes and the Jews.

Men of good will, active for humane and enlightened causes, had long had faith that all that was required was a raising of the level of education in all classes and an improvement of the economic status of those whom insecurity and dread had made the eager, even the hysterically eager, pupils of hate propaganda. It was assumed, not without ground, that as the habit of critical intelligence was promoted, the slogans and shibboleths of race and class hate could be gradually eradicated. It will be remembered that Wendell Willkie, who save for his untimely death might have been President of the United States, had managed to persuade even some of the most provincial middle-western isolationists that all men were members of one world, and the feeling against foreigners had begun, for a time, to die down, even the feeling against Russians. And progress was being made in the decades immediately following the Second World War in Negro-White and Gentile-Jewish relations. It was becoming harder to poison a generation which had the ever-present antidote of critical intelligence. They were immune to the traditional clichés: that there was such a thing as white supremacy, or that the Jews were a separate kind of infrahuman doers of secret and sinister evil. As for Catholics, there was as yet no great likelihood of a Catholic becoming President of the United States, it is true. But the notion that had been spread during one campaign, when a Catholic was running for President, that the Pope was planning to govern our country through the agency of a Catholic President, was, save in the most illiterate quarters of Georgia, laughed to scorn.

Gradually, too, with the spread of public interest in general or philosophical ideas, some of the sane and liberating concepts that had animated the founders of the Republic came back into currency, and proved safeguards against the invidious and poisonous prejudices and provincialisms that were always threatening to corrupt the good sense of the population. The ideals of universal brotherhood, of the intrinsic dignity of the individual, of the equality of men whatever their race, color, or creed, of the rights of minorities, of the justice due each man in his capacity as a human being—all these notions began to capture the general imagination as education spread and as Americans came to know their own noble and liberal heritage. In schools, in colleges, and through reprints in pocket form of some of the great classics of human freedom and human justice, even ordinary men, who might otherwise have been the victims of their local and tribal tabus, were led gradually from the barbarities which lingered from their simian heritage. They were educated to a feeling, amounting almost to instinct, of the humane integrity of the great liberal tradition. The Greek ideas of equality, the Stoic and Christian notion of brotherhood, the concept of natural law descended from the Romans through Thomas Aquinas, the English passion for liberty and its statement, clear and quietly passionate, in John Stuart Mill, the equalitarianism of the French Revolution and of Walt Whitman, the Emersonian emphasis on the dignity and even the divinity of the individual—these grand and yet tender themes had been gradually seeping their way into the general awareness of Americans.

Obviously not *all* Americans had read the works in which these democratic philosophies found their original expression. But it is true that with the spread especially of adult education these basic philosophies, these leading "great ideas," were beginning to influence millions of Americans who were thus made less easy prey to the obscene primitivisms of illiterate senators from the Deep South and elsewhere. It was a significant symptom that more and more educators were emphasizing the importance of the "great books" as sources of education, and that many of these books were those expressing the central ideas of equality, freedom, and justice.

It has been pointed out already how these pivotal books were removed from the curricula of schools and colleges, and anything like a philosophic idea, including the fundamental themes of democracy, could no longer be taught. When some savage or sinister demagogue began to fan the now already-mounting flames of racial hatreds and talk the old dangerous nonsense of racial superiorities, larger and larger groups of the population were at his mercy, lacking the critical habit, induced by training in logic, which might have enabled them to resist him. They lacked also the fortification of those wide and saving perspectives which come by exposure to the liberating philosophies of the long humane tradition. Serious students of the American past were increasingly alarmed to see how utterly unknown to the average Americans were the very basic hypotheses of human life for which, at every crisis in its history, this Republic had laid down its lives and treasures. There was scarcely a young American, even among the university-bred, who now had the critical capacity or the philosophic education to enable him to reply to even the filthiest sort of libel and canard on human dignity. More than one leading citizen was heard to say privately, and a few began to dare to say publicly, at the risk of their own reputations, that the moods of violence, of prejudice, of hysteria, that were assailing the country, if not due to the prohibition of philosophy, were seriously exacerbated thereby. With the absence of faith in human intelligence came a return to savage and deep-seated violence. Lynchings grew in number, strikes grew in brutality on both sides; and, despite the perils, constantly preached, of the almost unbelievable horror of a third world war, there began to be those who talked in terms of blood baths and a blood-letting to save the world. Even the government agents did not suspect that this itself was, although perverse, a philosophy.

Finally, those concerned with the public health began to note certain alarming symptoms, always present in a society, but now greatly aggravated by the Great Purgation. In the old pre-abolition days, those who had a tincture of philosophy in them had, in times of personal crisis or of national emergency when civilization seemed to have no prospect and personal life no safety, the refuge of contemplation, the taking of the long view, which served as both an anodyne and an exhilaration. Such a capacity for detached contemplation eased the tension and distress of the immediate present. Many a man had been saved from melancholia and even from suicide by being able, if only for the time being, to take the perspective of eternity. In the past there had been a wonderful exhilaration in the ability to look at events and at the whole of existence itself in categories different from those currently in fashion, in terms diverse from those imposed by the brutalities and barbarisms and urgencies of present national and international chaos. The mere traversing of other views of life gave one access to worlds elsewhere. Especially during the Second World War years this had been noted. For at that period travel had been greatly curtailed, and those confined through the whole anxious war period to their own villages and their own jobs had found the glorious wanderings of the spirit it was possible to take by reading in the great thinkers and accompanying them on their intellectual pilgrimages. And, if blood-letting was wanted, bad blood could be got rid of harmlessly in debate. Moreover, the arguments and controversies of philosophy were harmless enough. Intellectual differences, intellectually taken, did not lead to literal bloodshed, or hatred. And many a naturally combative temperament, at least among the educated classes, had learned the technique of unembittered argument—and often, in the course of argument, the healthy pleasure of discussion for the sake not of victory, of making a debater's point, but of co-operative intellectual light.

All this, the guardians of psychic health observed, was no longer feasible. Nor was it any longer possible to have the always quieting sense that even in the present madness of the world an individual might work out for himself principles of sanity by which he might live. It used to be possible not to join, or to join with mental reservations, the dominant lunacies.

Meanwhile, as these eminent public health experts pointed out, since the authentic article under accredited auspices could not be secured, there was recourse to all sorts of substitutes and quackery. They agreed that philosophy had led to abuses, and that contemplation and escape into unfamiliar views of life might lead people to intellectual debauchery and to moral paralysis. But a *little* of the stimulus of philosophy, at least, was good for man, and a little of the narcosis it sometimes provided. Neither the stimulation nor the soothing was now available. But cheap and sometimes highly dangerous substitutes were being vended, under the counter, as philosophy. They were not the real article, as any trained practitioner would have known. They were often thin vaporous mysticisms from the East, or allegedly from the East, though it was clear that some of them, whatever their labels said, were manufactured in Hollywood or New York. There were revivals of ancient nostrums, of transmigrations, of ghostly immortalities, of schemes of physical exercise that were palmed off as avenues to meditative peace. There were fantastic, apparently new concoctions of literary sensibility labeled schematic philosophies of life.

All these somber testimonies from various unimpeachable sources, technical and moral, were bound eventually to have their effect. It was clear that people had begun to laugh at the Purgation and to circumvent it in every possible way, sometimes as a public duty. They would ostentatiously indulge in philosophy though they personally had no use for the stuff. It was a long time, however, before any well-known and respectable leader would come out publicly against the Purgation Amendment and publicly demand its repeal. The first strong voice raised for Repeal was that of a veteran university president whose utterances on public questions had acquired something of the character and force of pronouncements from the ancient Oracle of Delphi, though it must be said for the old gentleman that he was much less ambiguous in his proclamations. The ancient educator was accustomed to issue his utterances in time for appearance on the front pages of the Monday papers. Dr. McKenna came out one dull summer week end, when the statement would be sure to be prominently printed, with a perfectly explicit recommendation that the Purgation be repealed for most of the reasons given above. He declared that the future of the country was otherwise hopeless. Especially did he emphasize that it was the death of democracy unless philosophy, the indispensable condition of independent thought, was revived. It was impossible to question the old gentleman's motives; he, personally, had never written a work of philosophy in his life, nor was he now likely to do so.

This matter was of such immediate concern by now to everyone (for various reasons) that the educator's case against Purgation and for Philosophy was read in detail. The League for

Common Sense, of course, promptly issued a statement castigating the old man, and indeed its chief secretary suggested that it was senility that had prompted him in the first place. But the unusual eloquence of the statement and the cogency of the old educator's arguments touched off a wide public response, especially as he was saying what many of the wiser heads had long come to believe. The Church might fulminate against him, and those, too, who had reason to fear that the revival of philosophy was a threat to the cults, the prejudices, or the follies by the exploitation and furtherance of which they lived. The black marketeers in ideas were, of course, solidly opposed to Repeal.

Very soon there was formed the League for Uncommon Sense, and the very title made many who had no particular claim to such a commodity desire to inscribe themselves as members. But most of the membership, which rapidly grew into the millions, was quite sincere and ardent. The organization worked step by step and state by state, and just as the Purgation had come as a surprise, so Repeal came with unexpected speed. Within a year after Dr. McKenna's utterance, philosophy was again permitted to be written and read, to be studied and taught, in the country. Some philosophers who had gone into hiding, or had busied themselves in other occupations (such as taking in the umbrellas in the museums, which had once been suggested as a fitting station for them), had begun—so sure were they that Repeal was coming—the writing of philosophical books again. One or two, who had always been interested in the development of ideas in private rather more than in their reception and propagation in public, had long been writing in secret, even during the great intellectual drought. They had tended their little garden oases in the universal desert.

The night of Repeal was almost as memorable as that of the

last day of legally permissible philosophy. A very ancient former professor, once eminent in the profession, and a past president of the vanished Philosophical Association, was guest of honor at a ball in Madison Square Garden at which there were five thousand people. Illuminated bookstore windows—some of them were even floodlighted—flaunted works that had not been seen in years. Passers-by, as a matter of fact, wondered where obviously brand-new copies of the works of John Dewey and Alfred North Whitehead had suddenly come from. The executive committee of the Eastern Division of the American Philosophical Association, which presumed it still had a mandate, met hastily to celebrate and to plan for prompt revival of meetings of the Association. Little groups which had informed the public that they were bridge clubs or religious societies now proudly displayed posters on the doors of the meetinghouses where they met, reading "Philosophy," or "Truth Crushed to Earth!"

The revival of philosophy was both more difficult and more rapid than had been expected. Almost the whole older generation had died out. A few had survived, but their ideas seemed either hopelessly outdated or quite unintelligible. And a few who had been very active and eminent in the teaching and propaganda of the subject when it had been legally respectable were now old and weary and disenchanted. They felt they could work up neither the enthusiasm to teach the young nor the energy to engage in argument with their contemporaries, for among those who survived were, naturally, some tough-skinned old controversialists. There had been a gap of two decades in the training of teachers of philosophy, and the demand for instruction was far larger than it had ever been even in boom times when young ladies of leisure and wealth had crowded afternoon extension courses in the subject. The colleges and universities were simply inundated. Anyone who could distinguish the name of Plato from that of Aristotle, or who could explain the Ontological Argument, was hastily impressed into service by the weaker institutions. Philosophy should ideally be taught in small groups and learned by discussion, as everyone knows. But that, under the circumstances, was quite impossible, and professors of philosophy, most of them now ancient and feeble and drawn from retirement as a public duty, lectured in some state universities to as many as five thousand students at a time. It was found that some professors of English had once long ago taught philosophy, and that some economists who had never taught the subject could use language quite as impressive in elaborateness as that of philosophers.

The problem of educating the millions of citizens past university age who wished to know about philosophy was almost insoluble. The radio was a great help, though the broadcasting companies proved very severe competition for the universities, for they could offer salaries for a fifteen-minute daily philosophical commentary that even the most disinterested lover of philosophic truth could not afford to reject. Many professors of the relatively few available were drawn off by the networks.

It was encouraging to see again on the drugstore counters reprints of the old familiar works. *The Critique of Pure Reason* could again be bought for twenty-five cents. It is true its enormous text had to be very closely printed in minute type, and that very little of it was understood by the general reader. But in due time simple expositions of it were available in large print, in smaller compass and in easier language, at fifteen cents.

Graduate schools revived, and within a remarkably few years things were much as normal again. By normal, it is not, of course, meant that philosophy was universally popular. The first flush of enthusiasm that had come with Repeal died down, and there were a good many who very soon found that they did not like the genuine article and preferred the substitutes that had been available during the official drought. Some foreign experts said the American taste in intellectual matters had been ruined by the cheap things they had been given as mental drink during the Purgation. It would take some time, they said—and indeed it did—to recover standards of intellectual judgment. But within ten years there were seven new systems of metaphysics; new moral philosophies began appearing. Within twenty years these found their way into novels and plays—for playwrights and tale-tellers are always, it will be remembered, a notable length of time behind fresh currents of philosophical thought. New ideas were again afoot in the educational world, and, so short is public memory, that actually the idea of teaching philosophy seemed itself to be a brilliant discovery. There were still some of the old outcries against philosophy, and in one or two states, Tennessee being one, there was talk of having a state prohibition. But the difficulties of keeping ideas outside a given state frontier were soon seen to be insuperable.

Some innocent people assumed that once philosophy was restored, all would be well, for in an almost hopelessly confused world it was felt not beyond possibility that some young thinker, cutting cleanly through the underbrush of perplexities, would have an answer that would resolve all issues and confusions. But everyone saw soon and plainly that, with slight variation of theme and vocabulary, the old multiple babble of doctrines was back.

"See," said some, "what did we tell you?" And the young people who loved to argue for argument's sake were back at it again, and the phrase-makers and the dialecticians. But, nonetheless, it was patent to almost everyone that things were really better and the country better off. The air was filled with the hint of unexplored possibilities in life and in politics, in education and in art. People were thinking and questioning and searching out rational answers again. The great drought was over. As always, there was no final answer. But the search itself focused people's energies and sharpened their awareness. Once more the infinite sensibilities and alternatives opened up by speculation, in a world that in every generation is too much with us, gave the reader and thinker another world to live in.

Audacious hypotheses again spurred people to try new ways of living and doing and experiencing. Everyone seemed to be on tiptoe for a glimpse of the fresh and the promising and the as yet unexplored. Europeans again began to say: "But westward, look, the land is bright!" No one, not even their propounders, thought these imaginative leaps of thought contained the final truth. But men turned to philosophy, as man had turned to it in the past, for a disciplined dream, a coherent vision of what men might make of the world and of themselves. The more varied the dreams, the more liberated the spirits of men, and the more exciting the vista opened up. Nor did it surprise anyone that some of the freshest speculations came, as they had come in earlier generations, from outside departments of philosophy, from outside universities altogether.

Mature minds found it not unbecoming their maturity to

play with the possibilities, frankly imaginary, that speculations of the more daring thinkers opened up to them. Such play with the infinite once more offered men, amid the oppressions of the actual, "a world elsewhere" in which, if only briefly and on occasion, men may spaciously and soaringly live.

SIX

The Undistracted

THE philosophers of the world have been those who have tried to be clear about what there is to be permanently absorbed in, what there is that one should not be distracted from. At various times in my life—it is an experience that must have been duplicated by others—I have been in contact with a few men who have known what it meant not to be put off the main issue. I have known just a few persons who have been able to resist distraction because they have known what the main issue is, because they have seen a clear road to a straight goal. Perhaps one or two of them have, like the classic mystics, occasionally seen that goal shining direct and immediate before their very eyes. Most of us most of the time are easily diverted because we are by no means certain that the alleged distraction is not after all, perhaps, the paramount thing we have been looking for. That is why so many of us vacillate from one goal to another, from one interest to another, and end up by being simply bewildered, or with a deep sense of having been ultimately defrauded.

I had been reflecting on these matters one winter evening when I lay in bed weakly recovering from an attack of the grippe. In our civilization, at least in cities, an attack of grippe, or rather the aftermath of an attack of grippe, is almost the only time when one has leisure and perspective. One is cut off from the usual commitments, interruptions, distractions. Even the telephone is, perhaps, forbidden. The whole of one's life appears for once unmistakably as the chaotic mélange it really is. All those stresses and pressures one has lived under: what are they for and what do they lead to, what do they mean, even to one's self? The tasks one has set one's self, the ambitions one has become involved in, the stream of society in which one has become immersed? Even the urgent news in the papers seems once removed from reality or significance. It is wartime, but there will be no peace even with victory. Or is it peacetime, and the victory has become ambiguous and the peace more distant than ever?

And for more immediate personal matters: the parties one might normally have felt one was missing seem to be more empty and repetitious than one had realized, and the plays and books one had been meaning to read, the exhibitions one had meant to see, the acquaintances one had hoped to visit, all seem an "expense of spirit in a waste of shame." Not only do the opportunities of life seem less seductive, the responsibilities seem less commanding—one lies languidly, exempt from all imperatives. Nothing is either winning or pressing enough to make one so much as try to rise from one's pillow.

Meanwhile, there is nothing like an aspirin or two—quinine and a hot drink do even better—to start the stream of free association going. With three aspirins, even a modern citizen, adult and metropolitan, finds the operation of fantasy going on within himself. In the usual responsible moments of mature life one would be ashamed to lie pliable to every wind of dream that played across one's imagination. The ever-intrusive telephone alone would be enough to cut short the flights of wish and of reverie. But during and directly after grippe one is protected, and it was during one of these post-influenza periods that the following modern equivalent or ersatz for a vision or a series of visions occurred to me. I offer them with due reservation. They are guaranteed, if at all, only by the integrity of the manufacturer of the aspirin which I used.

It was morning. It was Greece. It was a headland above the sea. The scene strongly resembled that beautiful point near the Mariner's Temple, some three hours from Athens. A Greek approached. He wore a robe somewhat like that familiar to me from pictures on Greek vases. There were, too, the classic sandals. Could it be? I seemed to recognize a figure that looked very much like one I had beheld before. It came back to me. It was in Rome, in the Vatican. This bearded man surely had stepped right out of the "School of Athens" by Raphael, and though his hand was not pointing upward, as Plato's is in the picture, he had the makings of a rapt expression. The brow was, as in the tradition, broad. I was somehow not surprised to hear him speak in clipped, melodious Oxford English, somewhat as Dr. Jowett of Balliol College, Oxford, his translator, might have supposed him to speak.

"I am afraid I am distracting you," he said, smiling.

I almost jumped, more astonished at his divining the theme on which I had been reflecting than at seeing him at all.

"Well, I have been *thinking* about distraction," I said. "But how did you know that?"

"There is," said Plato, "a kinship of the mind, a sense of understanding that lies below the words one uses and beyond the century one lives in. I was correct, wasn't I? You really *had* been thinking about distraction?"

"Yes," I said, "and I had been wondering why there are so few undistracted people in the world—a saint here, a fanatic there, a conqueror there. But most people are lethargic or hysterical. They are a cave of whirling winds, or they are dead calms. They are confusedly excited about everything, and they have clear dedications to nothing at all. They are promiscuously tempted by anything, and they love nothing deeply, or dearly, or well."

"Noncommittal," said Plato, "is, I think, your modern English word for it."

"Yes, exactly, Plato." I blushed, for I was not quite clear as to how I ought to address him. "But you, too, are noncommittal, aren't you?"

"I see you pay attention to what you read, or at any rate to what I write, especially to the way in which my dialogues close," said Plato. "Yes, I suppose I am noncommittal, if you take Socrates' opinions to be mine, as, on the whole, I think you may properly do. But I am not *distracted*. There *is* a difference."

"Well, since you are apparently still in the world, Plato, you must observe now as keenly as you used to do. You are undistracted, Plato, but from what? And how can you remain so?"

"I have been wandering up and down your world a good deal," said Plato, "and I myself have not been observed. I have been on the whole a mere wandering presence; I have been a spirit felt rather than a palpable presence perceived. Sometimes when I have been walking in places touched with poetry or, what is near it, memory, I have heard people, especially young people, say suddenly: 'A spirit haunts this place.' Sometimes I have dropped in on a lecture in philosophy, and at the close of the discourse I have heard some of the listeners say of the speaker: 'The spirit of Plato broods over him.' I have sometimes understood what they meant. But it is not when the professors lecture on my alleged teaching that I most recognize my own spirit. I have felt a kindred soul oftenest when young philosophers have not been talking about my doctrines at all, but when they have been speaking about time and eternity, appearance and reality, with something of the temper in which I might have wished to speak myself. When I have heard in the speaker's tones a hunger for the eternal and a sadness either at the imperfections or the transience of the visual and tactual and audible beauties they have known, then I have felt myself in the presence of a friend in spirit. I have felt myself most intimately present in the thoughts of a writer or a speaker when he least had me or my writings in his mind. I stood over Shelley's shoulder when he wrote:

> The One remains, the many change and pass;
> Heaven's light forever shines, Earth's shadows fly;
> Life, like a dome of many-coloured glass,
> Stains the white radiance of Eternity.

I have recognized friends among the mystics who have felt an Absolute Radiance, and among mathematicians who have been absorbed by the timeless relations of numbers. And they have felt an unseen friendly presence hovering near them. It was I."

I looked at his broad brow, his serene eyes, his modeled hand, fitted, one somehow guessed, to produce proportions in music or in line. Plato was not looking at me, nor, as in Raphael's picture, toward Heaven. He was looking straight ahead, fixedly and quietly, or perhaps looking inward. He seemed to be listening to an unheard music, seeing unseen forms.

"You say you are undistracted," I continued, "and I believe you are and always were. But what makes, what made, you so undistracted in your own time? Surely there were disturbing and unsettling events even then, and private life itself could not have been free from shock, from torment, and from disillusion. The city-state which you knew was full of corruption and menaced by ruthless conquerors both without and within. You saw good men turn bad—there was Alcibiades, for instance—and men full of good intentions, perhaps, but not in the least knowing what the good was, or not knowing how to translate their vision into action. You yourself started with political idealism, and turned to philosophy, I think, out of the shock and disillusion that came with the execution of Socrates, the noblest citizen in Athens. I suspect, moreover, private life was just as filled with crises and disappointments in your time as in ours. You must have seen how others or you yourself, perhaps, were distracted by a growing faintness or weariness in your own soul, by the seductions or the frustrations or the fatuities of the flesh. You saw reforms fail, when you tried them yourself as tutor to a king in Sicily. You saw wars and the equal failures of defeat and of victory."

Plato looked at me and smiled, a little indulgently, a little gravely.

"Only those are distracted," he said, "who live in time; those only are undistracted who live in eternity. For they only can be anxious who live in the suspense of a future sought for precariously and cared for uneasily. It is only in time that there is hope, uncertainty, expectation. Only in time is there a future in which expectation can be disappointed, in which uncertainty can swell into disaster, and dreams become corrupted by actuality. Only those who live *beyond* time are exempt from distraction."

"But surely," I said, "you yourself were not exempt from the more seductive distractions of time. Your writings constantly remind us of the varying succession of the beautiful, the diversity and recurrence of beauties in the constantly shifting here and now. What other writings are fuller than your dialogues of the lovely things in Athens: youths in the first flush of manhood, temples on shining hills, racing steeds, summer noon by the river outside Athens, the buzz of court and market place? No one knew better than you how natural and how absorbing is distraction by the senses. No one could write so exactly and so passionately about all the forms of beauty present to the eyes, the ears, and the fingertips who had not been, shall we say, distracted by them."

"I should be the last to argue," said Plato, "that there is no seduction in the sensuous and passionate surfaces of things, or that I had not myself succumbed to their suasion. One yields to the beckoning arms of appearance. The soul may be corrupted and even destroyed by those material and fleshly beauties which first awaken it. Because I knew all too well in my heart and from my own experience what power the senses have, I felt that there must be some security against them. There is only one guarantee against them: the disciplined awareness of the mind that knows all these beauties are but a passing show. The ordered soul has learned that the whole realm of appearance half veils and half discloses the beauty that does not pass, the good that moth and rust (to use a phrase I have come across in my post-mortal reading) cannot corrupt."

"You mean what the Christian calls treasures in Heaven?" I asked.

"I suppose so, though some of what Christians call treasures in Heaven are earthly enough, I gather," Plato replied. "One of your Christian writers, the author of the Fourth Gospel, seems to have had an inkling of what I mean. I mean, of course, the world of changeless and eternal forms, ultimately of the single absolute good which is a single absolute beauty. It is this which is disclosed to the truly disciplined spirit. The clear mind (possible only to those with a clear heart) perceives the beauty that is the source of all other beauties. The soul is gradually educated so that it comes at last, through an ordering of the senses, of feeling and thought, to a union with Absolute Beauty itself. And though such mystical union with the timeless occurs to very few, very seldom throughout their lives, those with some measure of order in their spirits have a standard by which they measure all things, a goal to which they are addressed, a vision of, or a memory of, beauty and good eternal. It is this by which their lives are given direction. Once one is so absorbed, nothing can prove distracting very long. The beauties of earth become a steppingstone to the beauties of Heaven. Once arrived, there will be no distraction then. Time will have a stop, and with the end of time, there will be no change and variation any more, no conflict, no confusion. There will be no anxiety about a future, for there will be no future; no regret for a past, for there will be no past and no memory of it. One will live in the eternal present. The beauties of earth and of the flesh tempt and taunt us, for we know they will not stay, and even in beholding or embracing them, we feel the inner secret pain of realizing intimately how subtly short of perfection they are. But he who in his ordered heart has an intimation of perfect and timeless beauty will be neither saddened nor gladdened too intensely or too long by the poor transient beauties of earth. He will know better, and he will be steadfast and undistracted in his knowledge, for his knowledge will be vision, and his vision will be that of eternal good. People in all ages have in their mortal moments had such immortal intimations. They have their interludes of temporal life when they are completely absorbed, when there is for them no change, no pause, no urgency, no disappointment; nothing but vision and fulfillment. Men fated, as all men are, to extinction have known such moments in friendship, in art, in knowledge, and in love."

Plato paused. I thought back to those moments in my own life in music, in affection, in drama, in the sudden perception of truth not true yesterday or tomorrow, but in all time, beyond all time. Plato watched my face for a moment.

"There are," he said, "in these days philosophers who call themselves naturalists and empiricists, who do not believe in changeless truth any more than they believe in changeless anything else; in changeless beauty, for instance. And yet even these, I notice—perhaps you are among their followers—feel a nostalgia for what they indulgently call Platonism, a homesickness for what they call 'the myth of the eternal.' Even the devotees of the illusion of progress must at a certain point grow sick of change, and long for a good that endures."

"But surely," I said, "a moment's absorption, however intense and complete, is not eternity. The music that absorbs me now does not last forever, nor do I. That is part of the tragedy, is it not? The moment vanishes and I with it. And even the master works of human genius, themselves, will vanish some day; and the human race, which among some small portion of its numbers worships beauty; and the earth itself, which contains the master works and their lovers, will some day vanish as well. The song ends, and the singer, too, and the listener sooner or later. No "now" lives to become its own hereafter. Perhaps that explains why, because of this sense of transience in the most intense moments of our experience, certain images have such poignant emblematic appeal: the picture of the insect dying in the noonday sun in an orgy of love that ends his little life of a day. One sees why in the Middle Ages, or for that matter in a well-known opera of our modern times [Plato nodded: "Tristan, you mean."] the ecstasy of love and death are identified."

Plato looked at me a little indulgently. "I note that eloquence, or at least rhetoric, exists in your world as it did in mine, though my good Socrates in *The Gorgias* tried to distinguish between the two. I rather liked your metaphor, though; that about the singer and the song. I was very fond, as you know, of myth as metaphor, though I make Socrates pretty careful to distinguish now and then between myth and the literal truth. But let us take your metaphor. The singer may die, the listener may die, but the song does not. The song itself may be lost or forgotten, but not that deathless form or phase of beauty, which, if it is the real thing, and not artifice, it inexpungably is. It is there, forever, in the timeless Heaven of Ideas. The heard song is a transcript of beauty, and so is the score from which it is sung. But the beauty of which the score and the singing are transcripts is deathless because they are out of time. You recognize what I mean, do you not?" said Plato. "Clearly you are one of the homesick ones."

"I recognize what you mean, Plato," I said, "but I am not quite convinced by it. The eternal by definition cannot die. But is 'eternal' anything more than a definition? Eternity, in that sense, is no more than an abstraction, and can abstraction win and hold one's love? As compared to such austere Euclidean beauty, will not the beauties of the world always be more persuasive? I, too, have felt the pang of what, saving your presence in our world, we now call Platonic beauty. But the pang has come intermittently and has not lasted too long. I have been distracted by the more urgent beauties of faces, colors, sounds, the almost painful brightness and glory of persons and things. I have known, too, now and then, something of the mathematical passion for eternity and the peace of knowing it briefly. I have known it in lighting on some idea in its purity or some melody in its line. I have known it sometimes in the midst of daily living. I have felt it on one of those days in midsummer when the sun is high in the sky, when the light seems for the moment to be a steady forever, when there is no wind or sound to indicate disturbance or change, when time itself seems to stand still. There is a steady silence, or a steady uninterrupted hum that is itself almost a silence. One is breathing quietly in what seems an undying noon. You have caught the note yourself, Plato, in your dialogue *The Phaedrus*, and it fascinates Socrates walking by the river Illisus in June.

"But," I continued, "the hum of an eternal noon grows monotonous, and one craves for time itself. One is distracted by the hunger for distraction, like those bred in a city who, after weeks of quietude in the country, crave for the conflicts and excitements and entertainments, even the fret and noise, of the city. If I remember, even Socrates by the Illisus rather wished he were back in the streets of Athens. I notice, by the way, all those urbane rusticators—Horace, for instance—talk of the city almost as much as they do of the country. Eternity, from the little I've known of it, Plato, may be less interesting than it sounds. Is not half the interest of life in the suspense of what is going to happen next? Games and races have thrived on contingency, and where all is vision and fulfillment there is nothing of the thrill of the possible, of *something* (life itself, perhaps) to be gained or lost. And, though I recall how in *The Republic* you scorn those who love novelty for its own sake, I must say one of the things that keeps one tautly alive is the expectation that there may be something new under the sun, a melody one has not heard, a dream one has not imagined, a pattern of light and color never seen or contrived before. I suspect, though you talk so much of the deathless beauty of the changeless, you loved change yourself, Plato. In the *Theatetus,* the dialogue in which you represent Socrates as having just come back from the wars, he inquires whether there is anyone notable for wisdom or beauty among the youths of Athens. And how you pause over the delicious detail of face or form, the unique, the individual (and, I may add, the perishing) looks of men and things! Variety, richness, detail, one would never find those in your geometric eternities."

"Variety, richness, detail," Plato mused. "One needs them in youth, when the senses and the passions are strong and the discipline of the mind is weak. The untutored in painting prefer ornament to design, and lusciousness of color to purity of line. The inexperienced in music prefer the luxurious in orchestration to the clarity of melodic movement. The young in mind prefer the flesh. But with training in perception, with discipline in understanding, comes a love for the form that defines beauty, the line that creates because it limits. The very young wallow in palpable beauty and thrill to the flesh. The older and wiser pierce beyond the surface to the structure and lineaments. They penetrate to the inner beauty by whose surface they have believed themselves moved. You are middle-aged," said Plato suddenly, looking at me sharply, "and I suspect you have already found that the surface of things known through the senses come to be less important and importunate than the firm and fine structure of ideas. And some day, perhaps, you will be led by the things of the mind to that realm beyond mind, pure light and pure being itself, with which you will be rapturously one."

Plato left me rather unceremoniously at this point. Left is not quite the word. He faded gradually into air. He became a luminously clear outline, a geometry of bone. And soon that, too, vanished.

I felt curiously mixed in my emotions. I felt a little illuminated, a little quieted, and not quite convinced. I had had this happen to me before, though I knew not when and could not remember where. Perhaps it was some now remote memory of undergraduate days when—yes, it came back now—there was that great man, Professor Woodbridge at Columbia, who left one, at the close of his lectures on Plato, treading on timeless air, beholding beauty itself, absolute and alone. But I had found in later life that absorption in the eternal was a temporary assuagement. Not cheerfulness, as in Doctor Johnson's story, but the world, as in Wordsworth's poem, kept breaking in. What is the use of telling one's self not to be distracted by the world of time, when time is the very element in which we move? As well tell a fish not to be distracted by the water. Perhaps the best way to be undistracted was to lie here as I seemed to be doing, utterly uncaring for either the goods or evils of the world, not caring about the future, only vaguely regretful of the past. Perhaps the only relief from confusion and defeat was to lapse, as I seemed to be doing now (as the Buddhists recommended trying to lapse always) into Nirvana.

Nirvana, Nirvana, I kept repeating the word to myself until its very sounds, always suggesting dreamless vastness and remoteness, became a hypnosis and a narcotic. Nirvana, Nirvana, I kept repeating the word to myself silently, and yet I could hear its murmurous syllables, which sounded almost like a hushed prelude to silence. There are sleeping pills known as hypnotics, but a word that by both sound and sense suggests sleep, dreamless and endless, is itself a species of opiate. Or phrases or lines of poetry: I tried to think of some. But by now I was so sleepy that I could not think of one, save the beginning of "The Splendors of the firmament of . . ." I drowsed now.

I was really still awake enough to have been, I should think, a little startled by another apparition that came quietly before my eyes, another scene, containing another person as its central figure. It is wonderful how, with a little relaxation of the practical and conventional mind, one is freed from the routine assumption of causes and comes to accept events as a child does, without too much expectation of a clear chain of necessity. The fine graven features of the man before me reminded me somehow of those I had seen on Roman coins in museums. As a matter of fact, I was certain I *had* seen that very face, on just such a coin. The face, though apparently living, looked hieratic and official, as if it were itself a museum piece. The voice that spoke was grave and musical, with a measured cadence, a little bit oratorical and as if it were more accustomed to pronouncing Latin orations than conversing in English. The costume, too, seemed to be that of a Roman military officer. The surrounding landscape reminded me vaguely and dreamily of the Roman campagna.

"Throw away your books; no longer distract yourself," the figure said almost as if he were quoting something, and it came to me that he was doing exactly that—he was quoting himself.

"But I have not been reading," I said. "It is not books that are distracting me or anyone else nowadays, for they are really not much read. It is the world that is disturbing, the people and things in it."

"Busy yourself with few things, and you will be tranquil," said Marcus Aurelius, and I wondered vaguely whether it was himself he was citing now or one of the philosophers to whom, in his *Meditations,* he constantly alluded.

"Well, it isn't as easy as that," I said, "for there aren't quiet spots to retire to any more, and no matter how one withdraws from events, they impinge themselves upon us. Our two world wars have taught us how very convulsing daily happenings can be, even to spirits that are most calm and most retired. I always admired you, Marcus, as a character even more than as a philosopher. For with all the vexations and disappointments of a conscientious and devoted life as an emperor and a husband and a father, you remained serene and calm and unconfused."

"Perhaps I was never quite as much all those things as I allowed myself to appear in my *Meditations,*" Marcus Aurelius replied, "for I was writing those to steady myself, and I put down, I suppose, what I had persuaded myself to believe. It is not hard to suffer chaos when one is persuaded that the chaos is purely superficial. It is possible to suffer even fools gladly, if their foolishness, one is certain, adds up to the wide reasonableness of all things. I remained disturbed by the evils of the world. I tried to feel that the evils were superficial, that all was disposed for the best, and that one could, at least within one's self, live in accordance with the true and clear nature of things.

"It is, I told myself, the illusions that distract the soul, and the chief illusion is the taking seriously and as ultimate what is trivial and purely passing. You remember perhaps that I once wrote: 'Even in a palace it is possible to live well,' and I suspect some of my readers have thought I was trying to be ironic and cynical—far from it. It is really easier to resist pain than it is to withstand pleasure. Instinctively, if one has any character at all, one tries to resist pain, to be a man under the pressure of misery. But pleasures are a subtler form of distraction, for they entice us with delight. I had more experience of and suffered more kinds of defeat in personal life and in war than most men meet. I had more opportunities, too, to be distracted by pleasure. I had experience, also, far more than most men could, of fame. And more and more, as I grew older and wiser to the ways of that large imperial life to which I was so carefully trained, I found out, I believe I truly did, that what beclouds most men and confuses them most is to move among externalities and illusions. They are made unhappy because they have lost something which is in any case illusory or transient, such as the applause of their contemporaries, vanishing and stupid, or the love of their doomed loved ones, or their precarious wealth, or their momentary power. One can be secure against the hurts and blows of loss and disillusion only if one can retire into the citadel of one's own self, to what is incorruptible, to the principle of reason which lies within one's self."

"But, Marcus," I ventured, "all you mean is that reason discovers the unreasonableness of the universe, then, and feels superior to it."

"Surely," Marcus replied, "you could not have read me carefully if you believe that I think all reason can do is to discover the unreasonableness of the illusions men cherish and yearn for and fight for and often die for. No, to be reasonable is to see below the illusions of the parts of things and to become aware, in the very core of the logic of one's own being, that all things, the so-called goods and the so-called evils of the world alike, are phases of universal reason itself, of which one's own reasonableness is a part."

"Do you mean to tell me, honestly, Marcus," I persisted, looking at him, "that merely to contemplate the alleged rationality of the whole universe is enough, while one sees daily all the particular evils in it, the fools and bores and liars and hypocrites one is to meet every day, as you yourself point out? There must have been something more to sustain you. What is the use of believing *everything* in the universe is reasonable if everything one meets in it is absurd?"

The Emperor looked at me and said: "I should have found the universe unbearable if I had not had the sustaining conviction that all in all it makes sense. Of this reasonableness one's own mind is the speaking voice and the rational conscience and consciousness. But I think I know what you mean; it is very hard to believe in cosmic sense in the midst of universal nonsense. I think it was doing my job that saved me from distraction. For I had the comforting conviction that my comfortless job of being an emperor made some coherence in the world, just as Epictetus found some sense in his being a slave. But I could not have maintained faith if I had not kept it fresh and burnished in action. I could not have suffered the outrageous humiliations of trying to be a wise ruler of fools if the task had not fully absorbed me in the details of doing it.

"A great many persons misinterpret my Stoicism as detachment. They forget that I speak again and again of the importance of doing one's part, playing one's role in the universal drama. While one is busy doing it, one can persuade one's self the more easily that it is worth the doing. For one has no time for doubts. And while one is doing one's job, it is far easier to believe that one is part of a universal commonwealth, mystically at one with all other reasonable men who share in the divine reason. This shared participation in the reason of the universe reveals good below apparent evils, order despite the chaos, such as I met at every turn in life and in the empire. I have watched many generations since my own time. I admit I am not so convinced now that the universe is reasonable, but I am more deeply convinced than ever that those alone are undistracted who do whatever they have to do with all their might, and live fully to the extent of their powers, like an eye that sees, a fire that burns, a flower that blossoms. Do not stop to ask yourself what to be absorbed by. Turn inward; examine your own nature, and if you find out what it is that you are, and if you do that which the nature of things meant you to be and do, you will never be distracted any more. And you will find yourself at one with all other reasonable men. Believe me, my latter-day friend, all your distractions come from the external world, from outside yourself. I am sure things must be the same in your time as in my own, for it is my belief now, as it was then, that there are eternal cycles and that there is nothing new under the sun. Now, as in my time, if all goes wrong, or seems to go wrong, it cannot be disastrous to a free spirit, nor can the excitement of success or the images bred of passion be distracting to an independent mind.

"The parallels between your time and mine are truly striking.

The old pattern of civilization, in your time as in mine, is showing signs of disintegration. The terror of war in the civilization of the West came twice in your generation, and, I need not tell you, threatens to come again. There was a strange new epidemic faith in my lifetime. I was mistaken about it, for Christianity was closer to my own beliefs than I realized. But it was, like the new epidemic religion of the communists, a threat to the great religion of established civilization. Educated men today, as in the days of my administration of the Roman empire, are turning as an alternate refuge to philosophy. But many of the voices of the great tradition seem to them to be speaking irrelevantly to their own living problems. And there is, as there was with us, a babble of strange new voices, and one hardly knows which to believe. Men are being asked to be satisfied with the bleak certainties of scientific materialism and the extinction it foresees ultimately for the race. They are being counseled, as we were, to grasp at any exquisite or passing pleasure, but that can hardly suffice for men with a sense of responsibility beyond the moment, nor can even the irresponsible quite enjoy themselves in a world where joy is itself always threatened by the imminent and already actual chaos. Men are being asked now—they were then—to preoccupy themselves with the fine distinctions of higher metaphysics or logic, or with the fine ecstasies of mysticism. But that will not satisfy men in your time, plagued even worse than were my contemporaries with entanglements and commitments of a vast uneasy empire that with you has become a vast uneasy world.

"Only a faith in the reasonableness of the universe, and a busy living in accordance with what one discovers to be one's reasonable place in it—only such a faith and such a steadfast activity in it, only such a conviction of order pervading everything, will enable one to face the disorder in the immediacies of one's life. Only by playing one's part in what seems a deeply reasonable game can one overcome the sense of fraud in one's life and futility in one's experience. A sense of duty saved me; it may save your generation from a sense of frivolity or vanity. And the sense of duty itself makes sense only when it is made part of the logical meaning of the whole universe, that logical order in which all reasonable men do their duty as part of the divine commonwealth. I understand that your generation is organizing a United Nations. We Stoics used to call it the City of Zeus. It is a step toward that order in affairs which approximates slowly the divine order of reality itself. Meanwhile, in your time as in mine, you must do your part toward reasonableness and be brave and tenacious when you are at moments discouraged. The discouragements will pass, and you also. But while you live you can do so as a reasonable man believing courageously against all the evidence in a reasonable world."

By almost imperceptible degrees I found the scene changing to another landscape, and there was another person before my eyes. There seemed to me nothing in the least out of the ordinary in the fact that I was, only a few seconds after Marcus Aurelius's vanishing, on a parched desert strip somewhere in Asia Minor. It looked a little like the country around Damascus which I had once seen. The sun beat down fiercely, and it was a somewhat fierce-looking, bearded, square-jawed, Eastern-looking man with intensely black hair and fanatic eyes who stared at me. But it was not at Damascus I had seen him. I knew just where it had been: at the Alte Pinakothek, now probably completely bombed out, in Munich. He was one of

Albrecht Dürer's pictures and I knew just where he hung on the wall. Yes, sure enough, here was Dürer's St. Paul looking at me intently as he stood there in the arid-looking landscape, mostly sand and a few plane trees, near Damascus. Neither he nor I looked surprised that I should be there.

He began to speak in tones which, if they had not been quite so hoarse—as if he had long been preaching to perhaps hostile crowds in the open air—might have resembled those of a Methodist preacher, full of pious, solemn comfort. His language had more than a trace of the King James version of the New Testament. But he began in words that did not sound like either the Epistles or the Book of Acts.

" 'The world,' " he said, looking at me with extraordinary intensity, " 'is trying the experiment of attempting to form a civilized but non-Christian mentality. The experiment will fail.' You recognize the quotation, perhaps."

It seemed the most natural thing in the world that Dürer's St. Paul should here, near Damascus, be quoting T. S. Eliot to me, though it crossed my mind that Eliot was not the contemporary thinker I should have imagined St. Paul would light upon for quotation. Reinhold Niebuhr, with his sense that the world can be saved only if it first revives a sense of sin, would have been a great deal nearer his line, I should have supposed.

St. Paul continued: "Meanwhile, T. S. Eliot tells us it is the Church that must save the world from suicide. But I think he meant the Anglican Church. There are others who agree with him except that they mean the Roman Catholic Church. Though historically, I should think, if one is to take the Church literally rather than mystically, it is clearly the Eastern Orthodox Church that is in the true order of succession. But I don't think it is by grand phrases or by Church institutions that civilization is to be saved. It is the mystical unity of the Church, not the politico-ecclesiastical institution, that I meant. And it was not civilization—whatever your grandiose modern phrase means—that *I* thought needed to be saved, but the unique, agonized, lost soul of the individual. But you are troubled, dear brother in Christ."

"I am not your dear brother in Christ," I said a little impatiently. "I do not believe in a city not made with hands, nor in a god made by the human imagination."

"But in any case, you *are* troubled," St. Paul said—very gently, come to think of it, considering how rude I had been.

"Troubled as to what it is I am troubled by," I said. "I am bothered by the distractions of this world. We are all led away, as we constantly admit, by triviality and by corruption, but we do not know what is not trivial, what is not corruptible."

"I recognize your plight," said St. Paul, "for I lived in a city not so different from New York as you might suppose. But you know something, yourself, about what Tarsus, my native city, was like. I seem to recall that you once wrote a little book about me, though there have been so many I cannot remember them all. I remember yours, though, for you did me the unusual justice to credit me with a mind. But to return to Tarsus and its resemblance to New York. Tarsus was *full* of distraction, moral, physical, and intellectual. It was the crossroads of the world, it was the point where East and West met, and where, one might say, flesh and spirit met, too. Every vice and every world-view were present in Tarsus, and there were constant temptations to the senses and the mind. Educated men felt, as educated men feel today, and as, in wandering about, I gather that even uneducated men feel, that a civilization is ending.

Greek civilization was ending, as, I gather, European civilization seems to be ending today. Meanwhile, in Tarsus, as in New York in your living day, all the winds of doctrine, all the inherited theories and philosophies and cults and religions, were there to tempt one, to confuse and corrupt. And it is not by ideas only that one was tempted then, nor is it now. The city was filled with all the coteries and cults of depravity as well as of philosophy. There was not an idea, Stoic or Epicurean or Platonic, that you could not find in Tarsus. There was not a delight, however exotic or perverse, that could not be discovered there. The old securities were fast going. The old proud boast and guarantee of being a citizen of a city-state were good no longer. The old consolations and supports of traditional religion, Greek or Roman or Hebrew, seemed valid no longer.

"It is easy to see why people sought escape into some magical salvation. The external world had no security to offer, nor did the philosophers provide any. After all, what did the Greek thinkers have to offer? The Stoics told you that you could be resigned to a reasonable but almost unbearable fate. Epicurus and his followers told you that, in a world where all was uncertain except eventual personal extinction, all you could count on was pleasure, discreetly and temperately indulged in, so that you did not die the sooner. What did the traditional religions offer? That of the Greeks gave you attractive enough pictures of gods living in endless celerity and grace, dwelling in a faraway Olympus. But the gods had neither care nor competence for earthly ills of human and dying beings. And what did my own Hebrew religion promise but a fantastic attempt, doomed to failure, to become righteous by fulfilling every jot and tittle of the Law of God?"

"You are quite right, Paul," I said. "It is not unlike our own world. Neither the pleasures nor the religions nor the philosophies of our time satisfy anybody either, and the choices open are bewildering. The scene is not very different. And we, too, have various vendors with magical schemes of salvation. I gather Tarsus was full of those."

"It was indeed," said Paul. "As in your own civilization, there were all sorts of nostrums from the East, schemes of magical rites and ritual formulas by which, once initiated into the strange cult, you could be saved. People seemed to have above all a horror of dying, a revulsion against obliteration. And there had developed all over the Near East a sort of universal life insurance society for salvation. There were immortal longings in everyone. I grew up in Tarsus and knew what the temptations were, the delights and distractions of the flesh and the spirit. But, as you know, I had a vision later in life on the way to Damascus and I saw at once in a flash that there is only one thing needful, and that there is only one way to be saved. Life is impossible without belief. And you cannot believe very long in pleasure or in any mere idea, or in any mere magic. You must believe not with your mind only, but with your soul. And there was in Tarsus, there is now, only one thing to believe and one thing necessary to believe. That is, in Christ crucified. You have only to believe in Him and have faith in Him, and you will be saved. The world will become as nothing, the flesh as nothing. You will leave carnality and corruption and become one with God in His eternity and His pure being."

"I don't know, Paul," I said, "whether you realize all the difficulties a modern mind has in accepting belief in Christ crucified, to begin with. You, if I may be so bold, before your vision at Damascus, yourself regarded it as a mad blasphemy.

But assuming that belief in Christ crucified is possible and even convincing—it certainly has been convincing to many and is so still—is it true that belief in one's own salvation really cures all other distraction, that all else vanishes away? Does not the passion for salvation, or even complacency in it, become an obsession? Were you not yourself in body subject to seizures, and, if you will forgive me, perhaps in spirit subject to them, too? And might not the same be said of your followers in all generations who destroyed heretics, as perhaps you yourself would not have been unwilling to do, in the name of Christ? Were not the inheritors of your vision, were not you yourself, perhaps, simply substituting another world to be worldly about? Are not the hungerers for salvation distracting themselves by the hope of another world even before life on this earth is over? Heaven, too, can be a corrupting prospect to those who are still alive."

Paul reflected a moment. "I was afraid," he said, "that many of my followers would take me literally, and they have done so for generations, though one would think they could read my words. But perhaps people need an education in Greek philosophy (which I did not have, but caught in the air at Tarsus) to see what I meant by salvation or by mystical union with Christ. How often did I tell them that it was not Jesus in the flesh but Christ in the spirit whom I was preaching? How often did I tell them that not law and ritual, but love, was the avenue by which the fires of the flesh were quenched, and by which one was translated into mystical and eternal union with the divine?"

"Love," I said, "is immensely resourceful and powerful, Paul; but why did you think that love could survive, if you took away its bodily sources, and its fleshly fires? And why, I have never been able to understand, did you think that the flesh, innocent enough, was such a vessel of corruption?"

"Innocent!" Paul's eyes flamed. "There are a few things I did mean literally. The body is death, and the flesh is corruption. And even you who do not call it corruption admit how distracting it can be. It infects even your purest arts and enters into your ambitions which are only apparently sexless. I think not only of those who become obsessed debauchees and who die or disintegrate out of sheer bestiality of sex. I think rather of the way in which sex confuses and torments you all, how it keeps even mature people confused and adolescent. I know there's been a good deal of modern explanation of these matters. Sex is supposed to nourish and color and lend vitality to the spirit. But it is the sign and archetype of death, you can believe me. It is the most crucial phase of man's natural selfishness, and woman's, too, for that matter, the core of the brute, the uncurbed will, the passionate ego. I would, as you may remember, have all live as I did, utterly celibate, though I admitted it was 'better to marry than to burn.' But there is no question in my mind, any more now than there was then, that until man renounces the flesh altogether he will never begin a new life, be a pure spirit, be a being exempt from destruction. Not love and death, as some of your modern poets seem to think, but sex and death, are identical. The flesh is by its very nature doomed to oblivion, and sex is flesh at its most assertive and unregenerate.

"I talked a good deal about sex, because sex was the temptation most current in the world of decay in which I grew up. But I meant something far wider and far deeper by my counsel of asceticism. I meant the power to say 'no' to all the worldliness and fleshliness that corrupts men and confuses them. To deny the world, to refuse the flesh, to mortify the body: it is only when one has separated one's self thus from distraction, that the spirit can shine pure and clear. The history of all the generations since my day have been illustrations of the truth of my doctrine, which is not mine, but God's own truth, vouchsafed to me through Christ.

"Show me a time, show me men and women in whom luxury, worldliness, and carnality are present, and you will show me an age in which authentic life languishes, you will show me men and women in whom spirit dies and is utterly and ultimately destroyed. And where, on the other hand, does one find those human beings who are paradigms of purity and goodness shining like bright beacons in a starless night? They are the saints who have suffered poverty, borne chastity, rejected power and its corruptions, denied their own private flesh and will. Only in such has spirit burned with a pure and deathless flame."

Paul paused, his face glowing with exultation.

"And in your world, to how many saints can you truly point?" he continued. "Most of your generation are tormented by the burden of desire, by the hunger for possession, by the lust for power. I know that the asceticism I preached is no longer fashionable, if it ever was. Nor is saintliness a mode; it rarely has been. Only material greeds, hysterical passions, the drive toward domination, only these have priority among the worldlings who constitute the majority of the world. The will of man on earth has always asserted itself over against the will of God. One would think that by this time men would have learned that only in God's will is peace. Instead they have followed their own will, and they wonder why there is no peace in their time. You devise all kinds of plans and schemes and leagues of peace and societies of nations. But until the private will is denied, until all men become brothers by being united in the mystical love of men for one another and of God, through whom in spirit they are one—until this transformation of men occurs, there will be no peace, either in the world or in the souls of men. Only when men have learned to transcend their wills and their bodies will they cease to be distracted, will they become one in themselves, and, by being one with one another, one with God; or (for it is the same thing) by being one with God, one with one another."

While Paul had been speaking of the evils of lust, greed, and the drive for power, his face had been a fire of hate. But his expression had changed now, and his eyes were a glow of pure love. The face soon vanished altogether, and only the glow remained. And that, too, soon faded into nothingness.

"Universal love," I murmured faintly, "universal sleep." And for what seemed quite a long while, I lay languidly half dreaming. I meditated, if so drowsy a brooding can be called meditation, upon the possibility of a new civilization, new chiefly because it would rest on a hitherto untried principle of human fellowship. I mused upon a society where all men might be bound together not simply by the necessities of fate, but by the mystical bond and willing chain of love. Men would then, and only then, be indissolubly united with one another, for gone would be the sharp divisions and the mutual destructiveness brought about by private lusts, personal greeds, the individual grasping for power. Mankind would not be distracted from universal justice by the distorting affections of class or family, or national or physical obsession. Men would be melted from their hard combativeness into a cosmic ecstasy of brotherhood.

These vague mystical apocalypses went through my mind, or at any rate my consciousness, like a vast choral climax of a romantic symphony. I almost heard, as a combined crescendo and obbligato to my thought, Beethoven's "Hymn to Joy" at the close of the Ninth. But like all crescendos, this one, too, died away, and left a sudden emptiness. What, I asked myself, would be left of each soul, if it melted into a universal orgy of brotherhood? How could one be one's self at all, if one were to lose one's self in a vast soft bog of world-wide affection? How could a radiant affirmation of joy and love in any case emerge out of the nay-saying to life that came from a bleak lifelong asceticism such as that counseled by Paul?

As I thus more mused than thought, I felt rather than saw a face that looked at me both gently and seriously.

I was standing now before a modest little house in The Hague. From a window on the ground floor there looked at me a face I recognized at once, the grave, saintly face so familiar from the steel engravings of it, the countenance of the philosopher whom the orthodox called an atheist, and whom Novalis called a God-intoxicated man. How lucky, I thought, that I had once lived in Holland for a season and understood Dutch fairly well. Spinoza beckoned to me to come in. I walked into the modest, almost bare room, and for some reason what most caught my eye were three slender white flowers in a white vase on a green baize-covered table. Spinoza, who was rather pale, coughed a little as if in some pain. He motioned me to a chair. I could not help noticing how pale and wan he looked.

"It is very kind of you to ask me in," I said.

"I had a feeling," he said, "that you were, perhaps without even knowing it, looking for me."

"In a way I have been," I said. "At least I've been talking with some of your predecessors about themes that were always on your mind, too. I've been talking with Plato and St. Paul and Marcus Aurelius."

"I am indebted to them all," said Spinoza, "and to the Old Testament prophets who have taught you as well as they have taught me. But in the long run one must think these matters out for one's self. If faith were enough, I should never have criticized the Jewish tradition nor been excommunicated by the Synagogue."

"Well, you have certainly thought these matters out, not only better than most men, but, as the philosophers are coming to recognize, better than most philosophers. You of all thinkers were utterly clear as to what the good is, the certain and indubitable good, and very lucid indeed (though not easy) as to what is the most certain way of attaining it. I used to know by heart the whole passage about the goal and your method in the essay *On the Improvement of the Human Understanding.* I can still quote parts of it in the English translation: 'After experience had taught me that all things which frequently take place in ordinary life are vain and futile; when I saw that all the things I feared and which feared me had nothing good or bad in them save insofar as the mind was affected by them, I determined at last to inquire whether there might be anything which might be truly good and able to communicate its goodness, and by which the mind might be affected to the exclusion of all other things. I determined, I say, to inquire whether I might discover and acquire the faculty of enjoying throughout eternity continual supreme happiness.'"

"I wrote that when I was quite young," Spinoza said, "and I fancy that many another philosopher began in much the same way. I suspect that most men when they begin to be reflective about life begin, as I did, by being dubious about the distractions of the world, and yet are not willing to give them up until they can be sure of something patently less illusory. Have you not gone along a similar path? Do not men of your century, all the more sensitive and meditative ones, go necessarily along a familiar road? Men's nature and the nature of things are the same in all generations; the path of men in their reflective search for the good in essence must be always the same.

"I judge you found a certain wisdom in the passage you have been quoting, and that you felt a fellowship with truth. Whenever we admire a paragraph by a philosopher, is it not because we admire what we have been silently, and perhaps unbeknownst to ourselves, wishing to say to ourselves?"

"Yes, Mynheer," I said warmly, "I did recognize a fellow truth and a permanent one. I recognized it in that curious way timeless truths have, of seeming suddenly of a peculiar and poignant timeliness. The truths are, as I have learned from you, always the same; they are innocent of our anxieties and our disasters. But certain kinds of experiences make it easy for us, as we say, to 'realize' them. It is clear why we now appreciate the emptiness of what you long ago saw was empty, for you, too, lived in an anarchic and revolutionary generation. I suppose we did not really need two wars in one generation in our time to become aware of the vacuity, the precariousness, the transience, and the absurdity, of wealth and position and fame and of purely sensuous pleasures. But the drastic spectacle of two wars (and it was only a few for whom war could remain simply a spectacle) helped us to see in brutal fact the lessons we had been taught in books by wise men from Ecclesiastes down. Two world wars taught the most secure and the most arrogant of us that if wealth and pleasure and fame are all we care for, these can all vanish. And even before they go, the world may press upon us so that our taste and enjoyment of them may be gone, before we or they are ended. But, as I said, one doesn't need a war to discover these things. It is easy enough to persuade even (perhaps especially) the most fortunate men in any generation to disillusionment with what they have held to be their dearest goods or possessions or enjoyments. It is harder to persuade, and impossible, I should think, to convince, them that there is a good, as you put it, difficult and rare, to which they may attain and which is less illusory than those they have left."

"But there is such a good," Spinoza said quietly, "and I thought you admitted that I had been clear as to what it is. But perhaps you have forgotten, or have confused it with notions of philosophers other than myself. You professors know so many systems (and often know nothing else), that I am not surprised that you mix them up. Where philosophies are mere words, the words easily become mumbo jumbo, or are altogether forgotten. I will take the liberty of reminding you: The only and the ultimate good is the union of one's own nature with the nature of things. It is not easy to understand what that means, I know, though if you read my *Ethics* carefully, I do think it is clear, even if difficult. But it is not enough that people understand it, they must feel it. And they will not be able to feel it until they do understand and have so affixed themselves to the eternal, to the true, nature of things that they are freed from bondage to temporality, to change, to illusion.

"Only when they have the perspective of eternity will they be free from the partial and provincial perspectives to which their passions attach them. 'Ripeness is all,' your English Shakespeare says. One ought not dare to paraphrase him. But I can't help thinking that what he meant could equally well be stated: 'Wholeness is all.' Wholeness of one's own soul, and an uncorroded oneness with the wholeness of things. You have correctly divined that distraction is the great enemy of wholeness, and that distraction comes because of that incomplete view which is a failure of reason. A Greek long before my own time saw the problem: 'To see life steadily and to see it whole.' Matthew Arnold was correct in thus defining Sophocles' ideal. But to see it steadily is to see with the intellectual eye, with the vision of reason. It is to see the chain of causes and consequences, it is to be one within one's self, and one with the one divine order of reason. It is error, partiality, incompleteness of vision, or partiality of passion, that makes the distractions of the world."

"Sometimes, Mynheer Spinoza," I said, "thoughts of you come into one's head when one is listening to moral systems or moral counsel that have a quite different vocabulary and a quite different origin. There are epidemic in our society at the present time (though you may not have come across them in your wanderings), a species of doctors of the spirit known as psychoanalysts. They have a kind of therapy which consists in no small measure of taking their patients out of their private worlds, their neurotic personal complexes, and gradually leading them to recognize the realities of their own nature and of the inescapable public world. They help them to persuade or convince themselves through the freed logic of their own utterance to live in consonance not with their own fantasies (which lead them to disaster), but with their own actual natures and the true nature of things."

"Very interesting," said Spinoza, "what you say about the freed logic of utterance. Are they led step by step by geometric proof, the only kind of proof really, to see what their own natures are and the nature of things also?"

"I don't pretend to understand it completely," I said to the philosopher placidly regarding me, "for the language of this new science—if it is a science—is not altogether clear. The patients arrive ultimately, I am told, when the cure is successful, at something very near what you prescribe as an ideal. They contemplate reality and are free from bondage to illusion. But they are not required—some of them would be thoroughly incompetent (and the doctors, themselves, who cure them would be incompetent)—to follow the arduous geometric method of your *Ethics*. It is the language of your book, by the way, that I fear has driven off many who might be most benefited by it. 'The best things,' as you yourself remark at the conclusion of the *Ethics*, 'are as difficult as they are rare.' "

"I never suggested," Spinoza said, "that liberation from the bondage of passion is easy, and the path of reason is notoriously an arduous one."

"But it is something more than the difficulties of mathematical method that has put people off, my dear philosopher," I said. "You make the good life itself a mere abstraction, and are not abstractions to most human beings oppressive and forbidding? An equation is not particularly winning or glamorous. What you seem to recommend is a sort of mathematical equation of the mind with the order of things. The order of ideas and the order of nature, you say, are one. The perfect philosopher is like a geometer perfectly understanding geometry, and at last becomes identified with the proofs he understands. But we are not all perfect philosophers, even those of us who have a touch of philosophy in us. It is easy to distract adolescents from the propositions of Euclid to the play of sunlight on the schoolroom desks, or to the drawings they make in their notebooks, or to the smiles and whispers of their neighbors. It is easy to distract adults, too, from the strict but bleak order of necessity to the warmer human incidents of the flesh and the world."

Spinoza looked at the white flowers in the tall vase on the table.

"But surely you remember," he said, "that I never anywhere suggest that emotion could be replaced by the intellect. I explicitly point out that an emotion can be replaced only by another and more powerful one. You call the ultimate good toward which my ethics points an abstraction. But is it, really? The union of one's whole clarified being with the whole of nature—that surely is not an abstraction. Nature is the whole of things, living and inclusive. The act of union with it is not an abstraction. It is an act of the most perfect realization, of the greatest vitality. The discipline by which one arrives at that union is intellectual, surely, for it is mathematical, and mathematics is the only avenue to true certainty. But the *fruit* of that discipline is not intellectual; it transcends intellect. It is life become completely whole, completely alive: experience, usually stumbling and blurred, becomes perspicuous as sunlight; action is transmuted to pure and radiant contemplation. It is the blessedness of insight. It is not intellect, halting and argumentative; it is an act of beholding, of clarity achieved and enhanced by love. It is the intellectual love of God. It is the rapt realization of, the rapturous merging with, nature. When we love a part of the whole, and love with partiality and fanaticism, we are distracted. Only when we see the whole and are one with it, are we at peace. Our life has become pure understanding, our understanding has become pure vision, our vision has become pure oneness with that Nature which, completely understood, is the whole substance of our knowledge, of our love, and of our transfigured selves. We have passed by way of the mind from time to eternity. And such a passage is possible in any era, however chaotic, for the chaos is chaos only to the imperfect intelligence. Properly understood, all is order, and if his soul is ordered, any man can, even in the most warlike and violent of times, be at peace."

The scene faded, and I and the room with it, and my own awareness. I seemed to be in a kind of nothingness again. Somehow by this time I expected another figure to appear, but here I was in my room at home, back in the world of the lingering slow time of convalescence. When my doctor, a former pupil, appeared that day, I asked him whether it was one of the properties of aspirin to give people complicated dreams. I remarked that such dreams always came to me after a tablet or two. I'd like to tell him of a long one I had had last night. There seemed to be a lot of grippe about town, and he said he had not time to listen. When I attempted to tell him the dream was philosophical—"Just your lecture notes," he said, "going through your head, and remember I once took your courses."

I waited until the following night with uneasy anticipation. I was quite sure my philosophical visions would in some form continue. They did; it seemed almost the instant I went to sleep, though I am informed by experts that one dreams chiefly just before awaking.

This time I strayed into a hotel dining room in Frankfurt in Germany. Sitting at the table alone was a rather moody, cold-looking, middle-aged man whose features I at once recognized. Sitting by him was a black poodle dog whom he looked at with an affection that contrasted with the glances of obvious disdain he cast at the other human beings in the room. The waiter placed me at the table next to his, and I kept on looking at him, but did not quite have the courage to address him, though I knew who he was beyond any doubt, and was sorely tempted. He seemed to be ordering an elaborate dinner with a great deal of care and a good deal of cautious apprehension.

"Be sure the fat is taken off the soup," I heard him say to the waiter. I watched my neighbor for a few moments and then I could refrain no longer.

"You are," I said with that directness and audacity one sometimes has in dreams, "Herr Artur Schopenhauer."

His look seemed to be mingled of vanity at being recognized, and of annoyance at being interrupted. "I am," he said, "but what is that to you?"

"I have long been a reader of your works."

"Millions have been," he said, "and often for the wrong reasons. They get an easy luxury of grief out of my work. But are my books read any more in your generation? My guess, frankly, is that they are. But I suspect most of those of my contemporaries are not. Does anyone still read that old pretender, Hegel, that pompous ass who thought history came to a culmination in his own philosophy, and that all evil dialectically transmogrified itself into the good?"

"No, Hegel is not much read," I said, "but of course *you* are widely read. I suppose you are one of the few philosophers whose works are sold at railway stations and in drugstores in cheap reprints."

"I imagine my philosophy has its healing properties," Schopenhauer said. "It has the saving power of truth at any rate; it helps people cut through the illusions by which they are possessed most of their lives. Are people as susceptible to illusions in your time? And are they as little aware of what it is that disturbs and destroys them?"

"People *are* distracted in our time," I said, "and they are seeking an escape, but they don't know exactly from what it is that they wish to escape, nor what it is that they wish to escape to."

"Naturally they don't know what it is from which they wish to escape," Schopenhauer replied. "They try every pleasure in turn, and are sated with it, and yet they return to try again, hoping this time, perhaps, ecstasy will last and not leave a bitter aftertaste. Or they try new pleasures only to have them turn to identical dust and ashes. They vaguely feel they wish to escape from boredom, from disillusion, from pain. But when they are free from some pain from which they suffer (or think they suffer) there is an emptiness of dullness, of no feeling at all. When they escape from one boredom it is but to see—and very rapidly—a new pleasure turn to an equal ennui. Look," he said, pointing to the respectable bourgeois crowd (I vaguely had a sense of the scene being somewhere about 1850) dining in this room. "They're comfortably well off, most of them, with no financial worries, with no miseries; but watch them, especially the husbands and wives, bored to death with each other and with the world. They were young lovers once, some of these couples, eager and ardent. And when they were young the men, here, had ambitions and in many cases their ambitions have been fulfilled. But their love has turned to habit and dullness, and their achievements, even, have no savor to them.

"Sometimes they escape, secretly, into vice and orgy, sometimes into drink. Once in a while you read of a happy, successful, domestically serene gentleman simply and suddenly disappearing. And he turns up, one hears, on some distant tropical shore. He seeks escape from civilization, from his accustomed life, from his familiar dullnesses, from his lifelong small anxieties. Sometimes one reads of the suicide of those who cannot face either the pains or the disappointing pleasures of life any longer, and a tiny thrill of envy is mingled with one's horror or pity. But often, their whole lives long, these persons do not realize what it is from which they seek escape."

"Aren't they trying to get away from the sense of vanity?" I said. "They all echo Ecclesiastes' theme: 'Vanity, all is vanity.' The overwhelming sense of futility is what distracts them and perhaps drives them on, as we say, to distraction."

"But their mistake," said Schopenhauer, "as I pointed out in *The World as Will and Idea* (a book, incidentally, for many years scorned by the professors, although I notice they have for a long time now been treating it quite seriously in their foolish academic lectures)—their mistake is that they have not found the source of the trouble. They blame the world, they blame luck, they accuse the disappointments of the flesh and the disillusions of the spirit. But they never stop to see that it is something most intimately in themselves by which they are distracted. It is their will which distracts them; it is their own desire from which unknowingly they are trying to escape. I think what the professors could not forgive in me was that I rejected their pompous idealism, their genteel optimism. I told human beings to face frankly the torment to which they were condemned, to recognize the perpetual oscillation between the pain of desire and the frustration of boredom and disillusion. I pointed out that as long as men allow themselves to assert their own will, their own desires, the world will remain a perpetual distraction to them. They will move from pleasure to pleasure in a perpetual cycle of hunger and satiation, of lust and satiety, of ambition and empty success. They will, almost like parodies of Midas, see everything they touch turn to dust."

"I remember, Herr Schopenhauer," I said. "No one has ever painted a more convincing picture than you have done of the emptiness of worldly success—though you always appeared to enjoy it; of the futility of carnal desire, about which you knew something, too, in your youth; of the endless longing for fulfillments that could never fulfill. And I know how plausible it seems to say that the way to escape unhappiness is to give up the desire for happiness. The way to be at peace is to cease to desire. But I was never quite convinced—I never thought you yourself were—that one could simply cease to desire. Nor was I ever persuaded that if one ceased to desire, the whole world with all its spectacle of misery and disillusion would disappear."

"I know," Schopenhauer replied, "it is the fashion now to say the will is an incident in the world, instead of the world's being, as I am convinced, a mirage which the will, cunningly aided by the brain, has contrived in the foolish hope of satisfying itself. I won't debate that point with you now. But surely you will admit, for you seem a cultivated man, that the will does find temporary assuagement in the blessed moments, brief enough, I admit, of the arts."

"I admit that one does even in an ugly world, or perhaps especially in an ugly one, enjoy the arts," I said, "but surely that does not mean that the will has ceased to assert itself. There are many unhappy aesthetes."

"Nonetheless, have you not yourself noticed," said Schopenhauer, "how, in standing before a picture in a museum, if you are really absorbed by the lines and the colors, you are at rest? You cease to be tormented by the disappointments of the past, or disquieted by the anxieties of the future. You are at one with what you behold; temporarily you are at least not unhappy, and you are, however briefly, for once tranquil, which is as near in ordinary life as one can come to felicity. You are neither filled with desire nor satiated with fulfillment. For these moments at least you, as we say, look at things disinterestedly. That still life before you is not fruit you hungrily crave to eat. It is line, color, and form, beheld for its own pure sake. If only we could look at life always as we look at pictures sometimes, we should be free from distraction. We should be at peace. We should be contemplating, somewhat as Plato imagined, essence, not in time and space, but eternal forms themselves. In beholding works of art, for those times at least, we have knowledge, not illusory knowledge trumped up by the fevered interest of the will. We know *not* that partial aspect of things which feeds the illusions and disillusions of desire; we rather have come to see forms in their timeless eternity. We see the changeless realities to which the genius of the artist has penetrated, and which for the absorbed beholder are present briefly also. We have lovely interludes of art in which the will is quieted, and contemplation is a tranquil moment of felicity. Surely those pauses of disinterested contemplation come to a fortunate few in your time, too?"

Despite the vague sense I had that I was somewhere in the 1850's, I yet had a deeper sense that I had not come into Schopenhauer's age, but that he had strayed into our own. "There is a good deal of talk in our day of art as an escape from the pressures and grimnesses of reality," I said.

"Rather the pressures and grimnesses of mere appearance,"

said Schopenhauer, "for the work of art brings you a revelation, brief though the revelation may be, of the reality of changeless forms which the artist has been able to envisage and to embody. You are quite right when you say people are lost in distraction. But reality is never distracting; it is the shadow that bewilders, and in the relatively few moments that we have of penetrating to reality in works of art, we are quieted. The world itself is but a projection of our desires; and when our desires cease, the world vanishes, and all the anxieties that come from involvement in it.

"Art is a chance to quiet the will, for an instant at least, to quit for a lucid moment the illusory world of things and time and space and apparent necessity. It is true enough that in the experience of art we escape from the world. But it is true, as I think you English-speaking people like to put it, in a Pickwickian sense only. The world itself is but a projection of our desires, and if we cease to will, the world that has tormented us with its many facets of seduction—that world is dead, and we dead to it. It were better if we could deny the will altogether, but that is an act of heroic renunciation it is not possible for most of us to achieve. It is a drastic *volte-face,* possible only when a sympathy infinitely widened turns us from willful brutes to selfless saints. It is for the morally gifted: in the West, alas, very few. But the arts are winsome even to the most assertive wills. Men of action, men of lust, are given pause by the beautiful suasion of art. In those occasional pauses of perception and sensibility we are released. Men of reflection, too, who are, when they think, troubled by all the ironies and contradictions and defeats of existence, find a solace, a *temporary* asylum, mind you, in art. For in art even defeat and tragedy themselves become pictures to be beheld, poems to be read, fictions to be followed for the sheer peace and delight of their essence and their form. Nothing hurts, for our will is in abeyance and cannot be roused or touched or disappointed. All, even the tragic, becomes beautiful. Beauty is the anodyne of the will, and art is the momentary flight from time, the rapt instantaneous glimpse of eternity."

Did I only imagine it, or did I actually see Plato standing silently over Schopenhauer's shoulder as he spoke these last sentences? And it could not have been purely coincidence that Schopenhauer should say at that exact moment: "You recall my saying in my great work"—he used the adjective quite naturally—"*The World as Will and Idea,* that it was Plato from whom I learned this truth."

"But you did not quite think art a permanent cure, a secure escape, did you?" I asked. "Nor is it, really; the absorption ends, the trance is over. One leaves the gallery and goes out into the restless traffic of the street. The concert concludes, one puts down the book, and the surcease (I seem to remember you admit as much) is over. I haven't noticed that those with the keenest aesthetic sensibility or the widest artistic interests are the happiest. Surely the contrast between the ideal forms of art and the ugliness and disorder of the actual world of daily experience constitutes a great source of unhappiness. Aesthetes have tried the path of art for art's sake in our own society. They have always returned to find it was the same old world, made none the better during their truancy. The irresponsible *precieux* of our civilization woke up twice from their opiates to find that the world was in the flames of war. And even in personal lives, the escapes into art solve no problems, cure no ills, bring only a temporary peace."

"I am no fool in these matters," said Schopenhauer sharply,

"and I hardly needed to have so late a comer as yourself teach me something that I myself have taught. There is only one permanent cure, one radical escape: that is to deny the will altogether. The path to Nirvana—the Buddhists knew it long ago—is the only escape from the inevitable burden of suffering, the penalty of sensibility. Happiness is impossible. It is a delusion of the uncurbed young, of the untamed will. The most that can be hoped for is inner peace, and that can come only when the self is ruthlessly expunged, the will firmly extirpated. To desire no longer is no longer to be. And only when one has merged one's self with non-being itself, only when one has one's self become nothingness, can one cease to be troubled by anything, by otherness. A dreamless sleep—that is the only perfection human beings have ever imagined truly, or that they have any possibility of attaining. The arts do not give us a dreamless sleep, but they enable us to live for a moment in a quiet dream of perfection, golden, clear, and free from the corruption of desire."

"The aesthete and the ascetic are then quite close in spirit," I ventured.

"Quite so," said Schopenhauer. "It takes some renunciation to see clearly, to behold cleanly, to see things in their own terms, for their own sake. The will must be, if not renounced, at least suspended, and practical interests transcended. In the midst of life the rare high moments of artistic experience enable us to step out of life and for the time being become liberated from its pressures. The true lover of the arts has escaped (insofar as he is a true lover) gross passions and vulgar tensions. Don't be misled by the fact that a great many people who gossip about the arts and move in what are called artistic circles seem, and often are, gross, vain, lustful, greedy. The arts, too, have their false adherents, and their politicians and their entrepreneurs. I am speaking of the authentic beholders, the genuine art-lovers, not the fashionable camp-follower of the arts. Only in contemplation is there freedom, and only works of art persuade those at least with trained eyes and ears to pause and behold. For once in a way the demands of action, the commands of the practical, are transcended. This immediate beauty is for the moment a man's absolute and intrinsic good. For the moment of beholding this rare form, this radiant light, he ceases to ask: What can this do for me? What does it threaten or promise? He demands nothing of life, he wills nothing, he is vulnerable to nothing. He is the soul of absorption, and while so absorbed, nothing can confuse or becloud or distract him."

"Well," I said, "there is hardly a doubt that art has been an intermittent salvation for the disturbed and bewildered in this world, though, as you may have gathered, if you have seen any contemporary art, there is enough to disturb and bewilder in art these days as well as in life. Painters seek to capture the very tone of chaos and writers the language of dream and hysteria. The classic clarities of art, of Greek sculpture, and of Greek tragedy, are your favorite instances of the golden peace you idealize. But modern painting and modern literature are hardly the realms to turn to for peace, even intermittent peace —nor, for that matter, modern music either."

"Music," Schopenhauer replied, "was always a different story. And I am not surprised to observe how favorite an art it is of your neurotic generation. For in music, as I once remarked, it is you yourself who are tortured with the strings. The will sobs most patently and poignantly in music; at least insofar as one is identified, one's self, with the music, one's own will is for the time being quite quieted and one surrenders to the will in nature, to the profound and blind desire in all reality. An adequate symphony, I have often thought, would be the most adequate metaphysics, for the will in nature would be overheard in the tensions, the risings and fallings, the developments and the crises and resolutions, of a symphony or a sonata. Perhaps modern music does peculiarly catch the note of reality. Its discords and dissonances, its broken melodies, its shattered harmonies—these are the very essence of the nature of things, the blind frustrations of the reasonless desire, the futile reiterations of the will always doomed to futility. Perhaps the music of your day is something like the music I have been waiting for. But, from the little I have heard of it, there is something missing: the touching quality of song, the poignance of feeling. It is the geometry of tragedy rather than the heartbreak of it that these cerebral young composers have caught. But if ever the great musician comes, he will have caught the very tone of world sorrow itself, and of human fatality, and in listening we will become one with it and our own little tragedies will find their fulfillment in transfigured union with the tragedy of all things."

"Ah, Herr Schopenhauer," I sighed, "there is, then, only one way out of distraction; that is, by giving up altogether the hopes, the yearnings, the desires, which give life its momentum and its excitement? The only way in which to be undistracted, I gather, is to give up personality altogether, to lose it in mysticism, or in music, or in art, to surrender one's own very being? —for it is quite true we are most ourselves when we are most desirous."

"Yes," said Schopenhauer, "and I am not surprised that a member of the modern world finds it so terrible a thought to give up one's own will. We hug ourselves to ourselves, we surround ourselves with veils of illusion. If the veils are torn away, and we are left embracing our own horrid tortured will, we think if the will, too, goes, there will be nothing. There will truly be nothing of illusion left. There will be nothing but nothingness, there will be peace. Isn't that what you, all of you in your generation, have been looking for, in the world, in yourselves? I have given you a way of finding it, and you shudder. In the West you resent this saving wisdom; perhaps some day you will learn from the East how to find it, to accept it, to find in it a quiet glory with which you will with pure and sacrificial passion merge yourselves."

I cannot say that the philosophers from among the illustrious dead continued to appear in my dreams. As I recovered my strength, the habit of fantasy ebbed. In the broad daylight world, in the pressure of ordinary affairs and the usual round of responsibility, one has no chance to indulge in musing conversation with the great deceased. One is too preoccupied with necessary or delightful conversation with the obscure and, once in a while, with the illustrious, living. But while, back at work at the university, I had not much time for musing—college teaching might improve if one did have leisure for such a free play of the spirit—I continued to be haunted by the themes that my shadowy interlocutors had broached in my aspirinate dreams. The busier I began to be, the more I resumed my contacts with other people no less busy, the more I kept asking myself what it meant to be undistracted, and who among my friends and acquaintances might be so described.

Well, there was, for one, Maria, who kept house for me, who kept faithfully to her duties to her God and her Church and to her job, who, without being very clear as to what was the ultimate good, was not confused by reflection upon the competing or the dubious excellences of life. Maria for one was undistracted. But Maria did not pretend to do any wide systematic or analytic thinking. Among my colleagues in academic life there were a few who did not insist on reflecting on the ultimate, partly because they assumed they had found it. These were men working in some very special field of knowledge. Their work and their families gave them a pattern and a stability which they never seemed to question. They never once asked ultimate questions, perhaps because those were not questions susceptible of scientific solution.

But among my friends in what are commonly called the humanities, the difficulties were more apparent. For them there were no clearly first or final things. They wavered between competing systems; they were blown about by contrary winds of doctrine. They were not certain that what they were doing was education, or, if it was, that it was worth doing. Among the publicists I knew, many of them learned, and all of them serious men and women, there, too, I found no clarity as to what were the purposes of society or of themselves. I was still haunted by the desire to find out what were the first things which various people I knew really put first; but I had come to the conclusion that for many men and women in our generation it was no use speaking of putting first things first, because no one would admit that he knew what things were first, or why he would place certain ones foremost.

I say I knew no one who had a sense or a conviction of something paramount. That is not quite true. I have formed the habit of watching my friends, and occasionally, at unguarded or unexpected moments, they will declare or reveal or diffidently admit what they do regard as ultimate. It really is not quite possible to get a man's views of the world by asking him point-blank what they are. In these days it is possible to get a man's views on Russia by asking what they are—because, while Russia is central enough in all conscience for the future of mankind, it seems more remote than a man's own immediate soul, and he will glibly toss out his favorite current clichés. But a man's deepest convictions are not generally elicited by a question, at least not by a question bearing directly on the point. No Gallup Poll will ever evoke the central convictions of America on the intimate concerns of the American psyche. But occasionally people do reveal what they regard as paramount and what keeps them from being distracted. It may take a long life of acquaintance to chance upon an occasion that will prompt a man to say what his views are. Sometimes, if two people meet in a remote place or in a crisis in the life of one of them, one may find out these things in the first half hour of conversation, as I did once from a young English lord when we were both caught in a bad storm in the interior of Sicily. His mask of good breeding dropped, and in the terror of despair appeared a frank avowal of an absolute inner emptiness of life. I was not surprised to read in the papers a year later of his suicide.

I had for a long time tried to guess what were the views of life of Mr. Talbot, the eminent financier I happened to know, who, as it also happened, had a taste for philosophy and for general ideas. Most of his political ideas one could predict from his fiscal interests and his personal associations. He was inclined, though a progressive enough spirit, to fear socialization of industry, and he believed with quiet sincerity in the system of free enterprise which had brought him, in the typical

American success story of an earlier generation, to the financial top. He was, not in the routine sense, one of our conquerors. He had a high sense of public duty; he exhibited none of the traits of a "robber baron," and I would not have expected ever to have him say in so many words that what absorbed him was *power*. I don't think, at the time he said it, he expected to say it, or so emphatically. That is why, I think, when he did speak, he seemed to be uttering what was most deep in his heart and character. And it was a heart and character that I had long admired, not least because Mr. Talbot seemed quietly at one with himself, not hard in any invidious sense, but hard as tempered steel is. I had a notion that he had not much use in his vocabulary for words like loneliness and regret or confusion or, my obsessional word, distraction. I had always felt it would be interesting to know what really was the *first* thing in Mr. Talbot's scale of values. I heard him declare what it was, quite offhand but with evident sincerity and gravity, over brandy and coffee in his paneled library one night after a dinner party.

Someone had just said, as he complimented our host upon the Napoleon brandy, "A good cognac certainly brings out the values of life."

"Perhaps our philosopher here could tell us something about that," said our host politely.

"Professional philosophers define values rather glibly," I said. "I should rather hear what a man of affairs like yourself thinks. Not about the theory of value—I read enough of that in the journals—but about what is valuable, and what is, above all, valuable to you in *your* life." I knew enough about Mr. Talbot to know that he would not say, nor did he actually believe, it was wealth. Millionaires generally do not, or do not consciously, hold such a belief.

"Well," said Mr. Talbot, who had apparently been reading my thoughts, "you might think a person like myself, who has been engaged in various forms of finance most of his life, would think the chief value of life is wealth. Mind you, I am not belittling possessions [and as I had looked around that noble mansion with its superb and expensive paintings, its Oriental rugs, its antique silver and eighteenth-century furniture, I thought it was just as well he didn't], but I think most of us, if we were honest, would answer that the chief value of life for us is the exercise of power. I confess that when I face myself in an attempt at honesty sometimes, I think that is what has absorbed me most. I have done a certain amount of good works and have, perhaps, given away a certain amount of money in the interest of good causes. But I would be lying if I said that I was not particularly pleased by seeing the sometimes beneficent differences that I, personally, could make. This check means a new building at my university, that endowment means that a serious scholar can work at a specialized project that even a first-rate institution has not the money to afford. I have seen, by a stroke of my pen or by a word from me at a committee meeting, a small vanishing New England village turn into a thriving little manufacturing town. I have been able to free a poet for a year to produce a classic long poem."

"But your exercise of power is beneficent," I said. "And are you not perhaps blackening yourself falsely when you say it is power that is your chief ideal? Is it not making possible good works that interests you?"

"We dread words with a certain sinister connotation," said Mr. Talbot. "We forget that power itself is neither good nor evil. There is power in a waterfall or a dynamo; there is power in a ruthless dictator; but I suspect that in most individuals, great and small, cruel or kind, it is power that is their good and their ideal. Power may be exercised in many ways. Love itself is the exercise of it, and so is art, and so is science. Knowledge itself—was it not Francis Bacon who said it?—is power. And so is all assertion of life or understanding or feeling or perception. Some of us are fortunate enough to discover clearly what our gifts are that enable us to come to the fulfillment of, as we say, our powers. And the major cause for unhappiness in the world, if I may hazard a guess, is that, in one way or another, powers are interfered with or frustrated, or people cannot learn what their true and possible capacities are."

"But has not the assertion of power," asked the very gentle young preacher present, "has it not been this which has brought about unhappiness? Men have competed for domination, and so have nations, and so they do now. Perhaps Gandhi is right, and until we surrender the gospel of power, we shall have and continue to have a distracted and miserable world."

"Gandhi himself illustrates the subtle varieties of power. And now, as a host, I must exercise domination myself. Let us join the ladies."

I had no difficulty deciding for myself what was the central absorption of my friend Fairdell. He was a painter, not without talent, though—he would have been the first to admit it—quite without genius. After some years as a businessman, he had retired on a small income. "What do you propose to do now?" friends had asked him. "Travel a little," he had said, "and perhaps paint a little." He had done a great deal of traveling, and those of us who had had the pleasure of meeting him at one time or another on his wanderings had felt ourselves to be lucky to have been allowed to benefit by his perceptions, exact and luminous and quietly intense. He was exquisitely responsive to the looks and tones of things, whether those things were pictures in a gallery, or the lights and color of a Paris street, or the facial expressions and gestures of an English couple glimpsed at a country inn. His perceptiveness extended to the arts, and though he never tried to impose his perceptions upon you, you could not go to a concert with him, or look at a Chinese bowl, without learning from some restrained observation of his to see what you had not seen at all, or wondered why you had not seen at once by yourself. You wondered why you had not come to see—come to see more accurately, like him, with something, for all his outward calm, of his own disciplined intensity—the light, the line, and the color of paintings and sculpture, the modulations and transitions of music, the deployment of sound and sense in words. He was very far, however, from being a mere exquisite. For his precise enjoyment of the world included the charms and nuances of social relationships, so that he could delight in the lights and shadows, the tones and overtones, of conversation as he might in the interplay of parts in a Mozart quartet; and the bright clean air of the Sierras delighted him quite as much as any exotic shore of Algiers or any Vale of Kashmir.

Occasionally his friends would discuss Fairdell. "I wonder what keeps him going, though?" some of them would say. "After all, you can't make a career just out of these scattered pleasant experiences. A life must have some point to it, must gather up into some meaning."

Fairdell's life did not seem to add up to very much. One would receive postcards from him from various parts of the world. He was, everyone admitted, a man of taste and impeccably just feeling in the presence of human relationships and of the arts. But one felt, as well, a detachment from life, for all his kindnesses, and a renunciation of it, for all his enjoyments. In addition to his apartment, he also had a small studio in New York, though he almost never invited anyone there. His friends were very curious to see what he had been painting, and he would, with his unfailing courtesy, say some day he would show them. People guessed as to what manner it would be, and since it was the French Impressionists he cherished, imagined it would be somewhat in their style. But no one knew, and with Fairdell one never asked what one suspected he would not like to be asked.

One evening he and I had been sitting in his apartment rather late. We had been discussing one of our friends who had been overworking and got himself run down, another whose marriage had gone on the rocks, a third who had become involved in a vast, and, as we thought, killing, administrative project in government.

"I often wonder why people get themselves so involved," I ventured. "After all, it may be banal, but we're here so short a time. I often wonder whether there's anything worth doing, even painting," I said, "except maybe for the fun of it, the way you're doing."

"But I don't do it for fun," said Fairdell with quiet emphasis.

"Well, what do you do it for?"

"Because I feel I must," he said. "Time is so short, as you said, and there comes a time when one feels one must get it down right, get the thing just exactly as it ought to be."

"You don't mean that you want to copy things exactly as they are? Surely that isn't the object of painting?"

Fairdell looked at one sometimes as if it were not quite worth bothering to correct a misstatement, since the utterer of it would not even understand what the correction would mean.

"No, not *copy* things," he said. "That, of course, isn't what I meant at all. But there is, I think, a deep compulsion just to do the thing, to get the painting itself just right, so that it adds up, so that it does have a meaning in itself. After all," he said, hazarding a generalization, which was very rare with him, "most lives do not add up to anything, though there are a great many people—we've been discussing some of them—who drive themselves and keep themselves busier and busier in the hope that they can persuade themselves and possibly a few others that their lives do mean something. But if one could do only one painting, and have it come out just right, just what one intended, just what it obviously was *meant* to be—well, that would be one up against chaos. I haven't done it yet. When I do, I think I'll let my friends come to see it. But not before! I don't imagine I'll be inviting you soon," he added, smiling.

"That's like an idea I've been playing with," I suggested. "I've been trying to write a paper on the subject." I looked at Fairdell out of the corner of my eye. "If it ever gets properly done, I'll tell you about it."

"You might as well tell me about it now," he said. "I don't want to wait that long."

"Well," I said, "I was trying to work out the idea that the philosophers have deluded themselves when they have sought in the universe a perfect logical coherence, when they have tried to show that nature or history added up to good sense, or to perfect form. The artist sometimes builds a little fortress against universal chaos, a little island of meaning in the epidemic contingency and futility of things. I think that is why these little discoveries of form and order delight us so, and why, if we have any talent at all, we feel we must achieve that just-rightness that you speak of, have the thing, the painting, the sonata, the sonnet, come out just right. One feels, on a small scale, I imagine, the way God must have felt when He was creating the universe. It had to look good to Him when it was finished. It did, too, if I remember. According to the story in Genesis, anyhow, creation came out right. And a writer writing a novel, a painter making a painting, a musician composing a quartet, is making a little cosmos. The universe doesn't look so good to any intelligent being, but at least one can say to one's self, 'Here, this at least has come out right.'"

"Have a little more brandy," said Fairdell, who would never commit himself on large generalizations.

No one I know of has yet seen Fairdell's paintings. But his life has begun to seem to make more sense to me than that of most people. His painting seems to absorb him more and more. He is *betting* his life, as it were, that something, at least, in the schemelessness of things, may be made to come out right. At least one may try, and the trying seems to render him one of the serenest men I know. Or perhaps he is kept tranquil by his delight in the various works of art and music and literature in which things *do* come out right. And even where the lives of his friends come out wrong, at least life itself, as he discriminatingly looks at it, composes into a kind of tragic spectacle or often a comic one. The way of art is, in a fashion different from that which Schopenhauer had suggested, one way of avoiding distraction. For in making a work of art, if one can, one has created a little logos; in enjoying a work of art, if one can, one has experienced a cosmos. For the time being, one has transcended anarchy and confusion. And each work of art is a different universe and a different order. I'd rather like to see Fairdell's painting-universe some day. Meanwhile, I am grateful to him for the many worlds to which he has introduced me, for the richness of meanings and values, the coherences, of which he has been the means of reminding me, continue to exist, and even to come into new being amid the incoherences of our age and our world.

Philosophers, I remarked back at the beginning of this chapter, have been concerned with what there is to be absorbed by, what not to be distracted from. Well, Fairdell's was one way of absorption, through a concentration of the senses, an ordering of perception. Without all the rhetoric of Schopenhauer, he was finding in the arts not so much escape as fulfillment. For a work of art in its fusion of vitality and design is what life and society might be always, with luck and intelligence on the part of the race. Talbot, too, had defined what the paramount engrossment of human beings might be. And it is hard to contest the fact that when human beings exercise power, in love, art, government, or personal relations, they feel a sense of engaged vitality, of enhanced awareness. What more does one need when the whole soul is preoccupied in the mere living of its own capacities? What could distract one from one's own fully engaged natural and dynamic energies?

I thought of Santayana's definition of a fanatic as one who has redoubled his energies after he has forgotten his aim. I remembered Balzac's wonderful sentence: "Although we do not in life know where we are going, we experience beyond a doubt the fatigues of the journey." But we experience the delights of the journey, too, as a less somber observer might have remarked. One way or another, delights or fatigues, it is not surprising that the obscure living should be so occupied—that the illustrious dead should have been so preoccupied, many of them—in trying to define what the purpose of the journey is, or for what goal one has set out. Several years ago, before the Second World War, some of the railway companies advertised a sort of ghost train, an excursion to an unannounced destination. Many subscribed for the excursion, and since it *was* an excursion were content not to know where they were going. And, since the companies were reliable and could be counted on not to disappoint their passengers, the surprise destination did not generally prove a letdown. But life itself seems headed to no goal, though its way stations are full of surprises, many of them unpleasant ones. There is no goal, perhaps, at all, and the course of existence itself is altogether accidental. But in this brief incidental interval, one must choose among goods, decide what, in the very urgency of the short mortal span, constitutes the best in art, in power, in love. Or could one, as some of my dream interlocutors suggested, find peace and undistractedness by escaping from life altogether, from time to eternity, from the flesh to the spirit, from the disillusioning search for happiness to the resigned and possible search for peace?

Perhaps in some future convalescence I will hear a more convincing voice and be given a more completely persuasive vision. Perhaps sometime, somewhere, among the living I will come across some wise and experienced soul, some exceptionally clear-minded thinker, who could define beyond peradventure what there is to be absorbed by, what there is not to be distracted from. So far, all that life, rather than the living or the dead, has taught me is that, willy-nilly, one can never be distracted very long from the search itself, from the philosopher's quest. That, I suspect, is what, in their various ways, has absorbed the thinkers, whatever their answers. There is no first or last thing, but first and last is the quest itself, to those not content to live in a mere miscellany, however delightful. To those who dream beyond the actual and think beyond their fingertips, there persists the search for order rather than a miscellany; and though the order is not found, the inquiry proves, itself, a goal.

The quest is for an answer as to what constitutes the first principles and the ultimate end. First and last, to those whose hearts have not been dulled by routine or crushed utterly by disaster, to those whose minds have not been paralyzed by habit and superstition and folly, the search continues and is itself, doubtless, what keeps the imagination and the spirit of man alive.

SEVEN

America's Own Philosopher:

A PARABLE

ACADEMIC philosophy has never been a popular subject in this country. There have been, it is true, some reflective men of letters, like Emerson and Thoreau, and there have been popular guides to success, from Benjamin Franklin down, both intellectually and chronologically. But the genuine academic philosopher has, in general, been relegated strictly to the campus where he has taught. He acquires a certain local fame and influence, a celebrity which flickeringly survives in the precarious memories of alumni, far-wandering and mortal. The names of these great teachers will crop up in spots on the globe remote from the ivy-towered college where they are oracles. Two alumni of some fabled eastern institution will meet in China or Peru and brighten a little with sentiment and nostalgia as they recall what the "old man" used to say in his classes in Philosophy 6. Often over the coffee cups at the home of an eminent banker in New York, a banker who is the product of a great—or numerically great—state university, you will hear the celebrated financier murmur: "Well do I remember dear old Professor So-and-So! He was not just a professor of philosophy. He was a true philosopher. I remember dozens of the things he used to say, and though I've met some distinguished minds here in the East, I have never met anyone who said as many wise things. I recall one of them: 'Well,' he used to say, looking dreamily out of the classroom window which gave a view of the University chapel, 'the little issues of life are the big ones.' It used to impress us all, and the more I go on in life the more I recognize it to be true."

Professor Wilkins was just such a philosopher. For thirty years at the great State University of X—— he had given a course regularly taken by six hundred young men and women, most of them destined, as one of the deans remarked in an unguarded moment, to return to the obscurity of the farms and garages from which they had emerged. The course was nearly always called "Man and the Universe," and it covered, as the title suggested, all the problems which can occur to the paragon of animals in that wide and complex realm in which he lives. The very title was enough to fire the imagination of the sophomore who, glancing through the catalogue of courses, wished to light on something that would meet all the vast troubling issues that come all of a rush to focus in the heads of reflective young men and women. The course was lent piquancy by the persistent rumors, not without foundation, that it would put dents into many of the biblical pieties with which so many students from that orthodox region came to the University. Occasionally the Professor would change the title of the offering and call it "Man's Eternal Horizons." His wife used to laugh at the change, and say he liked the variation because, as she put it, it gave him "room for scope." "Man's Eternal Horizons" was just the right note, too, to capture the dreaming mind of the poetic young. The very name of the course suggested a ship plowing through unknown seas to ever-new vistas on a voyage perpetually new, eternally fresh.

The Professor had begun to give the course when he was a very young man, and it had almost immediately become one of the most popular electives of the University. There had been something about the Professor even when he was a fledgling that had breathed an ageless wisdom and a modest, earnest concern. He seemed as devoted as a conscientious parish preacher, but with no unction and with no theological ax to grind. Two years after he had begun to teach "Man and the Universe" it was one of the "big" courses on the campus. From then on it was regularly taken by six hundred young men and women. No one knew quite why they all took it, or what they all got out of it, except three things. The first was the transparent moral sincerity of the lecturer, the second was the homeliness of his illustrations, the third was the complexity of his vocabulary. The illustrations were always simple and homespun, the very tone of the Middle West. "American Gothic in philosophy" the Professor had been dubbed by a sophisticated young man in the English department who had taken his Ph.D. at Harvard. The burden of the lecture, however, was in the forbidding technical vocabulary of philosophy; the Professor had studied in Germany and had never quite got over the Hegelian jargon, though he long since had recovered from German world views. The students did not mind the vocabulary, however, for they got the general drift, a warm, sensible, kindly humanism, gently antitheological, pro-democratic, pro-future, and pro-youth. It was a declaration of the rights of man, a manifesto of the hopes of mankind.

Not many of the students went on with philosophy. A few,

however, did so, and pursued graduate study elsewhere, whither they carried the name of the Professor and intimated what a pity it was that his System, for so the course came to be called, had not been written down. It was said that if the System ever *were* written down, it would render the Wilkins philosophy world-making, world-shaking, world-redeeming. The Professor's name had indeed begun to spread more than locally. Rumors of the System had reached the gossip corners of the annual meetings of the Western Division of the American Philosophical Association, and fainter rumors of it had even reached New York. The Professor had published an article or two every five years in one of the journals, and it was commonly said these were competent enough but really rather commonplace. "I hear, though," people would say, "that he's a most remarkable teacher. *Hordes* come to listen to him, and he does a fine job of humanistic missionary work in the Bible-reading Middle West." Occasionally at meetings of the Eastern Division of the Association, the Professor would rise to comment on a paper (he seldom read one of his own). There was a kind of simple honesty about the mild, gray-haired little man, or rather the majesty of honest simplicity. It was as if a self-enlightened backwoodsman had risen to speak, and the image of Lincoln the rail splitter, or perhaps of Mark Hopkins on one end of a log and a student on the other, would rush to people's minds as they listened to him. One disgruntled member of the Association, when for the hundredth time he heard the comparison with Mark Hopkins, said glumly: "There aren't any logs in the state he comes from—just lone prairie." "*His* classes aren't lonely," replied a staunch admirer, "nearly a thousand now, I'm told!"

Everyone at the great State University of X—— was certain

that if the System were ever written down (and they had no doubt that some day it would be) it would render the Professor's fame secure as one of the world's great philosophers, and, what was more, distinctively America's own. Even the notes which one student gifted with stenography had taken down verbatim, almost complete, were impressive to those who saw them, the student's roommate, for example, and his family. But the System never *was* written down, and the Professor himself was half haunted, half relieved by the fact that he had never got around to doing it. He was relieved when he thought of all the technical criticisms his colleagues would make; the barbed shafts that he heard leveled at some quite good papers at the Philosophical Association did not make him eager to subject himself to such onslaughts, at once trivial and virulent. He reminded himself, too, that Socrates, the prototype of all great teachers, had not written any system either. The great thing, he told himself, was to teach the young and open horizons to them, not to write books to be buried in libraries and consulted, in a short time, not even by scholars.

Yet he was haunted as he thought how transient was the influence of a teacher. Who, now, knew his own great teachers at the small college in Ohio which he had attended? And how long would his ideas continue to be current after his retirement and death? He was haunted by conscience, too, for while he thought of himself as no more than a faithful voice of a sound tradition, he felt that it was his duty to state that tradition as he understood it. Perhaps he had caught an aspect of it that others, far greater men, no doubt, had missed. He promised himself each year that he would write out the System. But the year never came when he had the time.

In the first place, teaching itself was an exhausting business, particularly lecturing now to six hundred students. For years he had done it without a public address system. Few people outside the profession and not many on the faculty ever realized the physical and spiritual drain it was to pour out three times a week to six hundred attentive listeners—for they were all attentive whether they understood the Professor or not—the accumulated moral energies and intellectual fruits of a whole devoted professional life. Only his wife knew what those lectures in the "big" course meant to Professor Wilkins. On lecture days, even after thirty years, he would still be nervous and distraught and preoccupied at breakfast, and would come home for lunch a mixture of weariness and aftermath of exhilaration. For on the days he lectured, Professor Wilkins could not bear to go to the Faculty Club and find himself at lunch with routineers, professors of Hog Husbandry, or professors of Methods of Teaching Fractions in the Fourth Grade from the School of Education, or even with the hard-boiled young professor of Symbolic Logic in his own department, a young man who even to the highly respected Wilkins would brashly dismiss all philosophy, save mathematical logic, as mere vision and moralizing. Usually the soul of kindness and domestic ease, he would hardly say a word at these post-lecture lunches, and his wife, whose life was absorbed in his career, had the good sense to let him alone. She would often turn down a dinner invitation for the night before the lecture or the evening after it on the ground that the Professor was going to be under a great strain, or just had been. Nor did anyone know better than she how much it took out of the Professor morally to lecture for an hour in his passionate defense of the possible eventual rationality of the universe which men might achieve by cooperative intelligence and good will. She knew what it cost him to continue his propaganda week after week for connivance with processes that, intelligently guided, flowered into the True, the Good, and the Beautiful.

These three lectures a week were psychic high water marks in the life of the Professor, and he paid for them. They were psychic high water marks in the lives of his students, too, and without any spiritual or physical expense on their part. His silver voice, his eloquent periods (even when the meaning of the eloquence was not clear), his impressive public concentration on the act of thinking, these were all memorable and absorbing. It was no wonder that very early the Professor became the official University Orator. Heaven knows how many eminent statesmen, industrialists and divines, artists, musicians, generals, and admirals had received all the rights and privileges appertaining to their honorary degrees in terms recited with gravity and music by the elder statesman of the Department of Philosophy.

He soon became, as was to be expected, one of the elder statesmen of the University, too. He was on the small inner council that determined University policy. He was the judge in conflicts in other departments. He came to be consulted also by state senators (many of whom had been his former pupils) on matters affecting the state quite outside the University, problems arising at the State Agricultural Experiment Stations and even at the State Hospital for the Insane. One of his former pupils (by no means the brightest) had become a senator in Washington, and at moments of international or national crisis he had been known (or at least so it was said) to call up his old teacher on the long-distance telephone to ask at great and expensive length the benefit of his wisdom. Former pupils, too, were scattered now, teaching in various junior colleges, and the Professor had to pay ceremonial visits and give in person and at first hand the philosophy which his disciples had been teaching in isolation at second hand. The women's clubs in the state, too, the more earnest and serious of them, would insist on having the Professor address them some time during the year. Meanwhile, the Professor took endless time with individual advanced students and also with any young student in the "big" course whom one of his eight or nine assistants commended as promising in philosophy or in life. And there was the constant stream of returning alumni. No one ever came back to the University of X—— without greeting the Professor and telling him what the course had meant in his life.

For many years the Professor had hoped to write down the System during the summers, which he generally spent on a small island in Lake Michigan. But the first month of his three-month vacation he needed, his wife correctly insisted, for recuperation. Thereafter, the summer was never as uninterrupted as he had hoped. He was regularly dragooned into giving two sermons at the Unitarian Church, where they felt that, whatever the Professor thought about *ordinary* religion, in their sense, at least, he did believe in God. There was also in the North Woods close by an annual meeting of the Liberal Students of the North and Central West, to which he was a spiritual father. The outstanding liberal-minded philosopher of the whole area could not decently refuse to join in the leading of conferences for a week, or decline to give both the key-note speech the first week and the summing up at the end.

There came in the middle of the summer, however, a few blessed weeks when the Professor was both rested and uninterrupted. It was at that time that he was always fresh enough and alert enough to realize the paramount obstacle to his writing down the System. Even in the very midst of his eloquence in class each year, he had felt inward twinges, not perceptible to the students. And by the middle of the summer each year he would rediscover the cause of these inward twinges, half-intellectual and half-moral. The System, he found anew each year, needed modification. And each year, as students found on trying to compare notes, or as lazy students found when they tried to borrow last year's notes for this year's examination, the course was never quite the same. The illustrations, maybe, but not always the points they illustrated. The Professor was conscientious enough to know that, while his System was thus in process of constant and necessary revision, it was more honest not to write it down and give it the deceptive finality of print. Had not Josiah Royce had to add a hundred pages in small print, after he had completed his two-volume work on *The World and the Individual,* in order to explain more accurately what he had meant to say? Would it not really be better to know what one had to say before saying it?

The Professor was getting older, and it began to look as if the System might never be written down at all. On his sixtieth birthday a book of essays by his former pupils was published, and a great dinner was held. John Dewey sent a telegram of congratulations. The admirers settled down to looking forward to the publication of his System posthumously or of founding a lectureship to keep his memory alive. They might indeed have had to resort to the last step. It looked, truly, as if the System might never be written; and it would not have been, had it not been for the great and moving impression the Professor and the course had left on a young student many years before. Save for him, the wholesome philosophy of Professor Wilkins would never have been completed, written out, and published at all; nor the whole direction of American intellectual history changed, at least for a season.

That student, Jerry Campbell, was now an eminent public relations counsel in New York. One spring afternoon he had been looking out of his fortieth-floor window in Rockefeller Center and reflecting in the soft spring air on his empty career. What had he done with his life, he asked himself, except sell (though it must be said with amazing success) other people's soap and soup and toothpaste? What had anyone done, in the cocktail-drinking, platinum-plated set he moved in in New York? They did nothing but gain wealth and waste leisure. Whose life was not wasted, of all the people he had ever known, or even known something about? He was not under the illusion that futility was a special vice of the rich. Now that working people had considerably more leisure, what did they do with it? The juke boxes and the mass mediocrity of the movies and radio told the story. But the real treason and the unpardonable sin was among the educated who knew the better and followed the worse. His memory roamed back over his life to try to think of one man who had done something with his life really worth doing. He had it!—it was Professor Wilkins who had most deeply of all impressed him, with an impression that had grown rather than faded through the years. Professor Wilkins had remained in his mind a touchstone by which to measure other men. For here was a human being who year after year, for a modest wage, with no thought of fame or profit, had devoted himself to teaching those young who had the good fortune to find their way into his classes—the way to a flowering of the True, the Good, and the Beautiful in their own lives and in civilization. Professor Wilkins had devoted himself to working out a system of understanding of life and of the universe which, properly applied, could transform our civilization, all ruins and chaos, into rational serenity and fruitfulness and peace—if it were properly disseminated.

Properly disseminated! Jerry Campbell smiled with sudden radiant perception, and at once his spirit experienced liberation and relief. An idea had dawned on him, and his ideas were worth millions to his clients. He could at one blow save the world, redeem his own soul, and bring recognition and perhaps even wealth to one of the wisest and most generous men he had ever known. Some advertising geniuses cherish the illusion that they could have done something great and original. Jerry was more honest with himself. He was, at best, simply a liaison officer. He had in the past been a missionary for the trivial and external. Here was a chance to promote something fine and noble and important that might otherwise, in the noisy dominance of the second-rate, be lost to this nation forever. Surely he, Jerry, who had made the country soap- and soup- and toothpaste-conscious, could make America conscious of the Wilkins System, and (his imagination soared more wildly still) make that System known and respected throughout the world. There was only one difficulty. The System was not yet written down. Jerry had thought of that. This was not the first time he had begun to think of ways of spreading an idea that had not yet even been put down clearly in a summary. He was not discouraged.

Jerry was a man of action. He pressed a button and told his secretary that he was leaving that night for the Middle West on urgent business. The next afternoon, almost unannounced, he was in the Professor's familiar book-lined study. The picture of the "School of Athens" was still over his old teacher's desk.

The Professor remembered Jerry well, though he had not seen nor heard from him since Jerry had left the University. Twenty-five years before, when the Professor was just beginning to be well known on the campus, Jerry had been editor of the *Daily Oriole,* the campus newspaper. It was a dull season for campus journalism—early spring; football long since over, campus politics in the doldrums, a sort of late winter dog-days of campus spirits. Jerry, who always wrote the leading editorial, was casting about for something to write about. He found it easily. The next day there had appeared in the *Oriole* an editorial with Jerry's initials attached to it. It was entitled *A Socrates Among Us.* It ran, in part, as follows:

"Too often a man's virtues are not recognized until he is dead. Probably if Socrates were to appear among us, either we should not be aware of it at all or we should soon come to take it for granted. Well, as a matter of fact, we do have a Socrates among us, a true teacher of wisdom, a tutor in the beautiful, the true, and the good. But students of this university, even when they take that great course, Philosophy 6 (as everyone does these days who has any claim to literacy at all), do not realize what they are getting. This is not just another lecture course; such come by the carload on this campus. This class of Professor Wilkins's, we say it without fear of offending his colleagues, who know it just as clearly as the students do, is an initiation into maturity, it is a path to freedom. It is, for many of us, though not all of us realize it, a liberation from the clichés of routine lip-service religion and conventional morality. It is a spacious avenue to a shining ideal in a wider life. Occasionally parents protest against what this course does to the traditional faith in which they have brought up their sons. What the *sons* come to realize, perhaps much later, is that they have been introduced to a more humane and generous faith, a more deeply felt religion. It is only later that most students who have taken this course appreciate that they have been made party to a system of thought which, if the evil world —committed to the notions of so-called practical men—would but, could but, follow, its cruelties, confusions, and barbarities would end, and the race would have a chart and franchise of felicity. But all this is imbibed so quietly and easily from this true scholar and gentleman that students are mostly unaware, even when they love him and applaud him at the end, what a healing renovation in their thought and their lives the course has brought about.

"It does not invalidate the truth of this estimate of Professor Wilkins's work that the world at large is ignorant of what is being taught here. Our elders tell us, though, that the professional philosophers do realize it, and there is even a rumor that Professor Wilkins is being tempted off by one of the great private eastern universities. (It would shame us, by the way, if this great state could not keep one of its greatest native thinkers here among us.) But whether the wide world knows the Wilkins System does not matter. Most people in Athens did not know about Socrates. Society kills its great thinkers, or their thoughts, by ignoring them. But some day when the System *is* written down, and rumor reaches us that some day it will be, the world will know. Meanwhile, it is for the students of the University of X—— to realize what it is they are learning in Philosophy 6—a new revelation. And they ought to carry that revelation into their future lives as scientists, statesmen, doctors, even as businessmen and farmers. We must vow that our lives will be living testimonies to the depths and grandeur of Professor Wilkins's philosophy. Our lives ought to be mirrors of truths which Professor Wilkins has taught us."

So widely acknowledged was the general sense of these observations that no one accused Jerry of currying favor with the Professor, though he was a student in the course at the time. The tone of the editorial persuaded so many students that the following autumn there were a hundred and fifty additional students in the course. Mrs. Wilkins had had the accolade engraved on parchment and hung, framed, on their parlor wall. It was still there now, twenty-five years later, Jerry noticed with a flush of pleasure as he passed through the parlor to the study.

The Professor was there sitting in his chair, grayer and older. But the same gentle homespun wisdom seemed to be in the eyes, the same hope for mankind, and the same look as of one who gazes far distances into dim futures and can speak with the accent and authority of a sage. "If only," Jerry thought, "the old man can be persuaded to write the System down."

He did all in his power, and not in vain. On the train he had rehearsed. He knew all the familiar objections, for he knew that others—he had never before had the courage to approach his old teacher—had tried to persuade him to write, and the Professor had regularly answered them all in about the same terms. The Professor greeted Jerry by saying he had heard of his great success in the world. "In worldliness," Jerry answered demurely. "It is you who have a life that justifies itself, Professor. You have been a messenger of illumination. You hardly need to be told what your great course has meant at the University. It is one of the things mentioned every year when the X—— Alumni Club meets in New York."

"It is most kind of you to say so," said the Professor.

"But I have come to ask you not to confine your benefits to the University," said Jerry. "The world should know your System, Professor."

"If it is any good, my pupils can convey it to others," said the Professor.

"But pupils, too, are mortal," replied Jerry. "'All men are mortal,'" he quoted the famous syllogism; "'Socrates is mortal.'" He bowed deeply to the Professor. "*Even* Socrates is mortal. And alumni are mortal, and their memories fail them even when they are alive. I say I remember your course, but I have to refresh myself with my notes now and then."

"I hope you don't use *those* old notes," said Professor Wilkins. "The course has improved since then."

"Ready, I am sure, to be written down finally," said Jerry.

"Alas," said the Professor, "I don't have the time, and with every year in the University my time gets more and more taken up. There are responsibilities one simply can't shirk. After all, the philosopher is a citizen, too."

Then Jerry sprang his surprise. He spoke very gently and deferentially. "We'll make time for you, Professor. It is not as a compliment to you personally, Professor, but as a necessary contribution to American culture, that I wish to make this proposal. Why don't you take a year off, say, go to St. Petersburg, and finish the System once and for all? I will gladly pay you your whole year's salary, and you can rely on it that the University would spare you for a year for so important a public service. The University owes you to the nation. I will also undertake to see that the manuscript is properly published, and, if I do say so myself, that it is given proper attention where such attention will be advantageous to its widest public influence."

"I have never sought notoriety," said the Professor.

"But you do not believe in concealing wisdom, do you?" said Jerry. "Wisdom, I heard you once say, is no private soliloquy. It must be published to the world!"

"But I am not sure I have wisdom," said the Professor. "I do happen to think my ideas are sound, but I should hate to put them in printed form when there are still points unsettled in my own mind. After all, one learns while one teaches, and I see difficulties I had not even suspected when you took the course, and reservations I should have to make, and changes."

Jerry was particularly prepared for that. He remembered how diffident, modest, and cautious the Professor had been, and how often at the end of a lecture he would suddenly say with honest avowal: "At least it seems to me" or "In my judgment."

"There is such a thing," Jerry found himself daring to say to his former professor, "as a disease of the will. Much wisdom might have been lost to the race forever if the great philosophers of the past had had the same kind of hesitation. Supposing Aristotle had never allowed himself to write his *Ethics* because there were a few controversial points; supposing Plato had never written down his dialogues; supposing Socrates . . ."

"But Socrates never wrote a line," the Professor pointed out somewhat sharply. "Perhaps he was the wisest of them all. He never wrote *anything*."

"Well, then, it's lucky he had a Plato to do it for him," said Jerry. "I'd do it for you, but I'm no Plato."

"And I no Socrates," said the Professor, "despite your kindness, Jerry."

Jerry persisted in explaining his scheme. He would give the Professor a check in advance for his whole year's salary. The Professor was to take the year off and go off to St. Petersburg in Florida or some other salubrious spot, in Arizona maybe, and write out the System.

"The book will fall stillborn from the press," said Professor Wilkins, and he at once blushed to think he had been comparing himself to David Hume, who had in his *Autobiography* so described the early fate of his *Treatise on Human Nature*.

"Oh, it *won't* fall stillborn, you may be sure of that," said Jerry, though he did not tell the Professor in detail what he proposed to do to prevent such a fatality. He was not an expert in publicity and promotion for nothing. But he knew how the Professor hated cheap notoriety. He kept his counsel. All he did was to repeat: "It *will not* fall stillborn from the press. You may be sure of that."

"But in any case," said Professor Wilkins, "I could not accept such a personal kindness and purely personal tribute."

"It is not a personal kindness or a personal tribute. It is a contribution to American culture, to American education," Jerry repeated firmly.

The Professor was complimented and touched, but he remained dubious. He said he must talk it over with his wife, whose whole life had been simply that of devotion to his. She was a good deal less hesitant than the Professor. She had been shocked the previous summer, when they had gone far afield to Maine instead of Michigan, to discover that the summer colony there hardly recognized the Professor's name—or, since most of them came from Boston, even the name of the state or the University where the Professor taught. She had always wished the System to be written down, for, though almost everywhere they went within a couple of hundred miles of home the Professor's name was known, she was aware that he had no national reputation. He had been "too long of proper fame defrauded." By the next day Professor Wilkins, whose fears were quieted and whose hopes were encouraged by his wife, was able to tell Jerry that he accepted the offer. He reminded Jerry that he must not expect too much and that it must be understood that he did not even promise to complete the System within the year.

"You have absolutely no obligation," said Jerry, "of *any* kind. But I do want you to have the chance to do this, and I want to improve the chances that the System will go down to posterity. You'll see, you'll finish it all right. You're full of it. It'll be like rolling off a log."

"I don't mean to be unkind, Jerry," said the Professor, "especially after *your* kindness, but have you ever really tried to think through to basic principles? Do you know how hard a thing it is to do that?"

"Well, at any rate, this year you'll have a chance to try," said Jerry cheerfully. He had no doubts that the Professor would finish the System, any more than he doubted that, through *his* efforts, America would rapidly become conscious of it.

The next year the Professor spent in Florida at a small resort near St. Petersburg. He worked hard and continuously at the manuscript. Meanwhile, Jerry lost no time. He started work immediately upon returning to New York. There began to appear curious hints, even in the most vulgar gossip columns, that a world-shaking system was being written by a quiet elderly professor on leave of absence from a great middle-western university for that express purpose. The *Journal of Philosophy* carried a more sober note: Professor Wilkins of the University of X—— was on leave of absence. The phrase "the System" began to appear in unexpected places; tantalizing references to the System were heard and seen everywhere. "In a work as yet unpublished," one of the more literate radio commentators would begin, and then some theme of the System would be cited. A good many people for a while thought the System referred to a new method in bridge.

Jerry had subtler devices for making the news percolate. He began to speak of it at the right cocktail parties and at the appropriate clubs. He found occasion to speak of it at a luncheon meeting in New York one day when an Arctic explorer was the speaker. "Wait till *next* year," he said, "I'll have someone to bring here who will *say* something." He talked of it in the East Room at the Century and at lunch at The Players. And, naturally, at the Advertising Club. He remembered enough of the course from his college days to be able to converse somewhat intelligently on its general themes. He was careful never to go on too long, nor was it ineffective to be as vague as he was compelled to be when his memory failed him (or often when it did not). As a matter of fact, most of his listeners were glad to accept Jerry's enthusiasm for the System without worrying too much or hearing too much about the details.

Jerry was also careful to mention the subject one evening shortly after his return to New York when he was dining at Mrs. Chapman's. That grand lady was the well-known wife of a steel magnate. She was known for her genuine though plodding interest in books and ideas. Her house was the natural haven for visiting English writers and thinkers, and Bergson, too, had once been entertained there. There wasn't a leading idea in the last forty years, or a leading thinker, at any rate, whom she had allowed herself to miss.

"Is there anything new in the intellectual line?" she asked Jerry. "You're always finding new ideas."

"You flatter me," said Jerry. "You are always the harbinger of the new ideas in this town, Mrs. Chapman, and you're the playmate of the great thinkers. But, as a matter of fact, I think I have beaten you to something." He had been waiting for this moment. It was just as well to enlist Mrs. Chapman's moral, and even financial, support for the System very early.

"Probably some new French vogue," said Mrs. Chapman.

"Oh, no, this is pure American. American Gothic, almost." Jerry proceeded to tell Mrs. Chapman about it. He spoke with such conviction and poetry and feeling that Mrs. Chapman was quickly convinced. "Professor Wilkins must stay with us when he comes to New York, and you must come to tea some day very soon and explain the System to me. I mustn't monopolize you now."

Jerry did come one day soon, and this is in substance what he told Mrs. Chapman: "There is, so runs the Professor's System, a World. But the World is frequently referred to throughout as the That, the Thereness, the So-Ness. This Thatness has discoverable principles of organization. There are regularities in it which can be studied. In the light of that study, men can control ('modulate,' the Professor sometimes calls it) those phases of the universe which concern their welfare. Intelligence is life understanding its own conditions. The mastery of things and of the self by reason the Professor calls Cosmic Apprenticeship. The activities of reason, insofar as they are used to modify nature and human nature, are called Control. But the System stresses the fact that the Cosmic Apprenticeship never becomes complete mastery, and that Control is always limited. But there is another aspect or use of reason. It is also a speculative contemplation of the whole of the universe. This is, in the System, called Intellection. The Professor makes clear the immense scope and adventure of Cosmic Apprenticeship, how little progress toward the fullness of possible Control man has thus far achieved. In his lectures, and his writing when he publishes it, will be found a most enthusiastic celebration of what man may make of nature and what man may make of himself when the regularities of nature are studied. These have been explored in the region of the physical sciences, but the fields of politics and economics, of industry and human relations, have been left all these hundreds of modern years to folly, fanaticism, and superstition.

"The Professor analyzes, too, the limits of Control. At best there are certain aspects of nature which are obviously obstacles to human good. Death ends all for individuals, and extinction will come eventually to the whole solar system itself. There are presumably incurable ills of body and mind, or irreducible miseries in personal relations which no social or medical programs could cure. What cannot be changed must be endured, what must be endured can and must be understood. One must not pamper or delude one's self, the Professor insists, by carrying on in the modern world the silly superstition that the world was made for man, who is an unforeseen accident in it. The System excludes a good many things, too, conventional purpose in the universe, cosmic justice, immortal life, irresponsible freedom. Man can learn to be well tutored in the ways of the universe, modify them to his uses where he can, contemplate them reasonably where he cannot."

Jerry told all this rather less briefly than it is told here. Mrs.

Chapman leaned forward, her cup of rare China tea in her hand, all eager attention. "But you *can* have some more tea," she said, "*and* crumpets."

Jerry brushed aside the crumpets and continued: "The systematic phases of the System come from the ways in which the Professor distinguishes the levels of regularity in the universe. He shows the Levels of Discoverable Order, from inanimate things up to the subtlest forms of the emotional and intellectual activities of man. The System, of course, leaves no place for God in the ordinary sense of divine purpose and intelligence, of a cosmic father. But it is filled with appreciation, eloquent, earnest, and documented, of the flowerings of nature and of life. Special creation is denied, but due justice is done to the fertility, the creativeness, the generous bloomings, of natural processes into the beauties of field and flower, bud and leaf, the marvels of the mind and imagination of man. So impressed is the Professor with the wonderful variety and richness of the natural world and its ever-burgeoning possibilities that perhaps nothing less than the word 'God' will do to name adequately the good which may flower out of nature, the energy which is the source of the flowering—the beauty nature generates, the truth of it, for good and evil, that observation and exploration of it discovers.

"People may ask why the Professor calls this view of nature, without any design in it, a *system* at all. Well, it is all bound together by cause and effect, from the movement of the stars in their courses to the two-part inventions of Bach. There is nothing *intended* by nature, but there is nothing purely accidental or capricious in it either. Is the System utopian? Well, it makes possible the entertainment of many generous hopes and makes possible also the fruition of many of them. But it excludes all sentimental escapisms as impossible for a mature mind. Whatever is to be done, the means must be studied in the inevitable regularities of nature; what cannot be done must be faced, for that, too, flows from the nexus of causes and effects. Does the System render man free? It does, though not in any romantic sense. Intelligence is man's franchise, and inquiry indicates that only through understanding can he be free at all, free to do what can be done, free to understand why he is not *absolutely* free, free to survey with detachment even the causes and effects of his own doom. Does the System provide for creativeness and spontaneity in man? It does, but creativeness, also, must trace the ways of nature, and spontaneity, in retrospect, is seen to involve the causal uses of the ways of nature. The flower may burst in unexpected glory upon the garden, but, like less beautiful blossoms, it, too, is dependent on the processes of sun and air."

This is, in substance, what Jerry explained to Mrs. Chapman over her delicious crumpets and her very special China tea before an open fireplace in New York, where firewood is worth its weight in gold. "It sounds too *wonderful*," said Mrs. Chapman. "Does the Professor ever come to New York?"

"Oh, he will," said Jerry. "You may be sure of that. I'll see to it."

"I must give a little dinner for him," said Jerry's hostess. Jerry thought to himself that it had better be a big one, but he knew that was what Mrs. Chapman meant. It was her brother-in-law who had said the little issues of life are the big ones.

It was the expansion of what Jerry had been telling Mrs. Chapman at tea that Professor Wilkins in Florida, in the meantime, had been trying to write down. It was even harder to say in writing than he had supposed it would be. He had had some bad moments of sudden terror in the middle of the night ever since he had made his promise to Jerry. At such times his wife heard him murmur, though she could not tell whether he was asleep or awake: "I'll never be able to do it." Sometimes he would repeat the same sentiment to her at breakfast. "Nonsense, darling," she would say. "You always accomplish what you intend to." She reminded him how he had pushed through his doctor's dissertation, though he had had to work eight hours a day as a Western Union clerk while he was doing it. "But I'm older, dear, and tired, and not so audacious any more," Professor Wilkins replied.

Now that he was in Florida, trying to write the System down, all his fears seemed to be justified. The problems and difficulties that he had always postponed or sometimes solved glibly (and guiltily) in the presence of a class seemed almost insuperable now that he struggled to put them into the finalities necessary for a book. Had he, for instance, really combined the chain of cause and effect in nature with his claim for human freedom, creation, and spontaneity? Was it true, really, that nature could be said to sustain the most generous hopes of man if, as the scientists seemed to tell us, the eventual destination of mankind (even assuming the atomic bomb were controlled) is extinction? How could something be called a system that was so full of miscellany as nature seemed to be, and ultimately so irrational at the core, so mysterious, so ultimately unpredictable, for all the scientific boasts of verifiability and predictability in the physical world? He rather wished now that he hadn't promised to finish the whole book in a year. No wonder his old teacher at college had resolutely refused to write anything down; no wonder Socrates had followed the same wise plan. To write things down was to pretend to have arrived at ultimate conclusions. What man with a tincture of modesty, a trace of understanding, in him could dare to do that, or presume that he had done it?

There were purely psychological difficulties, too, connected with his long years of teaching. The Professor had often wished for the leisure to write down the things he had, year after year, said with such clarified passion to his succeeding classes in the "big" course. He had been warmed to eloquence, and his ideas had been warmed to significance, by the cordial and respectful attention of six hundred upturned eager faces. In the momentum of his lectures, and in the friendliness of their reception, he had come often to forget that he was not saying these things for the first time. They had seemed to well up spontaneous and fresh from the deep recesses of his mind and heart. But now, in the little cottage in Florida, with nothing but the warmth of an electric stove in a Florida cold snap, all these ideas that had once seemed so grand and compelling seemed cold turkey. Perhaps that was one of the consequences of not teaching. While one was actually talking to students, the bleakness and thinness of one's own ideas came back radiant with the enthusiasm of the impressionable young men and young women to whom they were addressed. But here he was speaking to his own unresponsive typewriter; and although his wife adored him and unhesitatingly approved all he wrote, she did not pretend to understand it.

There was something else which others had long realized, judging by the little writing he had done, and which the Professor realized now. He spoke better than he wrote. In class he sounded good even when he wasn't clear. He had sometimes thought of dictating his book, but he had tried it once and it seemed too artificial. A stenographer was not a class, and, in any case, who could have imagined one of the great philosophers dictating a major work? Moreover, he used to pause so much in dictation that he was expensively wasting the time of a stenographer. He decided a philosopher did most of his writing in the pauses; that was when he did his *actual* thinking. In a class, moreover, the sense of the presence of hundreds of inexperienced youngsters made him humanely forgo technical jargon whenever he could; and even where he used it, the sincerity and human dedication of the man himself served to light the darkness of the verbal jungle, and his personality blazed a trail through it. But here at his writing table he felt obliged to be precise and to eschew the concessions to ordinary language that he made when the spirit moved him and when he felt a surge of obligation to his young hearers. Here, in writing, he felt a higher obligation: to the intricacies of the analysis, to his professional colleagues, to the severe demands of truth. He found himself inventing new words or using old ones in deliberately unfamiliar ways.

The Professor reread the pages he had written, and, since he loved good writing, he winced as he saw the fearful jargon into which he had fallen. But how else was he to expound accurately, responsibly, intellectually, well? Sometimes he was tempted to forget all the hesitancies, reservations, doubts, and ambiguities and speak frankly and from the heart as he did sometimes in his classes. Once in a while he allowed himself to write that way. But dully or fluently, eloquently or loosely, one way or another, the book moved forward. He finished it, as his wife and Jerry both had known he would, by the end of the year. He was used to meeting dates in an academic calendar.

The System, largely because of Jerry, was already familiar to the public influential in such matters long before it appeared in actual print. Jerry was terribly disappointed when it was *not* chosen, from advance proofs, by the judges of the Book-of-the-Month Club. One of the judges told him confidentially that they had almost risked it. But the vocabulary was really *too* unintelligible for even its one million highly literate readers, and, truth to tell, the judges had had some difficulty with it themselves. They could risk a "hard" book *once* in a while, for prestige reasons, but their subscribers could not live off prestige spiritually; they were, after all, entitled to something they could *read*. The failure of the book to be chosen was a minor disaster from Jerry's point of view, but he correctly did not regard it as fatal. He had entrusted it to a very enterprising firm for publication. This concern had once sold about five hundred thousand copies of a book that unblushingly used philosophy in the title. The title of the System as published was *A World Philosophy—for Americans.*

Jerry knew that a hundred thousand books placed in the hands of the sort of readers who not only read but discussed it, would do the trick he wanted done. It would even suffice if it got into their hands only and not into their heads, or if these hundred thousand didn't read quite all the book, which would run to five hundred and fifty closely printed pages. It would not hurt if they did not understand all that they read. The mood created, of a new intellectual revelation; the atmosphere produced, of high cerebral excitement, that was all that was really wanted, at first anyway.

Jerry himself, several months before publication, took additional steps. He invited to lunch a young man then making his mark as a distinguished literary critic. That is to say, the youth was a daily book reviewer for an evening newspaper. He rather prided himself on bringing some of the standards of the "little magazine" for which he had written, to the general market place. Even in a daily column of a conservative newspaper, he would pay attention to revolutionary and "difficult" books, and he had been known to make obscure foreign essayists popular. Jerry invited him to lunch at his club.

"I've got something to tell you that will interest you," said Jerry. "You admire Santayana, don't you?"

"Yes. He isn't writing a new book, is he?" said the young critic. "I surely should have heard of it."

"Oh, no," said Jerry. "Nothing Old World, decadent, and ivory tower like that. This is a philosophy that's going to be sprung on the world next fall. It belongs in the great tradition all right, as you'll be one of the first to recognize. But it's true-blue, one-hundred-per-cent American. Straight out of the Middle West. American Gothic in philosophy they'll be calling it. I wouldn't mention it to most of the critics; they're purely literary men. But you're philosophical, you have a head for ideas."

The young man was deeply interested. It was just the beginning of the vogue of Americana. This was worth hearing about. He could not only make a column of it for his newspaper; he could write a long article about it for one of the little reviews. He very soon did.

Jerry talked about the System to a very able economist with philosophical leanings who was now running a big department store. There were a couple of presidents of the more liberal colleges whom he interested, and the director of humanities at one of the foundations. He had an eye, too, to the larger public. He luckily had an old friend who was an editor on *Life* and one on *Fortune*. He cornered the director of the *New York Times Sunday Magazine* and gave him a brief digest and answered one or two of his penetrating, pointed questions, though none too well. Many people asked him to produce the philosopher in person, but he could not persuade Professor Wilkins to leave his work to come to New York. "To be a philosopher in New York," the Professor wrote him, "has always seemed to me like trying to sing in a boiler factory."

By the time the book appeared, its reception was as widespread as it was cordial. During the week of its publication, a work which ordinarily might have been covered in a few paragraphs on the back pages of the book reviews months late, and then only in metropolitan centers, was reviewed instantaneously all over the country. The day of publication there was an editorial about it in the *New York Herald Tribune* which said it was fine to have, out of the very heart of the country, the Middle West which had seemed to some stupidly isolationist, so world-wide and searching and sensible a philosophy as that of the Wilkins System. A few crackpots, the editorial continued, thought the great philosophers were always revolutionary. Wilkins showed not only that the Middle West—the breadbasket of America—could produce spirit as well as bread, but that spirit here was sober and sensible. *The Nation* seized on the antireligiousness of the System, its secular humanism. The columnists who reviewed it on the day of publication tried to select the easier paragraphs, to say that they didn't quite understand it all but that it made very good sense, and that it was the intellectual event of the century. *Time* had a four-page review with a biography of the author, stressing his simple, homespun character, his humble origins, his popularity at the University, and his American good sense; and a very American Gothic-looking picture of the author was on the cover. Under his picture it said simply: "Plato, Cornbelt, American Sense." It predicted "hundreds of thousands will buy, some few hundred will read, and some millions will be talking about this book in the next six months." They were quite right.

There had to be a sound-proof room, a wit soon suggested, for anyone to be able to live without hearing the System mentioned. In the barber shops one would pick up *Life* and find a picture of the Professor's study, and, reproduced in large type, Jerry's undergraduate editorial about him. Nothing was said about Jerry's connection with the completion or the publicizing of the System. The popular radio comedians referred to the System. The Professor, much to his embarrassment and thanks to Jerry's contrivance, was made to appear in a movie news short reading a paragraph of his work.

There was something else, too, that Jerry had arranged, in connection with radio. There was a very popular current program on the air waves called "What This Country Needs." Every week there would be a representative of art or science or industry or government to tell what this country needed in art, in science, in business, in government. There had never been an evening devoted to What This Country Needs in Philosophy. This year there was to be such an evening. It coincided with the week of the publication of the book, and Professor Wilkins was to explain what it was that this country needed in wisdom. At first he could not be prevailed upon to appear in so immodest a pronouncement. But Jerry scolded him for his false diffidence, and said it was important to do everything he could to promote the widest public knowledge of his System. He noted, among other things, that there were lots of people already undertaking to explain the System on the air, and in lectures and in pamphlets. It would be best said and least betrayed if it were explained by the originator himself.

On the night of the broadcast Jerry, though he had tried sincerely to avoid it, was chairman. Behind the scenes he had already done a good deal. It was one of the most extraordinary audiences that had ever gathered in Carnegie Hall. The Russian and British ambassadors were present, and an observer from the State Department. There was hardly a name in arts, letters, finance, or education that was not to be seen there, and the more intellectual of the movie colony were well up front in the parquet. The *Saturday Review of Literature* had sent John Mason Brown, who knew that drama is found not only in the theater but among ideas.

The murmur of the audience before the event had the note both of excitement and decorum: the excitement because of the expected revelation, the spiritual unveiling; the decorum because this was no vulgar first-night audience, though there was a gossip columnist present. This was a group that consisted, in no small part, of the leaders of American life, though tickets had fallen through speculators into the hands of blackmarketeers. They and their gay-looking lady friends appeared odd seated next the dowager wives of celebrated university presidents. But the serious part of the audience predominated, and these knew that a spiritual revelation was impending; they knew, too, what this evening might portend. The most enlightened of those present knew, also, how badly and how deeply America needed leadership. As one newspaper publisher put it at the little dinner he had given the party he had arranged to take, en masse, to the occasion: "There was a time when Pericles spoke the mind of Athens. It's been a long time since there's been a leading mind to speak for the intelligence of America."

Some of the older people among the audience remembered that Bergson had once filled Carnegie Hall, and, though he spoke in French, had thrilled even those who knew not a word of that tongue. John Dewey had, in his heyday, too, commanded a wide popular hearing. But there were very few who could recall when so notable a crowd had awaited with so intense an expectation nothing other than a revelation in the form of a system of philosophy. Nor was it the audience in Carnegie Hall alone that waited. Two (not one) national networks were carrying the address, and for the unprecedented time of an hour and a quarter. The *Reader's Digest* had already printed a long digest of the philosophy, and the *Reader's Digest* was sponsoring this broadcast. In homes all over the country millions of families were tuned in, and even at bars and restaurants people were listening.

Jerry, modestly, and with consideration also of the limits of radio time, took only a very few minutes. But he did take the time to boast with piety that Professor Wilkins had been his teacher once, and said simply that he was happy now to present him as the teacher of the nation.

The Professor arose and walked to the microphone almost as in a trance. He had come to realize what a national event his System had become, and the obligation and responsibility it entailed for him. And while he had been waiting in the Speaker's Room he had felt a twinge of uneasiness. Somehow, the scene, the occasion, the public excitement about his "new" ideas, reminded him of nothing so much as the days when the Sophists had been fashionable in Greece. He knew that, since the Greeks, many shams in the way of ideas had had a brief vogue, and how often that happened in America, and how much worse it would have been, possibly, if any vogue in ideas had really lasted. Yet the thought crossed his mind that here, after all, was an opportunity. He knew that at least he was *not* a *sham*. He had the more confidence in himself because he knew that he was not trying to palm off some new-fangled oddity of his own. He was simply trying to restate for modern American minds the essence of the sane orthodoxy of Western philosophical thought, not the orthodoxy of the religions, but of the candid and realistic minds in all ages who spoke common sense for, and essentially the common sense of, all mankind. But would the general public understand? Would they care? Could he make himself clear? He found himself having something of the same nervousness with which he had first faced a small class at the University a generation ago, the same slight tension which he, like any good and conscientious teacher, feels, even after many years, just before a class. But his tension was many times multiplied now as he realized he was being, for this hour—exactly the time (counting out the time of Jerry's introduction) of a class at the University—the teacher of the nation.

There was a murmur as the lecturer arose. A good many of those present, especially those who had come for the show, had never seen a philosopher before, and they expected something weird and exotic, possibly Oriental-looking. But this man, for all his proper evening dress, looked homespun. He was a typical little middle-western college professor. And there was a general murmured comment on his obvious honesty, not always the most patent trait of popular lecturers, his simplicity and earnestness. When he began to speak, from his very first words his accent was revealed as what a wag present called a mixture of Middle West and Highbrow, of cornfield and professorese. It was noted, not without sympathy, that the Professor began rather nervously. Some of those who had known arrogant professors in the past sighed with relief.

"Ladies and gentlemen," began the Professor (and the silence was absolute), "I am afraid I have been brought to you under false pretenses, and I want to save you from any further illusion. I bring you no philosophical revelation, no Manna from Heaven." (A shrewd radio executive in the second row murmured to his wife: "He *couldn't* be more disarming. That's very shrewd technique.") The Professor continued: "I have not much use for originality in philosophy, and I would have less confidence in what I am about to expound to you did I not have the feeling that I am merely modulating freshly a long, sound tradition, begun with Aristotle himself. The Greeks were sound philosophers because they had no philosophers before them whose teachings they learned to recite by rote. They looked at the world clearly and candidly, and at the human beings in the world. The world has not changed *essentially*, whatever surface transformations there are, and human nature remains in essence the same. A sound philosophy today will not and cannot be very different from what it was in Greece. There is still the world of nature and that wonderful product of nature, man, equipped, if he is honest and persistent, to understand nature and, within measure, to control both it and himself, who is a part of it. The only excuse for my being here tonight is that in every generation, in every intellectual climate, the old truths need fresh statement, the old insights need to be re-expressed in terms of our own problems and the new knowledge of our own day. I have a further excuse; there are many attempts these days to give us folly or superstition in the name of philosophy, invitations to turn our backs on life and nature, to escape to some eternity beyond time, to fly to the supernatural, to glory in defeat or agony or despair. And, as you all know, the world was never so desperately in need of facing actuality, of organizing its intelligence and good will, never faced by so acute a challenge to turn the resources of nature to the most generous uses open to the mind and imagination of man. This is not only one world, as two world wars have made painfully clear; there is only one possibility of that world's saving itself: through intelligence, or life understanding its own conditions. In general, that conception of intelligence has been recognized flickeringly since the Greeks. It is my honorable privilege to try to restate that theme to you tonight. I shall try to be simple, but the issues of philosophy are not easy. You will forgive me if I indulge in some technical terms. But I shall try to be as free from jargon as possible."

The Professor's nervousness disappeared as he went on, and within five minutes he might have been in his own classroom, and this large audience of sophisticated national figures his cornfed young pupils at the University of X——. The speaker forgot the national networks, he was oblivious to the maturity of the faces before him. He forgot everything but his message and the fact that there were eager upturned faces to receive it. It was indeed remarkable that many of the countenances before him were eager and upturned, and some usually hard, cynical faces were turned toward him as if hungry for a new gospel.

A study of the expressions on the faces of that audience would have revealed, as some flash photographs taken during the lecture did reveal, bepuzzlement about some of the Professor's terms. Some looked grimly determined to understand. Some seemed lost in a beatific vision, as if it were the music of the voice and the melody of the themes that bemused them so that they did not care whether they understood or not. For the Professor, despite a slight mid-western nasality, had a winning softness and, for all his jargon, his sentences had cadence.

In substance he expounded, though with more complications and more reservations, what Jerry had explained to Mrs. Chapman at tea. Toward the close, he said one thing that Jerry had not said, and had perhaps not anticipated. It got into the first paragraph of all the front-page news stories the next morning: "There *is* one world and one human nature, and there is only one method, that of intelligent inquiry, by which it can be saved. If this is so, there is," said the Professor, "no *American* philosophy, *no* AMERICAN view of the world. Nor is it possible to practice wisdom in isolation from the remainder of the planet. If we are to be wise, it can only be by discovering what St. Paul once long ago and for different reasons told us: we are all members of one another. I don't like to draw political morals, but this one is too urgent not to be mentioned: a United Nations is the practical equivalent of what I have been saying, and a nation that sets up to be wise and reasonable *by itself* is courting folly and disaster."

In a bar in the Loop in Chicago, where the radio, almost unattended, had been broadcasting the Professor's words for an hour, someone was heard to say: "I don't know what this guy has been talking about for the last half hour, but he's for the United Nations; I get that. A New Dealer probably, one of those professors."

"Make that the lead item, that United Nations business,

on the eleven o'clock news report," said the radio news editor at the CBS studios.

Some interesting comments might have been heard by some universal listeners at various crucial radio receivers in New York. They were not unlike those made by the audience that filed out of Carnegie Hall, which, judging by some scattered comments in the lobby, was very much impressed. There was almost universal approbation of the Professor. He was clearly the real article. There were different grounds on which this was alleged. "Nobody but an authentic human being," one socially prominent lady declared, "would dare to be so careless in the tying of his bow tie." Others were awed and convinced by the very fact that most of the lecture was unintelligible: "No playing to popularity there!" Many seized on the notion of a world society. "The man has his head in the clouds, like any other philosopher, but he's clearly a sincere idealist," said some. "There is some obvious sense and applicability in his philosophy," said others. There was only one dissident observation, that from a professional colleague who had come to the hall out of morbid curiosity: "Wilkins is still a sophomore speaking to sophomores," he said, "and he still packs them in here in New York as he did at the University of X——."

There was (and it was quite unusual for a radio broadcast and unprecedented for a broadcast on philosophy) a good deal of editorial comment the next day or two. The *New York Times* had words of sober praise. "A great many people," ran its editorial, "think of philosophers as profoundly radical and revolutionary, or they think of thinkers in general as being Olympian and remote. Anyone who heard Professor Wilkins the other evening at Carnegie Hall must have been cured of such a notion. Here is a typical American; he might have been photographed as a prize winner in a 'typical American grandfather' contest. He bears in his speech the accent of the Midwest. His illustrations are homely: pigs stuck in mud, droughts in wheat country, stalks of corn. He is to American philosophy in the Midwest what Robert Frost is to American poetry in New England. He does not pretend, either, to have a new revelation. He tells us what the Greeks and the prophets have told us. He is the voice of the great tradition, with a Cornbelt cadence. And the listener in person or over the radio must have been heartened to hear so authentic a voice in our land speak for the security and peace and brotherhood of all lands. Some of Professor Wilkins's technical terms may have transcended the training of his listeners, but no one could mistake the honesty, the simplicity, and the truth of his message. Hail to the new American philosophy, which, as always, contains as no small ingredient the best of the Old World."

A woman columnist gave an almost hysterical picture of the Philosopher. She had not been so moved, she said, since she had first seen Toscanini conduct, and the Philosopher (as she called him) used his hands almost as eloquently as Toscanini uses his.

Only the *Chicago Tribune,* Jerry noted (he could not persuade the Professor to read *all* the clippings), dissented. It was a betrayal of the Professor's middle-western heritage, the *Chicago Tribune* commented, to have him deliberately exploit his position in the educational and philosophical world to utter the silly internationalist nonsense of the cosmopolitan East. It would be better for him and for our national safety if the Professor returned to his native midwestern soil and recovered the perspective of his own country, uncorrupted by New York and Europe. The *Tribune* added it was not surprised to note that the British and Russian ambassadors were there, expecting to hear the sort of thing they might want to hear. As a matter of fact, whenever *anyone* talked this internationalist gibberish he was talking either British imperialism or Russian revolution. It was a shame for a man who was being everywhere called "America's own philosopher" to talk such dangerous and treacherous nonsense. America's own philosopher should talk America's own interests. It was all the more alarming since the President had been photographed the other day with a copy of the System under his arm. The rest of the world had better realize that no philosopher spoke for America. Any middle-western farmer more accurately voiced the spirit of this nation than this university professor who had been catapulted into fame by rootless polyglot intellectuals on the eastern seaboard.

There were the usual articles in the *Nation* and *New Republic* explaining the System. The *Nation* sent the book for review to a recently converted Anglo-Catholic—he had been made over from an earlier phase of his life when Communism had been his ruling passion. Obviously, said his review, this System wasn't reliable at all, since it took its Aristotle directly from Aristotle; its Greeks from the Greeks. St. Thomas Aquinas was the only sound basis for a philosophy, certainly for one that could save the world. The *New Republic's* reviewer, having been brought up as a naturalist and empiricist at Columbia, was much more favorable, though he found a few disturbing references to eternal truths and a little too much tendency to both moralizing and systematizing to please him, for he had been brought up to believe that preaching and system-making had been a curse to philosophy.

The preachers in the liberal churches had a field day. Here

was a philosopher now being widely read—the highest expectations of the publishers had long been transcended by a sale of some six hundred thousand copies—who, while he did not, it is true, believe the conventional conception of God, repeatedly suggested that the word "divine" might properly be applied to the energies of nature which flower into man's highest ideals and achievements, to the goodness which is potential in nature, and to the truth which the mind of man can find in it. The System, they had to admit, seemed to deny immortality, but it did talk about "eternal things." At one point even the term "nature" seemed to be used with such reverence for its manifold and miraculous possibilities that, it was said in the text of the System itself, the word "*super*natural" might do almost as well.

This last was exactly what the liberal preachers of both Judaism and Protestantism, and a few daring Catholics, even, had been looking for. Here was a thinker who (though in his own special way) believed in God. Many secular-minded writers, too, found a wonderful opportunity and an exhilarating escape here. Many liberals hated to be classed with the unimaginative and literal atheists of the nineteenth century and earlier. They loved much of the poetry of the older religions without being able to believe it. Here was a man who, never moving beyond nature, still could talk without tears or pretense about the divine. It looked for a little while as if the atheists and the religionists were going to lie down together like lambs. For a time the System had a wide sale in the bookstores of the theological seminaries, except in one Seminary where the most popular professor, having revived Sin, objected to the emphasis in the System on the natural goodness of man.

The State Department asked the Professor to go to Argentina

on a good-will mission. There were rumors that he might be asked to give the Gifford Lectures at Edinburgh, and the *Times of London* gave a long serious analysis of the American edition of the System even before the book was published in London. Somewhat naïve, they said, like so many American philosophical works, but marked, as was to be expected from gallant allies, by fine feeling and a generous hope for mankind.

There were, of course, all sorts of dialectical defects found in the System by the philosophical journals, though they all recognized at least that there was enough technical jargon to argue with. But Jerry, who was interested in the wide spread of the Professor's ideas, was not too worried about that. The symbolic logicians, whose periodical had a circulation of about two hundred and fifty subscribers, were, of course, filled with contempt for a work that had so vulgarly wide an appeal and was, for the most part, unbecomingly intelligible.

By the time the book was published, Professor Wilkins was teaching at the University again, and his course, naturally, now had a thousand students. What was more, even some of his colleagues came to hear what on earth it was that their students and the newspapers all seemed to be talking about all the time. It became the fashion for stars en route from Hollywood to New York, or writers en route from New York to Hollywood, to break their journey at the campus of the University of X—— to listen to one of the Professor's lectures. It came to be the habit of students to try to guess who were the celebrities gathered in the back row. Edward G. Robinson, of course, was recognized at once. But the attendance of strangers grew rapidly; the fashion developed among ordinary tourists, too, so that eventually those not registered in the course could attend only by very special permission. The bureaucratic little Assistant Secretary of the University, it was said, had flatly refused a ticket to a famous ballet dancer.

The Professor through all this remained his familiar simple self, as far as circumstances permitted. Even his wife, who gloried in his fame, found it almost impossible to protect the Professor from all the demands on his time. A Czechoslovak journalist came all the way from Washington to interview the Professor. Nobody would leave him alone. The fan mail became an enormous problem. Not simply gushing letters of enthusiasm. Those, as Jerry explained to his old teacher, could be answered by a form letter or even a postcard. But there were letters of poignant and obviously sincere human questions. Thousands upon thousands of human beings seemed honestly to believe that the author of the System could answer all questions, and that somewhere concealed in the doctrine was a solution for all human ambiguities and issues and miseries. There came, for instance, a letter from a lady in South Dakota who was on the verge of divorce. What did the System have to say about divorce? The teachers' colleges all flooded the Professor with questions as to the implications of the System in "the area of secondary education." Textbooks began to be rewritten in terms of the System, and one teachers' college announced a course for the following year in "Methods of Teaching the Wilkins System." The Professor was inundated with requests to appear before women's clubs. He rejected most of them, though Jerry urged him to accept as many as possible. "After all," he said, "it is the women who influence the children of the next generation and begin to influence them earliest." The Professor did accept a few invitations and regretted it. He did not know which were worse, the earnest women or the frivolous ones. Both failed equally to understand; and the luncheons before his lectures and the teas after were simply too exhausting, even though the University, considering the special strain he was under and the kudos he had brought it, had cut down his teaching program considerably and released him from all committees.

The worst experience he had with forums, however, was not a women's club. It was called the Cup and Plate Club. He had been persuaded to address it largely through his own too-good and innocent heart. After about ten lectures at women's clubs he had resolutely turned down any further invitations. A lecture bureau had tried to persuade him to leave the University for a highly paid tour all over the country. Jerry had urged him to consider it seriously, on the ground that the System must be propagated as widely as possible. But the Professor felt his first duty was to the University, and, besides, the System, in all conscience, was being propagated enough. No, he would not and could not make such a tour. Then would he consider at least *one* lecture? There was one club in a big midwestern industrial city known as the Cup and Plate Club. It consisted of four hundred of the leading professional men from all over the region. They had expressed the most earnest desire to hear the Professor. They were his own fellow prairie-dwellers. The Professor could not resist. After all, a serious group of leading professional men could sow the seed of free wisdom throughout the whole territory. And the Professor could not resist the earnestness with which they seemed to desire his presence.

He arrived at the bleak chromium-plated hotel in this bustling freezing-cold midwinter western industrial city. He rather liked the idea of introducing the note of idealism into this town, famous for its practicality; it was noted for the manufacture of refrigerators. He had scarcely settled down to rest for a few minutes in an armchair when the phone rang, and picking it up he heard a brisk, businesslike voice: "This is Mr. Kenyon," the voice said. "I am the Chairman of the First National Bank here and also Chairman of the Cup and Plate Club. Glad to welcome you here, Professor. I just wanted to call to tell you that the speaker always dresses; the rest of us don't. I'll call for you at a quarter to seven."

When the brisk Mr. Kenyon called for the Professor, now attired in evening clothes, he greeted him with cordiality. But the Professor gathered somehow as they rode in the Chairman's car to the meeting that, considering all the earnest desire that had been expressed for his presence, the Chairman clearly appeared to know very little about him. "Your line's philosophy, isn't it, Doc?" said Mr. Kenyon. When they walked into the bare, badly lighted Masonic hall where the dinner meeting was to be held, the Professor received a second shock. "We've saved you for the climax," said the Chairman; "you're the second of the two events."

"Events?" repeated the Professor, raising his eyebrows. "I did not *know* I was an event, and that there was another one this evening. What is the other *event*?" he asked with mingled curiosity and uneasiness.

"Oh, we always have two events," said the Chairman. "The lecture bureau always sends us two events, one evening a month. We have a steak dinner and then the two events. They told us the two items were particularly good this time, you and the magician. But we thought we'd save you for the last."

The Professor never forgot that evening; the long dinner through which he sat making conversation with the Chairman, who had clearly not the least notion of what he or philosophy was, the conversation with the minister on his right who also did not know much more about either matter. Then the humorous introduction to the parlor magician, read from a script. Then the forty minutes of the most ordinary producing-an-egg-out-of-air, milk-inventing, rabbit-emerging parlor tricks decked out with the sort of sophomoric pseudo-Oriental mumbo jumbo such as might have entertained one of the less intellectual of college fraternities. Then, worst of all, the halting introduction by the Chairman, who had copied his data erroneously out of *Who's Who,* and who called the Professor "one of the most currently topflight psychologists in the country" and corrected himself to say "philosopher." (He added, "whatever that is.") There was a mumbling recital of the anecdote from Dr. Johnson, though it was credited to Mark Twain, about how a certain man had studied philosophy in his youth and the cheerfulness always kept breaking in.

The Professor had always prided himself on the easy rapport he had with audiences. He remembered distinctly the few occasions when it was clear from the first moment that there could be no rapport at all. This was, he very soon found, one of them. He began with one of the gentle anecdotes, half-humorous, half-serious, for which he was famous at the University. The audience had been relatively lethargic toward the magician. They were obviously dead cold to the Professor. By the middle of his address, a cold sweat was pouring from the Professor's face. These men looked at him as if they *challenged* him to hold their attention. It was all he could do not to say he would gladly refund the large fee they had promised him if only they would let him and themselves go home. The four hundred stolid leading professionals applauded politely at the end. The magician told the Professor if he would wait a minute they would share his car going back to town. He treated Professor Wilkins as a professional colleague, and remarked on the way back to the hotel on the coldness of the audience. "I don't think they liked either of us too well, but you've got to expect it sometimes. Audiences differ. It'll be better tomorrow night. Who's booking you?" The Professor replied primly that he was *not* on tour.

The Professor did not like to feel he was an intellectual snob, but the evening rankled in him. It was not only that he had been treated as so much merchandise. It was clear that the lecture bureau had lied and that these four hundred leading professionals of this prairie region had never so much as heard of him. There was something else that decided him from then on to do no popular lecturing, something that this evening had made symbolically and patently clear. Philosophy for America was, at least for such a group as this, simply a form of parlor magic and on a level with it. And the vogue of the System was, itself, simply another form of magic, with few clever enough to try to guess the technique of the illusions by which they felt themselves half entertained and half defrauded, or even to suspect what in the case of parlor magic they knew, that they were illusions.

The Professor was to have another lesson in the incidence of ideas in America. Jerry very firmly insisted that he must come to New York to a large dinner party that Mrs. Chapman wished to arrange for him. The Professor pleaded academic duties, fatigue, his weariness with even the little of New York society to which he had been exposed. But this was important, said Jerry. Mrs. Chapman was to have forty-eight of the most eminent and representative men and women from all the arts and sciences and professions and the varied aspects of life and culture and society in America. She knew everybody, and could count on her invitations being cherished, especially when they announced as the guest of honor the author of the System. It would be a telling evening in the career of the Wilkins influence. Professor Wilkins, though he had begun to suspect the accuracy of Jerry's judgment in these matters, felt deeply grateful to him for his work, his support, and his patently good intentions and filial piety. He agreed to come.

The dinner at the Chapmans' was a splendid affair, including the actual dinner itself. It was splendid in other ways, too: white tie, of course, and the ladies' dinner gowns worthy of so important an event. The roster of guests was a small *Who's Who* of New York, America, and the world. There were two four-star generals and a full admiral, the presidents of two eastern universities, a fashionable bishop of the Episcopal Church, a prominent liberal lay Catholic (the Cardinal had refused to come), an eminent rabbi, three newspaper publishers, a visiting French philosopher, and a transient English novelist returning to the French Riviera from Hollywood. There were two well-known psychiatrists, of different schools, one of the most learned of the biochemists from one of the big foundations, a Federal judge, a noted decorator, the Undersecretary of the Treasury, and the British Ambassador (the Russian Ambassador was rumored to have declined on the ground that he was weary of this bourgeois ideology). Added to these was a scattering of the more literate of Mrs. Chapman's *Social Register* friends, a couple of curators from the museums, and one European orchestra conductor. All these, and their wives, added up to forty-eight, seated at eight small tables of six each—the placing of people at which had been no small problem for Mrs. Chapman's social secretary. Except for Jerry, who, of course, was present, Professor Wilkins knew hardly anyone, and by the time, over the cocktails and the canapés, he had had most of them presented to him for a moment or two, his head was a whirl of confusion and modest embarrassment. At dinner he sat at the table with Mrs. Chapman and the fashionable bishop, one newspaper publisher and his wife, and the psychiatrist and his wife, who was a well-known sculptress.

There was only one reference to the guest of honor in any way embarrassing at dinner: "Let us drink a toast," said Mrs. Chapman, rising, "to the world's greatest philosopher, and America's own!" Then she said, "We won't bother the Professor about his ideas over dinner. That can wait."

The bother began when the forty-eight assembled guests sat in the grand drawing room. "Most of us here were at the Professor's lecture in Carnegie Hall," said Mrs. Chapman, "so we won't ask him to give an exposition of his philosophy. But I am sure he will be glad to answer any questions that any of you may have."

For a few minutes there was an embarrassed silence.

The first person to speak up was an earnest youngish matron who had once been president of the League of Women Voters and was well known for her combination of simple charm and enterprising activity in the public welfare. And for all her quiet manner, everyone knew how she efficiently got things done. She had once made laggard city administrations do something with eventual promptness about the cleaning up of the parks.

"When," she asked quietly, "is the System going into *effect*?"

One of the generals wished to know whether any possible

enemy would be likely to share this philosophy, or whether, if the System should come to dominate public opinion in this country, it would provoke enmity on the part of rival powers. The Professor said he hoped it would not be immodest if he said he thought his philosophy might help to promote world unity.

There was present another young matron who had been very active in Child Guidance work. "Professor," she said, "do you mind my making a suggestion? I have been so entranced and elevated by the truth and beauty of the System that I have not the slightest doubt it could transform the nation and the world. But I wonder whether it might not be possible to have a sort of junior version of it in simpler form. Not for adults; I think grownups should have to wrestle with the difficulties of your thought. But for children. After all, basic attitudes are formed long before people learn to think. In your work you quote Plato himself on the importance of early persuading the young to sound ideas. By the time people are old enough to read your philosophy, they are hopelessly conditioned to older, outmoded ways of thought. I should think a primer of the subject that might be put in the hands of a seven-year-old child could do incalculable good. It might even be illustrated."

The Professor murmured politely that while he saw certain difficulties in making philosophical distinctions on the level of a child's mind, perhaps it could be done, and possibly with illustrations.

Mrs. Chapman interrupted to ask the fashionable bishop if he would not favor the group with some comments on the System. The Bishop had been known for a generation as an ecclesiastic who spoke his mind firmly on dangerous new doctrines in religion and in philosophy that seemed to him pernicious, or immoral new books or dance crazes. Mrs. Chapman had reason to know that the Bishop thought rather well of the System, and that, even if he did not, he was even more a gentleman than he was a man of God and an experienced ecclesiastical politician, and that he would not say sharp or insulting things about the work of her guest. Or, for that matter, anything very penetrating, either.

"Hm," said the Bishop, a small man who had once been defined as a mathematician's conception of a point—that which has position without size. "It's what the Church has been standing for for the past two thousand years," he said simply. The Bishop looked his most professionally benign tonight.

One of the two eminent publishers present had excused himself for a few moments on the ground that he must get in touch with his office. He came back beaming. "They tell me at the office," he said, "that the most recent Gallup Poll shows that ninety-seven per cent of the people of the United States are in favor of the System."

"How would the System affect art?" asked one of the museum curators, and the other one said that what the Professor had been teaching was exactly what modernistic painters had been trying to paint for the last three decades. The novelist on the way to the Riviera said he had been much impressed by the System, by its lucidity, its truly philosophical spirit. "You will not misunderstand me," he said, "for I regard it as a great compliment when I say your book reads as interestingly as a good novel." A wealthy Communist present wanted to know what was the relationship of the Professor's doctrine to those of Marx.

The Professor answered all these questions as best he could, and his modesty and clarity were admired by all. Mrs. Chapman tried to pin him down about God, and the novelist tried to find out whether he thought, in the light of contemporary astronomy, there was, in the long run, in the *ultimate* finality, anything really hopeful, anything other than futility, for man and civilization. Professor Wilkins never gave glib answers. He tried to be as honest as he could. He would not grant for a moment that, in the ordinary sense, he believed in God, though the Bishop murmured that it was clear he really did. As for the futile end of all things, there was, he said, a *long* meanwhile in which much could be made of man and nature.

There were a good many people present, especially among the wives, who could not be expected, even for so distinguished a guest of honor, to keep their minds on high philosophical questions all evening. Moreover, after so plentiful and rich a dinner, the intellects even of some of the most eminent people present were not functioning too briskly. The questions languished and, by this time, so did the Professor. The large audience broke up into smaller groups who discussed themes more familiar and fascinating to many of those present: inflation, taxes, recent marriages and divorces. The Professor engaged Jerry in conversation, and most of the guests, either from shyness or diminishing interest, did not venture to address the philosopher. The Professor pleaded to Jerry and to Mrs. Chapman exhaustion from the long conversation and questions and begged to be excused. As the butler handed him his hat and coat and opened the door, he was reminded of something in the history of philosophy. Had not Protagoras once expounded his philosophy to just such a group in Athens? But there had been no Socrates here tonight to ask him penetrating questions.

Several people murmured in their little groups that they felt that Socrates had been among them. Most of them had not even noticed that he had left.

When the Professor had come back to the University—he had been away only a week—he found an extraordinary amount of fan mail and telegrams. He had employed a special secretary for the purpose, but she no longer sufficed. He sat down exhausted to reflect on the events of the past year. Probably his System was more widely talked about than almost any other reflective book in America since Bellamy's *Looking Backward*. There were even Wilkins societies being formed all over the country to expound the principles of the System. But, the Professor reflected, where were the Browning Societies now? What did such a dinner party as Mrs. Chapman's mean? What did the readers of his book, who, judging from most of the letters, clearly did not understand it, get out of it? The Professor wearily sat down at his desk, grimly pressed his lips, and wrote the following letter to Jerry.

"Dear Jerry: I know you meant well, but oh, that mine enemy would write a book! You innocently supposed, and so did I, that a sound philosophy widely read would transform the country, and even be understood. I think you are wrong, and I do not think the way you and I have chosen is the way to educate people philosophically.

"Philosophy is a long slow growth. It must germinate in the soul of man, in isolation. It is the product of meditation, winter and summer, of brooding in silence to the deepest recesses of the mind and heart. The best that a teacher can do is to foster habits of analysis and meditation that a young man will continue them the remainder of his life. If a thinker has the root of the matter in him, and he brings to some articulation thoughts about the nature of things, about society and about life, perhaps his system will come to be known and, what is a longer process, felt and lived, by a considerable and influential portion of mankind. Thus Plato was influential ultimately, not so much through the direct impact of his works as through the fact that the forms and rites of Christian tradition and Christian worship and Christian feeling embodied, often in passionate images, his ideas. John Locke's ideas filtered slowly into the economics and politics of democratic societies in the hundred to two hundred years after his death. But these things cannot be hastened. One can't convert a nation instantaneously to philosophy, or to *a* philosophy. I do not know why I ever believed, or, if you don't mind my putting it this way, ever let you persuade me, that my philosophy would be any different. Such truths as it contains have, most of them, been known many hundred years to a few. The world has never been among any large portion of its inhabitants converted to these truths, though, in their honest and candid hearts and practice, men have believed some of my principles, whatever inherited or established or fashionable current follies they subscribed to.

"I wonder if you remember that once, long ago, when you were a pupil of mine, I read a page or two from Plato's *Phaedrus,* that part in which he says the written word can never compare in power and truth with the spoken one. I should never have tried to write down my thoughts. Something evaporates from the thinker when the living voice is gone. It is as if readers get the words but not the music nor the temper in which the words are uttered, the tone of voice which modulates the very meaning. Written words give readers at best an opiate, not a challenge.

"I should have had the sense to stay in my own bailiwick, to speak to my own people, the young people of this region. They understand me essentially, though they may not understand everything I say. They have no ax to grind; they are ingenuous; they are malleable; they have enthusiasm still; they still have hope. They are not middle-aged people who have been disillusioned of a dozen fashionable revelations and in every new one find only the titillation of a temporary new excitement in their bored lives. A new philosophy is for these older people like a new gadget or a new toy. Or it is a desperately clutched-at magic formula. They'll tire of the toy very soon, or discover that the System is not any magic at all. It is simply a modest suggestion of what, by co-operative effort and sustained discipline, mankind may achieve. Those people gathered at Mrs. Chapman's or at my broadcast really do not, most of them, want a program for action or a faith to live by. They want a new salvation without cost to themselves in effort or renunciation or ardor or endurance.

"Socrates, whom I have always regarded as the model for all teachers, had, I am now certain, the right idea. He never wrote; he gathered together a few promising young men. He thought if he could make a difference in their characters and introduce some discipline into their minds; give them the habit of critical understanding, they would know both themselves and what their intentions meant, and thus, and only thus, understand the world. Perhaps even my big lecture course has been a mistake. Even the spoken word becomes a hollow sound if it is not the meeting of minds in the exchange of words. A small seminar, the give and take of ideas—maybe that is the way I really ought to have been 'teaching' philosophy all these years. Though there is a place for my big course, I think. These youngsters here in the Middle West are hungry for a moral challenge, a suggestion of what the free minds of free men can do with freedom, freedom from the conventional stereotypes in which so many of them have been brought up. I seem to be able to kindle their imaginations, because they are young and idealistic and because I do not try to give them magic, and they respond to an old man who still has faith in the young adventure of mankind.

"Next year I shall go back to the University exclusively. For a few years more I shall be an 'influence' at the great State University of X——. Then I shall retire, and in a few years I shall be dead. And it will be remembered perhaps, and mentioned occasionally that once I was a good teacher at the University of X——."

Professor Wilkins was right. Within a year the celebrity of the System had vanished. Copies of it were sold at a very large discount in the department stores. Mrs. Chapman was entertaining other celebrities, and a new form of Yoga, presented by an able young British novelist, had captured the imagination of the more literate. The more popular taste reverted to a new *Guide for the Uneasy* that had just been published.

The Professor's big course was still crowded, for it was said all over the campus that *last* year he had been a national celebrity. But there were no longer any visiting eminences, and no faculty members came any longer, out of curiosity both morbid and envious, to see what it actually was that the Professor taught. Three years later students coming to the University vaguely knew that Professor Wilkins was important, and that once, some time ago, he had written a book. People began to say that his lectures lacked his old fire. It suddenly became clear to everyone, students and colleagues alike, that he was a tired old man. At the age of sixty-five he retired. Four years later he was dead. He long remained a great legend at the great State University of X——. And occasionally it was remarked of a senator in Washington or a writer in New York that a touch of wisdom or poetry he had came from his old philosophy professor, a wise old man named Wilkins. The System soon ceased to be the subject even of Ph.D. dissertations.

EIGHT

The Unconvinced

LATE one afternoon at the Millennium Club, a short time after I had listened there to the psychiatrist's story recounted earlier in these pages, I found myself sitting in the Lounge beside MacNerny, the genial retired newspaper editor whom everyone loved for his generous sallies, his humane wit, and his realistic sense of the world, untinctured by disillusion or worldliness. MacNerny had been a city editor in the old, less streamlined days. He was always full of stories, and not of this country only, for in his early days as a roving reporter he had roamed the world. What impressed people most about him was how he had kept, through all the trivia of events with which, as a city editor, he had dealt, a sense of the longer meanings of things, an awareness of the larger tides that determined the doings of men. "How did you manage to remain so philosophical in a newspaper office?" I once asked him.

"But where else?" he replied. "Where so good a spot to observe the chance in human affairs, or the ruthless operations of Fate?"

MacNerny usually had all the good stories, so that (though I loved to listen to him), on the few occasions when I thought I had a tale that ranked fairly with his, I could not refrain from passing it on to him. "Jamieson, the psychiatrist," I said, "was telling me quite a story the other night about a man who had a curious neurosis: the philosophic neurosis, he called it. The fellow had a singular compulsion to have a clear and consistent view of the world."

"Jamieson cured him, no doubt," said MacNerny. "Psychiatrists are pretty suspicious of that sort of thing."

"Oh, yes," I said, "he cured him, but the really interesting part of the story is how the man got that way and how he tried to cure himself first. He thought there was some philosophy somewhere in the books that would show everything added up to the True, the Good, and the Beautiful. Jamieson said the desire to have a clear and consistent view of the world was what he called a compulsion." And I told MacNerny the story as well as I could remember it. He listened with his usual cordial interest; MacNerny had a wonderful gift of giving you his whole live attention. He listened with the same vivacity with which he talked.

When I was through, he looked reflective for a moment. "Very good story," he said, "but I wonder if Jamieson was right in his diagnosis. A desire to have a clear and consistent view of the world is not a neurosis. There *is* a philosophic neurosis, I believe one might call it the *typical* philosophic neurosis. But I think it takes a rather different form. I knew a man who had it once. Except that Jamieson's patient went to extremes, he really was philosophically, which is to say humanly, quite normal. Maybe the man I am speaking of was also. But it didn't look that way to me, nor to his other friends. He didn't come to me to be cured. He told me his story one night in London when I was at the London office of the Associated Press. He had a job with us for a few months, though I never felt he was really committed to newspaper work. You can tell at once the man with a true vocation for it. I felt he had taken the job chiefly because he wanted to be in Europe for a while. He wasn't sold on newspaper work; he was never convinced it was worth doing. Never was convinced of anything his whole life long. That was his story, and it might have been a tragic one. But I never felt, somehow, however moody he was, that Warren was headed for disaster. Some people have the certificate of that written all over them. He did not.

"We used to tease him around the office. Most newspapermen are skeptics. They have reason to be. They see what the public men say, and they see, more intimately than most people, what the public men do. They are accustomed to knowing the lowdown on things, so that they can't have too highfalutin a notion of human beings. It drives some of them, out of sheer self-defense, to the sheerest sentimentalism."

I smiled inwardly, for a kindly Hibernian sentimentalism was part of the charm of the speaker himself.

"Yes, most newspapermen are skeptical, but Warren outdistanced us all. We'd tell him that the Prime Minister had just promised to do something about Irish independence. He would smile as he sat down at his typewriter. And I must say I couldn't blame him for that. He'd read aloud the campaign promises that the Republican or any candidate had just made. He'd call our attention to the genteel obituary of one of the most eminent men and notorious rotters in England. He came to be known as "Doubting Thomas" around the office, and we used to say that he wouldn't believe it had stopped raining, if he heard it on somebody else's report, without first going to the window to see for himself. He was one of the kindliest of men and would lend money, deeply doubtful that he would ever get it back. When he had just made some acerbous and skeptical comment on human nature, one of us would point out to him his own conscientiousness at his work, for he *was* very conscientious, and his own generosities. 'I wonder if that's what those things really are,' he would say, and point out what doubts he had that he ever did anything out of real kindness, or that his conscientiousness was anything other than fear.

"One night we met at a bar frequented by American newspapermen in London. Over a Scotch and soda I found myself saying to Tom Warren: 'Tom, where did you ever learn to be, when did you ever *start* to be, so completely skeptical? It's a sort of mania with you, isn't it? You seem to enjoy it so much. I'll bet you looked skeptically at the milk in your bottle.'

"Warren was a moody chap, and this evening he was particularly so. He looked at me darkly. 'What makes you think I *like* being skeptical? Good God!' he said with sudden intensity, 'I wish I weren't. I've been longing more than I can tell you, ever since I was eight years old, to be *convinced.* The trouble with me is I'm one of the permanently unconvinced.'

" 'Unconvinced of what?' I asked.

" 'Of anything, of everything,' said Tom, ordering another Scotch. 'Ever since I was eight. Never could quite believe. I remember the first time I heard the phrase: *Seeing is Believing.* It was at school. On my way home, I found myself staring at things, shops, buses, people, with a new and critical eye. *Supposing I don't believe,* I said to myself, *and I don't. I wonder if those things are really there? Maybe it's like a magic lantern show.* I used to close my eyes in bed at night and in the darkness ask myself what proof I had that there was anything there. I sometimes doubted even myself, and pinched myself to make sure. But even though pinching hurt me, it didn't convince me.

"'Well,' he said, taking the second drink, 'I went on from there. I found it harder and harder to believe what my contemporaries seemed to believe. The Sunday school lessons, for one. I kept on wondering how on earth they knew all this stuff about Jesus, though I never dared to mention my doubts at home. And about God being everywhere. I used to wonder if He was in the slum I passed on the way home.

"'And then, I'd hear my mother at home say so-and-so was such a good man. But I knew how mean he could be to children. Or that it was right to give money to the poor, and wrong to speak in a loud voice. But I knew many fine football players with loud voices. Well, I don't suppose I was the only kid who would ask *Why*? But I think I was less ready than any child I know about, to accept at face value any explanation I was given. *He has a curious way of looking at you out of the corner of his eye,* mother would say, *whenever you try to tell him anything.* At prep school I found myself, when the preacher spoke of immortal life, inwardly asking myself how he could possibly prove it, and wondering how it could be proved that the Lord maketh me to lie down in green pastures. He never had, and I doubted that He ever made anyone else do it.

"'Don't think,' Warren said, 'that I was just a smart-aleck kid. I can't tell you how eager I was to be convinced. How eager I still am.'

"'What do you want to be convinced of now?' I asked him.

"'Oh, of anything important, really. If there were just one proposition about life that really mattered that I could be convinced of! But I never have been convinced of anything but the relatively trivial. I believe two and two make four, and that the sun rises every day, but that's as far as it goes. I can't believe anything *important* is proved; not God, not immortality, nor simpler things; that anything is provably important or beautiful or good—*anything!* There's always a doubt that lingers in my mind. Wasn't there an old chap named Protagoras who said: *Man is the Measure of all things?* Well,' Warren went on, 'I doubt right now that I'll ever have life proved to me, or the world, or human ideals. I wish I could.'"

MacNerny paused in his tale of his skeptical friend.

"I don't remember the details of what he said in his own words. But this, as I gathered it, was his story. At college he had continued to feel curiously apart, as if he were the most unconvinced of men, or the only unconvinced one. The rest, most of them, seemed to take the mores of the college quite seriously. They wrote down the doctrines of the professors. They believed they were in love. They were taken in by the theater, by wealth, by glamour, by sex, by success. Warren wished he could be. He tried hard. But always there was something that seemed to him to demand *proof*. His roommate at college was interested in social revolution. Warren found himself questioning it altogether. And he hated his questioning. He wished to Heaven he might be convinced that life or anything in it logically justified itself. David Hume seemed to him to be only a half-hearted and not quite honest skeptic. He is doubtful and analytic just so far, and then recommends that the reader go back to his chess and backgammon after dinner as usual.

"Well, Warren didn't worry too much about the reality of the external world, or of causation, but he did worry a good deal because he could not believe very much more: conscience, patriotism, love, or religion. And the gap between his skepticism and his desire to be convinced grew wider. He simply couldn't believe; and he simply could not live without belief. He came very near to being converted, as some of his friends had been, to Roman Catholicism. But he found it impossible to accept the initial premise of God, from which all else followed. He could not even be converted to a profession; his family had early intended that he should be a lawyer. He had thought of being a doctor, an engineer. He finally drifted into newspaper work. 'I thought it would be a good place for a cynic or at least a skeptic,' he said. He never wanted to be a cynic or even a skeptic. Well, that's how he got to be with us in London. He liked proof, and he had a great respect for facts, and he was a fine one for ferreting them out; all that helped to make him a good reporter. And there was something about him that prompted Cabinet ministers, even, to tell him the truth—he would just look at them penetratingly when they made grandiose statements or magniloquent promises.

"At the home office they congratulated us on having found a man who had such a gift for getting at the inside stories of things. But Warren didn't stay with us very long. He told me one day he was going to leave, that he had saved up a little money and that he was going to see the world. 'Well, not exactly the world,' he said, 'but certain people in it. I've got questions to ask them. Did you ever read Plato's *Apology*?' he said. 'If you did, you remember how Socrates had been told by the Oracle of Delphi that he was the wisest man in Athens. He simply couldn't believe it, so he decided to ask the poets, the generals, and all the celebrated men of Athens what their wisdom consisted in. He found he was wiser than they were. He was the only one in Athens who *knew* he didn't know anything.

Well,' said Warren, 'I've decided to conduct a similar inquiry. There seem to be people in the world who have a belief by which they have been convinced; they think they have a valid ideal, a rational standard, by which they can live. They seem to have found for themselves convincing answers. I'm going to try to find out if they're *really* convinced. Maybe they'll take the trouble to convince *me*. I talked to Ramsay MacDonald at 10 Downing Street the other day at the end of an interview I had with him. It was toward the close of the afternoon, and he seemed tired to the point of relaxation and apparently in the mood for a little talk. "You are convinced of the soundness of Socialism," I said, "aren't you?"

"'"Why, of course—aren't you?" he said.

"'"Not quite," I said, "or of any political system."

"'"Socialism is the one thing there is that can be proved logically," he said. And I must say as he went on he seemed to be pretty well convinced by his own logic. He had been a Fabian when young and had been touched by the whole Shaw-Wells gospel. He's never had a doubt since. He honestly believes in the future of mankind and in Socialism as *the* way of achieving the welfare of mankind. I pointed out what seemed to be happening to Socialism in Russia, and what regimentation in a planned society would be, and how, despite my good will and my sympathy with all the criticisms the Socialists make of capitalist society, I doubted that it could be proved that it would work. I pointed out the dangers of bureaucracy which he seemed to have forgotten, the limits to human nature and to generosity, even under the most auspicious conditions. I don't mean that I knew more than the Prime Minister, but I knew enough to know that the answers were certainly less certain, less clear, less cogent and coherent than he supposed.

" 'The other day a big banker arrived from America in connection with some big international loan, or international utilities, or something—I forget what. Well, I had a talk with him, too, and I couldn't help raising similar questions about free enterprise. I pointed out all the usual things, how free enterprise had broken down and landed us in a world-wide depression. I pointed out that business uncontrolled had led us into disaster. One could hardly believe that relapsing into that old free world would work any better now, or marshal any arguments to validate such a whimsical conviction.

" 'I've got a list of people whom I want to see in America and Europe. They have various kinds of allegedly rational belief, or faith, in success, in the revolution, in the paramount importance of love or sex or nonresistance or violence or whatnot. I'm going to try to see if they'll give me a clue as to why they're convinced of the ultimacy of their special passion or program or salvation.'

"Warren quit his job shortly, and I did not see him until a few years later when he walked into my office in New York," MacNerny said.

" 'Well,' I said 'have you found anything yet you regard as proved?'

" 'Quite the contrary,' he said. 'If you'll come out for a drink, which at least makes the necessity of proof less urgent, I think I may have an interesting story to tell you.'

"We went to a bar close by, and Warren's story ran about as follows.

"He had managed, first, he related, to get a Russian he knew in London to talk freely, a Russian newspaperman. He plied him with vodka first. The man continued, even after the sixth drink, to seem a convinced revolutionary. He was one of the two men he did meet, he said, who was sure, was *really* convinced, of anything. He had it all straight from Marx and Lenin, it seemed. On authority. And Warren met a Catholic friend of his, a convert in New York who had become a distinguished lay writer on Catholic belief. He, too, seemed convinced. Otherwise, he found most of those he went to see really not much more convinced of anything than himself. 'In London,' said Warren, 'I talked with a good many people, mostly conservatives, who thought they had everything proved. It was amusing to see some diehard Tories in a world so visibly changing who thought that the soundness of the British empire had been demonstrated, and that of laissez-faire and individualism. And when I got back to the United States, I found similar people. I discovered that there are people (they are usually economically secure) who, with the aid of economists, so-called, prove that free enterprise is the only system. And there are those (some of them pretty secure, too)—parlor pinks—who think that only they can demonstrate a perfect logical system, that only in a planned economy is it possible for civilization to survive.

"'I talked to a good many of the most eminent practitioners of these doctrines, and some of them, I must say, seemed fairly well self-convinced anyway. And as I listened to them, I could not help admiring the lucidity with which they marshaled their arguments, the coherence with which they passed from their unexamined axioms to their inescapable conclusions. I felt in every case, though, that the axioms were questionable and, though it was harder to detect, I thought I saw flaws in the steps toward the conclusions. But I could never tell just what the flaws were, nor could I tell why *I* was so sure I could not really accept the axioms to begin with.

"'But, as I said, only a few of all these people seemed to be without inner doubts, and I had a feeling that these were, to persuade themselves, whistling on a sort of penny logical whistle to keep up their courage. The world was obviously changing; the securities, moral and financial, of their lives were very precarious, and they were looking for proofs to sustain them in what they could no longer wholeheartedly believe. The more the traditional free enterprise economy failed to function, the more they would seek, and learn by rote, proofs that it was the only thing that did function. In the same way I noticed that those were most emphatic in their proof that national sovereignties were the only possible form of international organization who saw with reluctant clarity that the world is becoming small and one. At just the moment when in an air age national sovereignties have become meaningless, they are being whooped up to blind and parochial nationalisms.

"'*I* was in the same boat as everyone else—with only one difference. We all wanted proof, and we all doubted. But these people, in respect to economic systems, talked themselves into believing they had found proof. And I, perhaps, with equal stubbornness, talked myself into being unconvinced.

"'I found the same passion for proof and precocious desire to find it in more personal matters. It suddenly dawned on me that psychoanalysis was an attempt to reduce the palpable chaos of human conduct to some clear logical pattern. Everything could be clearly explained, and it was possible, the addicts claimed, if you talked long enough under proper guidance, to prove to yourself what were the sources of your agonies and discontents. Or, if you talked long enough without guidance, you could prove to yourself whatever you most deeply desired; rationalization, they call it.

" 'Well, I seemed to find that most of the people who thought they had proved God or Free Enterprise, or Planned Economy, or Non-Violence to themselves were really simply rationalizing. Below the loud and garrulous proofs, I would note (it was not very hard) the profoundest insecurities. Reason, logic, this is the protesting-too-much of the uneasy and uncertain human creature. In his secret heart, everyone knows that proof is not possible for the things one most deeply cherishes or most deeply wants. The most profoundly religious people found that out centuries ago—St. Augustine and John Donne and Pascal. It was the agony of nineteenth-century intellectuals like Matthew Arnold and Amiel. It is the agony and crucifixion of spirit of many thinkers today. The emancipated shudder at their emancipation. The liberals do not trust their liberalism, the saints their saintliness. The passion for proof is the passion of those who doubt most intimately in their heart of hearts. I'm one of them.

" 'I went off to India for a while and managed to get an interview with Gandhi, and I was almost convinced that he was convinced. But I came away wondering how much his saintliness and nonviolence were devices and political tools. And somehow, it seemed impertinent to ask a saint for proof. The heart, as Pascal said, has its reasons. But I am not quite sure that the heart's reasons are really reasonable. I still wanted proof. I still do want it.'

"I can't reproduce all that Warren told me," said MacNerny. "I'm reconstructing a little from memory. But I think I am giving you in substance what he told me. As I understand it, his money gave out, and he returned to the United States, where he got various odd jobs, partly because he couldn't bring himself to settle down to any one profession, and partly because he began to feel that he might find among the insecure people he would run into the sign of ultimate conviction he sought: passion or devotion buttressed by proof. Well, he found varying degrees of emotional conviction, all right, but not much support for it. He worked on a ranch in Montana, and on a fruit farm in California. He went off to Brazil for a while and taught English for a time in a remote village in the tropical northern part of that country. He got a job for a few months as a purser on a ship, and in the long days at sea he would, at one time or another, find a passenger who thought he could prove some faith he deeply lived, or thought he lived by. There was an engineer on the small passenger vessel on which he was purser who proved to him almost mathematically that sex was the one meaning that life had. In Rio de Janeiro, he ran into a small group who had a religion inherited from Auguste Comte. They all belonged to a Positivist church where they had a religion which depended, they thought, on pure science. But there were very few members of the congregation.

"He roamed around for a while among half a dozen different jobs, as far from intellectuals as possible. And he did find a few people who had, as it were, a natural, unargued, unarguable conviction that they had found a truth. There were a few simple, pious people he worked with in a shipping office. There was the young rake who thought it quite clear that men lived by sex and liquor; there were those who lived for their families or for success. Some of these had no definite proof at all. They lived by habit. If one could so drug one's self, perhaps one would not need conviction. He found some of the followers of Father Divine among the Negroes who worked for him for a while in a bottling plant; he found some simple, believing Catholics. He had a young friend who was a sort of acolyte in a Buddhist center in New York. He seemed convinced, too. He came to the conclusion that all those who were not simply hypnotized were either fooling themselves or too narrow in their logic, or living simply by stereotypes as machines existed, or, like animals, by habit.

"He had a letter to a distinguished English novelist now living in retirement in Florence. He had heard that this man had come to be, as he grew older, more and more interested in philosophy. His books were full of a worldly wisdom, and he clearly had a well-ordered head. He told the novelist how he had been seeking something that was absolutely foolproof and logic-tight. They were sitting on the terrace of the writer's villa above the city of Florence at Settignano. Mallen, the novelist, looked at Warren and smiled. 'I think you're rather absurd to look for proof in life,' he said. 'It can't be found. There's a pathetic fallacy in human nature, seeking to prove to itself that the world makes as much sense as a good mind would have it make. I see very little evidence that a good mind made the universe, or for any sensible reason, or that life fulfills any sensible purpose or could do so long.'

" 'But that realization doesn't seem to have upset you very much,' said Warren.

" 'It used to depress me in my youth when I put logical demands upon the universe,' said the novelist, 'but with maturity I think one learns to do so no longer. You know the old saying that to understand is to forgive. Well, to understand is to be resigned. One of the things one must learn to understand is that from the point of view of pure logic, everything is absurd, which, translated into moral terms, means futile. And certainly everything, as you have apparently found out, is dubious.'

"'And that doesn't bother you either?' asked Warren.

"'No,' answered the novelist, 'because I found out something about life very early; both that it is absurd and that it must be taken for granted. You assume the universe, you accept the nature of things. As Carlyle said of Margaret Fuller's acceptance of it: Gad, she'd better! To live is an act of faith in a universe in which you don't really believe in any case. Such a discovery is a wonderful liberation. All that is destroyed comes to life again, all that is dubious becomes a convenient illusion. That's not as cynical as it sounds, either. It's really the way in which everyone lives, plain men and sophisticates alike. And it's what makes possible the adventure of mankind. I used to be quite upset when I was very young because I was, with reason, skeptical of everything. Because life clearly was absurd, I could not believe anything anyone told me that aimed to prove it had a meaning or reality. An adolescent begins to observe the shocking incongruities between people's actions and their pretensions. He begins to notice the cruelties and blindnesses in nature and contrast them with the stories he has been taught about the meaning of the universe and the high intentions of God. Well, I was a typical sensitive adolescent. A good many people never get beyond that. They turn into sentimentalists, trying to believe what they can't intellectually credit, or into cynics, guarding themselves by hardness from being hurt any longer, because they can't believe what the evidence disproves. I discovered the meaning of a phrase whose significance has been rubbed away by cliché. I learned that life is only a passing show, and that one can only accept the scene before one as what it is for one's eyes, or one's other senses, or what it can be for one's pleasures.

"'It is a wonderful liberation, too,' the novelist repeated to Warren, 'a marvelous release from despair. You no longer feel you have to live up to any system laid down by morality or religion. You are no longer shocked that other people don't live up to them either.'

"'You mean you just become a cynical aesthete?' Warren asked him.

"'No, not at all,' Mallen replied. 'You not only accept the world of the senses, but you accept the rest of the world, its conventions, its rules, its hypothetical knowledge, its conventional expectations. You learn to play the game of existence by rules which cannot be proved but are simply good working techniques. It's easier to live by assuming the conventions of the world than by waiting until they can be proved watertight to you, as they never can be. You learn to live by the unreal fictions of ordinary social life, but you are never taken in by them. You know conventions are merely conventional; you neither despair if you violate them nor think it worth your while to upset them. I was, with reason, skeptical of everything when I was young. I'm still skeptical, but serenely so. Even that vast, generous gamble: the United Nations. That's our only hope. We've got to believe in that or accept it as a working plausible chance, or we are lost for good and all.'

"'But don't you feel the *need* of proof?' Warren asked him. 'Can you go on living simply knowing you are walking on illusions? I should think it would make you seasick.'

"'Quite the contrary,' replied the novelist. 'It gives one an extraordinary sense of stability. You no longer have the sense that you've been defrauded or are about to be. And you no longer feel the pressure of, the strain of, finding some absolute logic for your actions or for those of other people.

" 'Take you and me here, talking on this pleasant terrace, drinking this first-rate brandy. The prospect may be a mirage, the brandy a dream, but we can act, can we not, as if these things were real?'

" 'Oh, I know all about that—a sort of romantic form of pragmatism,' Warren said. 'But pains and evils, are these mirages, too? And should one go on living *as if* they, too, were real?'

" 'My dear fellow, it is a comfort and a relief, when things go wrong, to insist that it is but a moment in a dream. But it doesn't help in the least to try to prove, as some people do, that these things don't exist. It really doesn't. The trouble with the human race is that we humans, most irrational creatures, pay lip-service to rationality. We want so desperately to be rational, and what's more we want to prove that the universe is rational, too. I confess it's a little disquieting to think that we are idiots in an idiotic universe. But I think we may as well face up to it and accept the absurdities, the appearances, the surfaces of things. If it is a veil of illusion, what of it? To understand that is to overcome the risk of being disillusioned any further. One is no longer shocked, disappointed, or surprised. Everything may vanish, including the devotion of one's friends, in a world where nothing can be proved. But while nothing can be proved, everything can be taken as a vivid fiction, a live hypothesis. In your heart of hearts, you remain what I take it you, too, have become: a skeptic, but not a tormented one. A humane and comfortable one.

" 'I wonder if you've ever read a story by Arthur Machen, whom no one reads nowadays? It's called *The Secret Glory.* It's the tale of a boy at an English boarding school who cannot take seriously for a moment the games, the cliques, the snobbish, cruel gossip of the other boys. There is something in his heart that is a secret glory that they can never see. He takes part in their games, in their chatter, in their cliques, but in his private awareness he lives apart with his esoteric splendor. Well, I have no secret glory in my heart. But I stay apart. My secret, perhaps, is that I am not taken in by the games people play. But I live by the rules, too. It's no use expecting practical arrangements to be proved to be the ultimate laws of morals and religion, for they cannot be. Or written in the very texture of reality, for that is difficult, even impossible, to demonstrate. But it's equally silly to assault the trivial assumptions, to quarrel with the foolish and transient ways, of the world.'

"For a while, I gathered, Warren tried to live by Mallen's rules. He went back for a while to New York, where he took a newspaper job again, and accepted the world about him as a convenient set of hypotheses. But he could not persuade himself ever that his whole life was founded on anything but fictions, and he could not fool himself into thinking that there was any truth absolutely proved. The war came, and it seemed to brush aside doubts and ambiguities for a while. The atomic bomb came. There was one issue; it seemed real enough and it had to be settled: the saving of the race itself from destruction. The United Nations seemed to him possibly a fiction, too. He thought of all the difficulties, the obstacles, the old fictions of nationalism, the slogans of class and creed and cultures and races that would make that fiction too transparent for ordinary shrewd men to live by. But the theme of the brotherhood of man was one fiction he decided to throw himself into, heart and soul. And he eventually did get a job with the educational branch of the United Nations. He's there now.

"The brotherhood of man is, you may think, a fiction, a dream. But it's worth trying to live by it, and accepting it as a fiction. Otherwise, even the doubters in the world will be wiped out. That's the conclusion Warren has come to. He's busy fighting skeptics now himself. He tries to tell them that they had better accept this hypothesis pro tem. He argues with those who want it *proved* that there *can* be a world government, that human nature is capable of living under it. He meets those who have had all the doubts that he had in the past about idealism and brotherhood, and about all the fine things people say about mankind and its hopes. But Warren doesn't demand proof any more. He asks us to accept the great dare that life itself is the risk that is involved in the adventure of mankind."

MacNerny stopped. "You know, I have my doubts about the brotherhood of man myself," he said. "But I see what accepting the idea has done for Warren. He's a different person. 'Can you prove,' I could not help asking him the other day, 'that the United Nations will work?'

"'Can you prove *anything* important?' he said. 'And must one really wait for proof? Life is full of uncertainty and unhappiness, but part of the uncertainty is the quest for happiness itself. Life is a risk and action a hypothesis. And now, with the atomic bomb, we cannot afford not to take the risk. There may not be *any* world if we do not take the off-chance of making one world.'"

"Would you say Warren is cured, then, of what you call his neurosis?" I asked, as MacNerny indicated his story was ended.

"Yes, but he is rather an exceptional instance. Most people, Professor," said MacNerny, "are not cured. They want to have certainty, they wish all things to be proved. But the scientists know better. They use no word stronger than 'hypothesis,' and they never think that things are proved more than pro tem. Suppose people are *not* convinced. What do they want to be convinced of? That life is a geometry? It clearly isn't. That it is like a contract? But the universe has never *promised* anyone anything at birth. Life is a precarious opportunity. And when the inviting possibilities beckon, you do not want to have them invalidated in advance. Whenever a human being falls in love, or plants a garden, or starts a creative act of any kind, or gets up in the morning, or sends a letter, it is an act of faith, not a demand for logical proof. The convinced people are really the dangerous ones, for they are the fanatics, the conquerors, the intolerant ones. They have the 'truth,' and they will not let others have their doubts. Let us drink a toast to the unconvinced who live for life and not for or by logic. But you must forgive me for lecturing you on these matters: I'm just an old newspaperman; I am not a professor."

"The unconvinced!" I mused aloud. "Aren't they really the ones that Dante puts in Hell, because they are the lethargic, the noncommittal, the people who will not risk a blow for either side? Surely you would not, MacNerny, drink a toast to those?"

"Oh, no, I don't mean those who wish they were *absolutely* unconvinced and are paralyzed because they cannot be anything else. I think the finest of human beings are the true humanists, the true relativists. They are those who, like Montaigne, see the possibilities of all human points of view, who are convinced only that there is no absolute single set of convictions that are absolutely provable and true. Perhaps another name would be better for the more benign species of the unconvinced. I'd rather call them the unchained. They subscribe to no orthodoxy, cling to no doctrine, cram no literal faith down other people's throats. But they have the tentative faith of the true humanist; they have the audacity of hope and the daring of adventure. They win converts by persuasion, by opening up horizons which they invite others to explore with them. They know [MacNerny was always quoting the poets] that:

> . . . All experience is an arch wherethrough
> Gleams that untravelled world whose margin fades
> For ever and for ever when I move.

Ulysses didn't wait for logic to force him to go on; he needed only a distant gleam. Drink to the gleam!"

I looked at my watch and rose to go to keep an appointment. "You ought to have been a philosopher, MacNerny," I said, "indeed, you are one."

"Oh, no," he said, "just an old newspaperman, and an Irishman. We're not philosophers, we Irish, we're romantic poets, and perhaps that's what the best philosophers are." He drained his glass. "They're all there, like Plato, in the dreamed-of Heaven of Ideas. Or like Adonais—you remember Adonais:

"*The soul of Adonais, like a star, beacons from the abode where the Eternal are.* He beacons, mind you, he does not prove. The gleam is enough. The absolutely convinced, the absolutely skeptical—steer clear of them both, my boy. The certain ones will kill you for what they will call your heresies; the skeptical ones will close their eyes to the possibility and the gleam. Range yourself with those who will *trust the soul's invincible surmise.* Or let me paraphrase an Irish poet, Arthur William Edgar O'Shaughnessy: *They are the movers and shakers of the world for ever, it seems.*"

I waved farewell to MacNerny, and as I started to walk down the stairs, I couldn't help looking back. There he was, in the late afternoon sunlight, and the rays of the sun made a kind of glow upon his head. And in his eyes, as he sat there smilingly meditating, was the gleam itself.

NINE

The Unawakened

I HAD come home from an evening of philosophical discussion with a group of diversified minds, all interested in those ultimate questions in the broaching of which poets and philosophers and scientists can meet. It was at one of those dinner clubs that still exist in the modern world where men of diverse professional interests come together once a month for a good dinner and for as good conversation as the assembled talents can produce. The talk is usually better for being allowed to wander where it will. There had been Higgins, the painter; Porter, the composer; Kelly, the biochemist from one of the foundations; a learned lawyer (one of those of whom people ask: "I wonder how he happened not to go into the ministry or philosophy?"), and a few others. The conversation had moved along on various topics through dinner, ranging from the Supreme Court to plastics. The quality of conversation on such occasions varies. It is sometimes best when one of the best minds is absent, for then there is more courage of conviction on the part of the others. The least theme can be a catalyst, and the mightiest idea can fall dull and dead.

It was later in the evening that, as so often happened, the talk, like a slow fire, finally caught flame. A theme came up that agitated this group a good deal more than many immediately urgent questions, for this issue was perennial. It was whether science or art or philosophy brought man nearer reality and nearer the truth. Higgins, the painter, was dubious of all abstractions; the musician sided with him, and the poet joined in, too. The scientist was sure that only through the analysis of verifiable data, carefully checked in the laboratory, could one expect anything entitled to be called knowledge. The rest was, he said, *mere* poetry, and the word "mere" as he used it had the sound of affectionate contempt. Nobody, as usual, convinced anybody else. A few bright things were said or sometimes, though unrecognized as quotations by either speaker or listeners, were quoted.

I walked home from the meeting pleasantly stimulated, though not too much enlightened. It is a nice question as to what one does get out of intellectual discussion, even with a good group. No answers, surely, and not even a sense always of just what questions are being asked. But some fresh breeze has been started in one's mind and imagination, and the wind has begun to stir up old memories and new ideas. Nor does the lively gust die down when one has left the conversation. It did not die down in me that night.

I came home alone and found that I was too stimulated to sleep, nor could I keep my mind on a book. I tried several that bore more or less on the themes we had been discussing. I looked up that passage in Plato in which he says there is an "ancient enmity between poetry and philosophy"; I took down the volume of Bergson's on *Morality and Religion* in which he looks to the saint and the prophet and the poet as alone able to bring us fresh revelations of living reality, always dead before it can be anatomized by the static intellect. I looked at the chapter in Eddington in which that Quaker physicist tries to show how science gives us simply pointer readings, and to show that only first-hand human experience gives us reality, that which we know in our hearts and in our eyes and fingertips. I began to think of other books and philosophers who had dealt with the "ancient enmity" between poetry and philosophy, between philosophy and all the arts. I thought of Shelley's noble "Defense of Poetry" and his eloquent demonstration that it is the legislator of mankind. I was reminded of Thomas Love Peacock's saucy essay which had provoked Shelley's enraptured and raging reply: that passage in which Peacock says that poetry is a childish pastime, a gewgaw and a rattle for the grown-up babies of the age. And I thought, too, of those poems which gave vistas of truth, like those of Lucretius and Dante, and philosophies that were poetic visions of reality, like that of Plato or even the geometrizing Spinoza.

"It's too late to try to think any more," I said to myself, and I got into bed and tried to stop thinking by reading in a long hack historical novel. But the themes of the evening still haunted me. I turned out the light and tried to sleep, without success. In my restless tossing about I began to imagine things a little incoherently, in that curious mood that sometimes at such moments possesses us—a state between waking and dreaming when one allows one's self to imagine things that one would not quite permit one's self in responsible daylight hours, and yet organizes them a little more coherently than one would if one were really dreaming. I began to think of the things that might have been said, and took for my interlocutors an imaginary group of immortals talking about the same things in essence that we had been discussing at the Conversation Club. I offer the reader this time, then, no apparition or half-slumber vision that came to me, but the fruits of a fancy, abnormally awake, in which I allowed myself to transcend the restrictive common sense of the daylight hours.

I found myself, then, imagining a group that in our secret hearts we members of the Conversation Club imagined ourselves to be. At least we liked to believe that our conversation, if not ourselves, moved among immortal things and that at our best moments we too inhabited the Heaven of Ideas. I found myself inventing a conversation that was taking place somewhere in the vague realm of eternity. It was a colloquy among the Poet, the Musician, the Painter, the Scientist, the Mystic, the Philosopher—I did not pause to give them more specific names. I finally switched on the light, arose, and wrote my imaginings down.

The group had been conversing in some vague Elysium at no particular time and no one knew for how long, for they were in eternity, quite beyond the harried preoccupation with days and hours.

"They are not awakened," said the elderly philosopher, "these humans. They live, as so many of their poets have told them, in a dream. But for most of them, a dull dream. Sometimes they awaken briefly at adolescence and love gilds their consciousness and vivifies it briefly. But they lapse, most of them, into torpor again. If one could only rouse the most promising of them! What a radiant and intensified awareness we might see lighted in them! Might we not make an experiment, at least in imagination? I've kept my eye on one of them. Let us choose a handsome, disciplined youth with a good mind and lively senses and feelings. I wonder what would happen if the arts and interests each of us represent could awaken him in turn? I wonder what steps of progress he would make from dullness to pellucid delight? Mark you, he's a sensitive mind and spirit to begin with, precociously stirred and eager to be fully awakened before he is extinguished as, despite the possible immortality of his works, he in his own person will be. I like to think that philosophy would most fully rouse our promising candidate to the richness and the flame of life. But I must not speak first simply because I am oldest. Our Poet here perhaps would like to say what he thinks his art might do for our Endymion who needs to be awakened."

The Poet thought for a moment. "The very image you use is a compliment to the art I here represent," he said, "for it is a picture, that of the beautiful sleeping youth, that has become so well known it is now a cliché in the mouths of mankind. I do truly believe that the art of poetry is the chief mode by which the torpid human being may be awakened to what you philosophers call reality, or, more simply, may be awakened at all. For it is the poet, when he is successful, who gives man eyes and ears and feelings, or restores them to him. Our imagined youth may even fail to respond to the beauties of the physical world about him, which seem so obvious, until after he has learned from the poet to see what they are, after he has found out through the caressive enumeration of poetic names to see what it is in the way of wonder that his eyes are beholding. The poet will restore to the youth innocence and immediacy of the eye. He breaks up the conventional molds which habit and practicality have imposed on the boy when he is growing up to become a citizen and a responsible human being. Poetry breaks up the patterns of genteel perception and respectable formalities. It finds the words that make things come alive again in their color and intensity and urgency. The poet helps the young man—otherwise so soon encased in habit that his emotions themselves become stereotypes—to feel freshly again. For make no mistake about it. As is well known, love itself can turn into habit, and even grief into a dull stupor. It is the poet who awakens us to the richness and intensity of what we see and hear and feel and even think. He gives, as Hegel (no poet) once put it, hands and feet even to ideas.

"There is another kind of sleep, too, from which the poet can awaken our promising youth, born to be fully aware. He rescues him from the abstractions in which the least abstract-minded of us live. By the time he is grown up, the young man will have come to live almost entirely in formulas. He will move, half dead, among logical conceptions. He thinks not of actual persons, with their induplicable voices, their individual gestures, their special note of comedy or pathos. He comes to think of peoples and polls and statistics; of populations and trends. He thinks not of actual hungering and suffering men and women, but of national groups, of geographical aggregations. It is not the water gleaming to the eye, soothing to the thirst, that he thinks of, but the chemical formula of H_2O by which its causes of production are identified; not the sadness and immediacy of death, but statistics and tables of mortality, occupy his mind. He sees not the actual processes of growth and life in flower or child, but the labels by which these are controlled and manipulated. He deals with the post-mortem formulas of a life he has never felt. It is the poet's function to waken him from these geometric torpors, to reinstate him in the living movement of nature itself, and the felt actuality of life. Poetry indeed reawakens rather than awakens. For when he was very young, the youth was once fully alive.

"'Our birth is but a sleep and a forgetting,' one of our company once said. Rather is it our growing up that is a falling asleep and a gradual forgetting. Before we are fully creatures of habit and lethargy, the poet can rearouse us. To be fully awakened would be to be fully and continuously aware of reality. And is not reality, is not what is 'really real,' that which comes to us through no abstraction, no formulas, but in the vital immediacy of experience itself? Is it not the poet's special magic to find the words which call this quality into awareness again by the shining specificity, the electric directness, of his words?

"The youth you speak of, good Philosopher, *listens* to the poet as well as reads him. He is awakened first by the very suasion of the language, the wine of song that begins to sing in his veins. He is captured by the rhythms even before he knows what they say, and by the 'goldsmith's work,' the seductive euphony of the syllables themselves. Accustomed as he is in daily life to the raucous, rhythmless way in which people say the necessary practical things of the world, the youth is enchanted suddenly by the very tones of voice in which the poet speaks to him and the jeweled colors of the words he uses. Then comes the deeper magic by which he is awakened, the wonderful images and pictures by which the world acquires new dimension, new color, new acuteness. Everything comes to have shape, line, hue, and the pathos of memory and the wistfulness of distance and dream and prophecy.

"The poet's metaphors rescue experience from the dead stereotypes of habit to the living world of memory and suggestion. Everything starts to sing and to become colorful and alive. It is not so much that the word becomes flesh, as that the flesh becomes word, and for the first time the enraptured youth knows what even the flesh really means to him."

The Painter had been listening not too patiently. "I doubt that the true awakening comes from words. Poetry is more to be compared to sleep than to wine. It is a soft caesura, a melodious hypnotic pause. It opens, as Keats said, faery casements. The pale moon gleams over poetry and gleams, too, over the readers of poetry. It is like the jingle of coral bells before savages, or as Peacock correctly said, the rattling of gewgaws before a baby. Words are never things, and I think can at best only vaguely evoke them. The fish peddler cries 'fish,' and I may be forgiven if I cry up painting as the real awakener to reality. For the painter forces the human being, sometimes for the first time in his life, to see. This promising youth you want us to awaken, Philosopher—what is it you wish us to awaken him from? What is it you want us to awaken him to? Save for us painters, your young man might busily stride through life without ever pausing to see what is actually there before him in the world. Things themselves are merely abstractions for him, outlines which signal him to action, contours which tell what things may be used for: this spoon, that table, this house, this bridge. Pattern becomes simply a blurred beckoning or warning; design a mere script or language to tell him what he may employ this for, what he may do with that.

"Dogs are said not to see color at all; at least they make up for it by a keen sense of smell. But many human beings go through life without noticing that color exists at all in the world. All grass is green to them, and all greens the same, even the thousand tints in a lake on an August day when the clouds in endless variations are reflected on the ring of mountains before their eyes.

They walk in cities, never once looking at the hues in the sky. They hurry past thousands of people, never noticing their endless uniqueness except when they are stirred momentarily by sex; they ignore the infinite nuances of color in the faces they meet. It is the same with line, too, and the shapes of things they encounter in their work and in their play, and the texture of things in the clothes they wear, the plates they dine off, the paper on which they write. Some spectacular vista on mountain or seascape momentarily shocks them into appreciation, but for the most part they have eyes and see not, or they see just as much as is useful for their urgencies of instinct or habit or practical *necessity*.

"The painter teaches them the realized, visual qualities of the world. He gives them not pictures of what they think they have seen, for they have not seen at all. He gives them light and line, and color and luminosity. He gives them the distances and designs, all more real, more intense, than these can be in what is commonly the world one sees. The painter awakens them to their fingertips, as we say, for he communicates at a distance what things are like to the touch as well as what they are to the concentrated and absorbed eye. The common man is said to be a sensualist, but, save in taste, and in touch during sexual excitement, he scarcely has sensuous awareness or intensity at all. The painter stirs the senses, and with that stirring comes a wonderful liberation. For the youth whom we imagine awakened will learn from the painter to turn back to the so-called actual world and perceive it freshly, variously, and sharply. Actuality becomes drenched with the qualities which the painter has discovered for him. People's faces make pictures and so do the routine scenes in which any youth spends his days. The dull city street through which he has hurried becomes a human landscape; the houses compose into a pattern, the idlers at the corner into a foreground, the clouds in the wintry sky a dramatic accent in the composition, and all drenched with pathos or pity or wonder, all making up a form, a pattern, an order.

"Perhaps never until he looks at a painting does the half-sleeping youth guess there is order in the world. Not abstract order in the mind of a philosopher or of a visionary prophet, but form, into which genius or, what is another name for it, gifted attention, can compose the actual world, can harmonize actual experience. In the business of life we tend to see things in fragments; we experience events in parts and shreds. It is only in painting or in sculpture that the senses are forced to recognize the immediate (which to human attention is the ultimate) and to recognize in it that pattern which the plastic arts alone can give. Once awakened to the arresting sensuous surface, to the impressive fact of design discoverable in the world about him, it will be impossible for our young man to fall victim to the abstractions of habit which alone make any two things seem alike, or to those abstracted systems which are formulas rather than the living forms of actual existence. A good painting renders matter rationalized and alive, not remote and dead as it seems through that bleak system of geometric symbols which things become for the practical and unpausing eye—the eye of those who have never been taught by looking at painting how to see."

The Musician had been drumming his fingers as he listened. He barely let the Painter end his sentence. "As if the eye were the road to reality, and as if the eye really could awaken anyone! It is only by an accident of evolution that the eye has become the practical organ, so that distances are measured by the contours of things defined in terms of line. You say the young man whom we are to awaken walks through the world unseeing. But we see, to an extent, all the time; we must. It is rather that our promising youth walks through the world not hearing, for he scarcely pays attention at all to the sounds that people's voices make, so much have practical life and biological necessity trained him to listen to what is said rather than to the cadence of the saying. Why is poetry so little popular in the world? Because the euphonies and rhythms that our Poet here has been talking about are not to the world's purposes, which require only the rough common sense of prose. The young man will hardly note the varying rises and falls of the voices of his elders, so keen is he to learn how to live in the world by what these mature talkers intentionally or unconsciously reveal. But if the young man, in the interest of sense, hardly listens to the *sounds* of words, he will, until he knows better, hardly listen to sounds themselves, sounds that have no 'practical' meaning at all. He will regard all sounds either as making sober sense or as constituting interruptions. Until one day he becomes happily aware through some gifted musician what it is that music can say to him, without words and without the vulgar necessity of shaped or colored things on canvas or in marble.

"Through sounds, bodiless in air, the soul may truly be awakened. In painting, lines and colors are always, even in the most abstract of painting, attached somehow to the things one knows in the practical world. Just so are the pleasures of touch always more or less directly tethered to sex, and those of taste to the bodily functions of eating and drinking. The pleasures of sound alone are pure, and through music the spirit is awakened to this clear and distilled pleasure. It is a strange and brilliant awakening. Suddenly the soul discovers the actuality, the blessed immediacy and intensity, of tones heard. Notes are no mere medium of information; they are ultimate glories in themselves. Our youth will awaken to the variations and nuances of rhythms, the deployment of notes in melody, the marshaling of melodies in harmonic developments; to the whole moving and vital geometry, the radiant logic and unfolding of sound. It is as if a deaf person had suddenly been given hearing.

"The musically awakened have been given a new and higher hearing. They have learned to be awakened to harmonies which they had long ignored, and rhythmic combinations to which their souls had been strangers. It is no wonder that sometimes human beings, trained to the finer distinctions of listening, feel in following the complex and bodiless life of a symphony or a sonata that they have been fully alive for the first time to an order of being that is more alive and more actual than the things they touch and see. They have such a feeling as one might have at the trumpet calling the Last Judgment—of being awakened from death to the most rapturous of psalmodies sung by the assembled angels of Heaven. No, my dear painter friend, if our young man is to be stirred to full awareness, it is, I think, through music that that stirring is most likely to come. For in listening to the pure internal world of sounds, the absorbed stripling will have passed altogether for the time being from that attachment to things in the external world which has dulled his ears. He will be a pure listener to pure joy. He will almost be free from the dross of the body; for the time of his listening he will share, and in essence be, the pure vitality of sound."

The Philosopher, who seemed to be a sort of chairman through all this, had been listening gravely and spoke, now, gravely, too. "All of us here belong to one or another," he said, "of the arts and devices by which men have been awakened from the great drowsiness, the lifelong lethargy, which is the lot of most of mankind through their brief and dull biographies. Children, as poets have so often reminded us, are nearest to being, within the limits of their sensibilities and intellectual powers, all alive. They see and hear directly, and for the sake of the seeing and hearing. They have an eager curiosity about the thousand new aspects of things, the colors, shapes, lines, sounds, movements, to which every new day introduces them freshly. But the pressures of habit and practical necessity close in upon the growing boy. By the time he becomes this once divinely promising youth you speak of, he is almost quenched. He has already entered the long dullness of adult routine. He is half-asleep before the final extinction, the big sleep. He is slumbering, as some of you have already pointed out, during what we flatteringly call his waking hours.

"Each of you present, in the art he has practiced, has done something to keep this youth awake, to startle him into awareness, to absorb him by the living movement of music, the ordered and rhythmic designs of painting, the euphony and cadence and freshening metaphors of poetry. But do you truly, any of you, think that poetry, painting, or music would wholly awaken the human being half-sleeping through his life, unaware of that ultimacy of which a full awareness would be the only complete consciousness? What has our friend the painter said? Merely that painting can rouse the dulled apprehension to the beauties of line and color, to those lineaments of design and rhythm in the visual aspects of things which the busy and anxious lives of human beings make them ignore. What has the musician said? He has told us simply that to ears sordidly trained simply to listen to sounds for what they portend as language, the glories of tone are dead. The poet has insisted, correctly, that poetry reminds us, like painting, of the colors and shapes, the feel of, and the feeling in, the presence of things. He has told of the lovely suasion of language itself. What have you all said but that the arts startle our senses and reinstate us in the heritage of the sensuous beauty of the world? But this is a very poor and limited awakening indeed.

"What would a full awakening be? Would it not, my friends, be a rich and complete awareness, a rounded consciousness, of what the whole meaning and impact of experience would be? Is it enough to be a listening ear, a seeing eye? Is it not the thinking mind of this thinking reed, man, that renders him completely alive, that is to say, completely conscious?

"Everyone here, even in this detached realm of timelessness we are now in, has argued for his own province. I am no exception. But I cannot forbear from saying that it is philosophy which is the sovereign awakener. For philosophy awakens men from those private worlds in which they drowse their lives away to the common world in which the fully aroused realize they are living. Philosophy awakens men to the intelligible, to those principles of thought and action to which reason leads all the fully alert.

"Perhaps this youth we are imagining, full of sensibility and intelligence, should (I am ready to admit it) come to philosophy last of all. It is the senses by which, as Plato long ago observed, he should be—and usually is—first roused. And I am sure it is the arts, poetry and music and painting and sculpture, which will stimulate him first to eager and startled observation. He will be sensuously alive, which is the first step in being alive at all. He will have learned to *perceive* form and design and order, to perceive them and to feel their beauty. And this is perhaps the first and best introduction to order itself, to that more difficult logic of abstract coherence which the mind can come to know. The arts will teach him to pause. Rather, they will not teach him; they will persuade him to linger, they will give him the delighted cue to leisure in which contemplation will begin. But I doubt that he will be *fully* awakened by these. Arts, too, are often opiates rather than stimulants—all the arts, not poetry simply. The entranced youth will come to move, and wantonly wish to move, in a dream of luminosity, a fantasy of images or a trance of melodious sound. The hypnosis will be delightful, but it will be a dream still, not a great awakening. That can come only with the mind. I think philosophy will do it.

"It will be well for our candidate first to go through various philosophies: these will challenge him out of that set of prejudices and assumptions to which his family and his class and his local culture have exposed him. He will be shocked into recognizing that there are many ways of looking at the world, and that his accustomed one is one only. He will be challenged by these to work toward some steady clarification of his own principles, he will learn above all to look beyond the event to the principle involved, beyond the instant to the long context of time and circumstance in which that instant is set. All experience will come to be shot through with larger meanings for him. He will regard life as being interesting just to the extent to which it is material for the mind to behold, for the mind to play with, for the mind to control or, where control is impossible, for the mind to understand and the free spirit to traverse. He will regard himself as fully awake just to the extent that nothing remains opaque and brutal but all becomes a living challenge to the intellect and an incandescence for contemplation. For pure actuality (Aristotle pointed it out once long ago), toward which all life aspires, is the body transmuted into awareness, the mind become completely luminous and the world completely intelligible. That is an ideal which the philosopher never quite attains. But it is the ideal toward which he moves. If there is a God, he would be such pure actuality. In his godlike moments, man's consciousness is such a divine pure theory or vision. In that vision, all things will be comprehended; the arts with their diverse loveliness, human experience with its comedy and tragedy, its griefs and hopes and sorrows. In the clear flame of theoretic vision everything will become part of man's collected and serene and yet passionate awareness. Such awareness, composed and cool, is what philosophy is. It is when the human being, always half sleeping, awakes completely that a philosophy, a comprehensive philosophy, emerges. He can participate in such awareness only in the brief moments of a rarely achieved awakening. But the history of thought is the history of the various great efforts toward such sustained alertness; the story of philosophy is the history of the more or less fully awakened among mankind. Those partial awarenesses that you others, you artists, have been describing are incorporated into that vision, that intense but conspect awareness which is philosophy.

"Sometimes, it is true, philosophers go into a private dream of their own, and then they declaim that they alone are the fully awakened. But even in their private, special vision, if it has any lineaments of logic, there will be some elements of awareness of the intelligible world. They will, if they are thinking at all, not be completely somnolent.

"This awakening through philosophy will save men from the follies and superstitions which have kept possessed the various sleepwalkers of the world. It will save man from narrowness and fanaticism. It will some day make men members of one another, and conscious and comprehending inhabitants of the same public world. For the fully awakened, and they alone, will recognize that they are brothers. Reason will have introduced them to one another in their true persons and actual brotherhood. This is what philosophy can do for our imagined youth and for all mankind."

The Mystic, with rapt countenance, began to speak: "We are not as far apart as I had supposed," he said, "especially in what you have been saying at the close. But I suspect you are one step short of the true insight, my philosopher friend. For it is not reason that will make men really aware that they are inhabitants of the same world, and are, more than that, themselves profoundly one. Reason will carry them as far (and it will be far) as reason can. You are quite right about that. The young man will discover the principles of things and the principles which animate all men and bind him to them. But by this discovery he will still not be completely open-eyed. Reason is always a discursive business. It argues, it demonstrates, it proves. It does not give immediate vision, which, in its intense and absolute form, alone is complete awareness. I think the artists in our company, the poet, the painter, the musician, were in some ways nearer the truth than the philosopher. Our young man whom we are trying to awaken was perhaps nearer the ultimate goal, complete aliveness, in his experience of the arts than he was in the dialectic of philosophy. For in the arts he is seeing directly, hearing immediately, knowing with his whole absorbed being. He has not discarded the flesh and blood of actual experience for the bloodless categories which he finds in Hegel or even in the modern empirical logicians. Where in the history of philosophy, save among the very greatest, is philosophy really an act of vision, a moment of complete and sustained awareness, not a dull traversing of the artifices of abstraction? But in the arts, the whole being is absorbed, and one feels, in the act of listening, in the moment of beholding, completely alive, in a state the exact opposite of sleep. At moments of artistic absorption, all one's faculties are not in the suspension of sleep, but in that acute suspended equilibrium of experience which is aesthetic delight, where everything becomes luminously clear and intensely immediate.

"Such an awareness, not of this painting or that music, but of the universe itself, is the goal of those who would be truly and completely awakened. If they are to have this, they must pass beyond the arts and beyond philosophy, even, though it is *through* philosophy they must pass. But they must not pause in the dialectic steps, the arguments and stages of thought. They must pass beyond to the act of vision itself. There the whole universe will become for them what a painting or a symphony is to the absorbed beholder or listener. It will all be marvelously and mystically clear. The youth come thus far will behold directly with his whole possessed spirit, he will be so awake to what it is that he beholds that his waking state will be a deliverance of himself sacrificially into the object of his vision. His rapture will resemble those moments in his carnal life when he feels himself most alive, in the act of love.

The arts have initiated him to intensity and clarity in the senses, love has initiated him to clarity and intensity of feeling; in the experience of great works of art the two are wonderfully joined. And that, too, is the experience ultimately (when it *is* experience and not merely words) of the greatest philosophies. In these the soul transcends philosophy itself and sees beyond it the whole universe, toward which it feels as toward a beautiful object passionately beheld, or a beautiful person intensely loved. One has become what we mystics call one with the One, when experience ceases to be of this or that. We *are* that. The All is we. Knowledge has become a fire of love and love a flame of knowledge. We are completely awake at last, if but briefly, and we know what eternal awareness would be. It would be to be divinity itself, it would be to be God always.

"No one has this experience long or often. But the imaginative youth you would educate may, through the arts, philosophy, and love, attain it briefly, and by that time he will doubtless no longer be a youth. He may be an aged philosopher, though some poets have miraculously arrived there very early by a species of precocious and preternatural insight. They have intuitively foreseen swiftly what philosophers must travel toward more slowly. But when philosophers do attain it, they have arrived where poets are tending, and painters and musicians, too. They have seen as a whole what these others have seen partially, and what, when philosophers do see, we cease to call them philosophers. We call them mystics, prophets, seers. We name them the Awakened, and if they have been able to say at all coherently what it is they have seen, they in turn become the awakeners of others. A few of us have been able to intimate the light to which we have been awakened, the light we have seen, the light we live in and by which and in which we are."

I was quite tired after writing all this down. It was late at night and I felt that perhaps I had not been altogether clear. But I am sure that this is what these men in eternity would have said, or something like it. And I am sure that the youth, grown not passionless in age, but the vehicle of a subtler passion, will have traversed such a path and will be awakened truly and enlightened. The "ancient enmity" of the arts and philosophy will have been resolved in him. For the truly awakened love with clarity, behold with passion, and their vision and their passion are suffused with understanding. They are awake at last to what each art and each episode of their experience has been struggling to say to them, still drowsing in the early dawn of anticipated knowledge.

TEN

High Thinking Below the Equator

IT HAS always been a favorite theme of mine, on which I have liked to expatiate whenever the opportunity offered, or whenever I could make it, that philosophy transcends time and frontiers and that men of metaphysical good will recognize one another at once, no matter where they are or what language they speak. I like to cite the French-speaking Negro from Haiti with his passion for post-Kantian theories of knowledge; I recall the French doctor, M. Platon, whom, as a patient, I found turning from physician to philosopher. I think of the scholar I know whom political barbarities of the Third Reich shifted, with his appreciation and learning of the Italian Renaissance, from Germany where he wrote in German, to Italy where he wrote in Italian, to America where he now writes happily—and well—in English, with his eye fixed still and always on themes no barbarity can quench. And there is an Irish metaphysician I once met in Galway whom Duns Scotus might have greatly liked.

I am by this time accustomed, therefore, to finding philosophy in remote spots and in unexpected accents. I should not have been surprised, therefore, to find it in Brazil. In some ways that abundant world is the proper place to be a philosopher. The material conditions of life are luxuriant. The air is wine, the sky is blue, and prejudice, at least, has been overcome, for divergent color and race in that mixed population is no bar to communication. Brazil is far enough away from the great intellectual centers. It takes some time, even in these days of air mail, for ideas to reach Rio. And that is not altogether a disadvantage. Ideas can develop uncorrupted and undeflected by sudden gusts of fashionable doctrine. There is a sense of size and distance, too, in Brazil: the backlands are still vast and unexplored; no one has counted all the population of Brazil or seen all its jungles. The inhabitants of the coastal cities constantly live with a sense of the great green unknown continent behind them. And in that country, too, lies every climate, from tropic Bahia in the north to the wintry chill of Porto Alegre in the south. Nor is it uninstructive to live in a land where baroque buildings of the eighteenth century jostle functional modern skyscrapers, where echoes of the past sound against the humming industries of the future, where Oro Preto eighteenth-century churches set one dreaming of European history, and São Paulo, mushrooming into an industrial metropolis, speaks only to and of a modern age, and calls up Kansas City and Chicago.

Brazil is a fine place to be a philosopher, not less because not much professional philosophy exists there. Thinking has not had a chance to be regimented in universities, for the universities there are very young, and a man who wishes to be a philosopher must persist in the face of every obstacle. Philosophy will not even bring him the barest living. There is hardly anyone to teach it to, for one thing: seventy per cent of the population are illiterate, and a philosopher is not in danger of having a cult made of his insights, since too few know how to read, and very few can be his pupils. All this I might have observed after three months in Brazil, where I had come to contribute my mite to good will by lecturing on the philosophy of art and on American philosophy at the young National University of Brazil under the auspices of that University and our own State Department.

Here is a country without professional philosophy, I observed, and I reflected, "What a rare opportunity for the native thinker!" My mind went back to an earlier world where there was also no class of academic thinkers, to early Greece. There thinkers had no previous thinking to study; they had but to look at life, to survey the world, to reflect "on the spectacle of men and cities, of birth and death, of wars and rumors of wars." They were free of the jargons of the schools and the vested interests of established doctrines. They spoke as free men in a free air. Above all, they were not teachers of philosophy herded into schools, nor were they shepherds of the young sheep of thought.

Well, it was not quite true that there was *no* professional philosophy in Brazil. For a century the educated class had been turning to France, and for over half a century France had been sending intellectual emissaries to South America. There were two or three French professors there at the very moment, who, having come for a brief guest appearance, had been caught by the war, and had stayed five years, lecturing on philosophy—and, true to their character as missionaries of French culture, still in French.

How vital an interest and a passion was philosophy, I wondered, and how would it thrive without professional tutelage, or economic support? I was to find out, for in the course of two or three months I came on a whole *cenacolo,* a little circle of philosophers who, in the face of every difficulty, remained passionately and pertinaciously addicted to the kind of questions which absorb philosophers. There was, for example, a little group, consisting, I think, of not more than half a dozen, who had been meeting once a week for more than four years in the home of one of them, a cultivated lady originally from Vienna and now domiciled some twenty years in Rio. They would meet and discuss from eight until midnight a section of the work of one of the great traditional philosophers. This particular year it chanced to be Kant.

The other members of the group included a government meteorologist, a civil engineer, a young and charming girl who at the University developed a passion for (among other things) ideas, and a middle-aged Russian lady. There was no Kant in Portuguese translation, and not all of them knew German, so from texts French, German, and English, and, if I remember, Russian, and in conversation mostly Portuguese but with admixtures of several other European tongues, they would eagerly try to resolve Kant's paradoxes and clarify his categories. There was passion and there was acuteness in the discussion, and as great seriousness and responsibility as if they had been working toward an examination in a seminar led by a distinguished savant. Later in the evening the high thinking was succeeded by a plain collation. Over the beer and sandwiches I could not help expressing my admiration for the tenacity with which in the midst of other works and distractions they persisted in their devotion to philosophical study. "Well," said our Austrian hostess, "nothing else seems to have much meaning."

"Life drives one to philosophy, ultimately—both its tragedies and its puzzles," said the Russian lady.

On the way back to town with the Brazilian meteorologist, as the open-air trolley bumbled along, I quizzed him a little as to his own devotion to philosophy. "I take it," I said, "meteorology doesn't interest you too much."

"Oh, yes," he said, "it does indeed, but after all there are questions arising in one's mind that meteorology really doesn't deal with. And it's good to study them at their sources, among the men who have really thought them through. Read Plato, read Kant, read Spinoza, and you are near the center of things, wherever you happen to live. Otherwise, I am afraid here in Rio I should feel very remote."

"Would you wish," I asked, "if it were possible for you, to make a profession of philosophy?"

"I don't think I would," he said, "and what's more, I don't think I could. I've studied Plato now for ten years, and Spinoza also. I'm not sure I'd be ready to teach them, or to teach philosophy at all. To teach, one must have made up one's mind, one must arrive at conclusions. But philosophy is a constant exploration, and I have just begun. One really shouldn't teach one's own confusions."

There were two other young amateur philosophers I met in Rio. I was struck by their appearance for weeks before I knew them. They sat in the first row at a series of lectures on North American Philosophy, as I had learned to call it, which I was giving at the University. They were perfectly regular attendants; occasionally they would stop at the end of the lecture and ask questions, always sharp, pointed, good ones. After a few weeks I became curious as to who they were and what their interest in philosophy was. I asked them to join me at a neighboring café over a *cafézinho,* one of those small cups of very strong black coffee which is the special Brazilian seal of a social occasion.

It turned out that the two young men, aged about twenty-five, had been friends since schooldays. They were both now chemists in the Air Ministry and would probably spend the remainder of their lives in technical engineering pursuits. But for years they had been interested in philosophy. One of them, the more dominant of the two, was the leader of a little group devoted to the study of the philosophy of science and of questions of logical theory. They both read the journals from England and the United States, which arrived sometimes as much as six months late. There was little in philosophy that existed in Portuguese, except some translations of the Greek classics made from English and French translations.

Their eyes opened almost with envy as, at their request, I told them of the journals, meetings, groups, associations, of professional philosophers in the United States.

"I don't suppose," said one of them sadly, "there are more than a hundred people in Brazil really interested in philosophy."

"Well, there are a good many tens of millions of people in the United States who are not interested in it either," I said consolingly.

"Ah, yes," said José, the older one, "but sometimes here in Brazil I feel as if we who are interested in philosophy were a small group of insane fanatics."

"You have a few unknown friends," I said, and I had the pleasure of bringing them together with the little circle with whom I had spent the seminar evening, and before I left Rio I had brought together a group of some twelve who, mostly unknown to one another, had been pursuing the same studies with the same interest for the same end: simply the delight in ideas and the satisfaction of clarifying their views on basic and ultimate things.

Some day, perhaps a hundred years from now, the University of Brazil will number its thousands rather than its handfuls. There will be hundreds of students in Introduction to Philosophy courses, as there are at the state universities in the United States. There will be—the scheme is already afoot—a journal of philosophy; there will be official meetings and professional pronouncements, but I am not sure that philosophy itself will be in a much healthier state than it is now. Ratisbona, the meteorologist, José, the Air Ministry chemist, Rita, the charming blond girl from the Oro Preto, are, not least because they are doing so practically alone and under difficulties, keeping it alive now. And philosophy below the equator turns out to be not very different from philosophy above it. Reasonable men following the paths of reason will not think very differently among the poinsettias and the mosaic pavements of Rio than they will think on the sidewalks of New York. I received a letter from José only yesterday. He had just lighted on Plato's *Philebus*. And Andy from Columbus, Ohio, who has had all the benefit of moving in a large circle of literate young men at a first-rate American university, had also, I learned in a letter last week, lighted on the *Philebus*. I hope he and José meet some day.

ELEVEN

End of the Term

THE class in Introduction to Philosophy had been meeting for a whole college year, three times a week, Monday, Wednesday, and Friday, at eleven. The group of forty had acquired that indefinable solidarity that a miscellany of students does sometimes achieve by the end of two terms. We all knew one another's intellectual quirks; we had met in all sorts of physical and intellectual weather. We had discussed Kant's proofs for the existence of God during a blizzard, and Bergson's *élan vital* on a lazy spring day. A crowd of young strangers had become, up to a certain point at least, a society of friends. Even the large football player could be roused from his lethargy, and quite on his own instigation ask and answer questions. Young men who at the beginning of the year had little more than suspected what the word philosophy meant, had come to move easily at least in the vocabulary that professional philosophers affect and had begun, I think, to guess what the terms more deeply portended. One youngster, much to the amused delight of the remainder of the class, had even casually one day, and as if he used the term every day and at the family dinner table, spoken of the "undifferentiated aesthetic continuum," which he had picked up in a book review of a recent widely noticed tome. Some of the members of the class had developed into agile dialecticians; others had, in the course of studying other people's philosophies, come to light on one of their own, or to recognize in a classic thinker a kindred spirit.

One of the chief pleasures of teaching, I suppose, is to watch ideas take root and flower in the minds of the young, to note the surprise and pleasure with which youngsters rediscover for themselves—though perhaps aided a little—notions, issues, problems, that have provoked and kindled the minds of men in generation after generation. It is one of the instructive sadnesses of teaching, too, to see how in the very young there begin to bud the intellectual and moral vices of their elders, and the intellectual and moral prejudices of their predecessors. Even at eighteen or nineteen it is possible to seek above all to make the worse appear the better cause. Cynicism, callousness, reactionary fears, and irresponsible hopes, can control the beginner in life and thought as well as the veteran. Some of these striplings had already been miseducated by their families or their friends far beyond redemption.

We had gone through the usual round of philosophical issues. By this time, as their quiz books showed, I could count on their knowing the characteristic problems, the typical answers, of the philosophical tradition. They knew what doubts and ambiguities resulted from reflection upon knowledge itself, how puzzling the meaning of such familiar terms as appearance and reality. They knew, too, that Right and Wrong were not as simple or unqualified as they had supposed, nor for that matter were Good and Evil. They could be expected to be able to explain—for examination purposes anyway—Plato's picture of the perfect state, Aristotle's notion of the middle way, Descartes's conception of clear and distinct ideas, Hume's notion of cause, and Mill's of the good as measured by utility. I suspect that some reader of these pages will remember, with a kind of nostalgia, how twenty or thirty or forty years ago he, too, once had some traffic with these things, and how, perhaps, certain images of philosophy and the philosophers cling to his mind: the *tabula rasa* of Locke as an image of the mind before it has received any knowledge, the notion of "better to be Socrates dissatisfied than a pig satisfied," John Stuart Mill's way of saying that some pleasures are better than others. The very mention of the names of philosophers will perhaps recall to the reader the doubts, the perplexities, the anxieties of his youth, and even revive these doubts at this late and yellowed now. Or, perhaps in self-defense and to protect the uneasy equilibrium he has established with life, the reader will brush all these things aside, as some of my students did, as the unnecessary refinements of philosophers and speculations fit for callow boys —or for professors.

Well, here we were, the class and I, facing each other for the last time in the academic year. It was late spring, and the minds of some of the students were undoubtedly already on other things, summer jobs, love, next year's courses, and for some whose last year at college it was, their future. Should it be law school, or business, or perhaps graduate work and teaching? But I flattered myself that some of them, at least, came to this last class with feelings of special interest and even excitement, of a little sadness, even of a little regret. And some of them, I knew, had saved up certain questions not dissimilar, perhaps, to those which they had asked on the very first day of the course, questions which neither I, nor, I was certain, anyone else, could solve, problems that would plague some of them their whole lives, though I suspected that very soon, all too soon, others would cease to be aware of them or troubled by the fact that there were no final answers, or even any clear ones.

I myself faced this concluding class in philosophy with very mingled feelings.

I had made it a point of pride during the course to present the various classic philosophies with almost aseptic detachment. It is not my business, as a teacher of philosophy, I feel, to inculcate students with my own point of view, to convert them to a doctrine, to give them a magic formula of wisdom. The best, I have always thought, that a philosopher can do is to awaken young minds to basic issues, to present with as much candor and clarity as possible the lineaments of those great visions of experience which the geniuses of thought have achieved, the clarification of ideas, the security of methods, they have worked out.

I say I aimed to present these with scrupulous objectivity. But at the end of the term I found myself reflecting on how easily one can deceive one's self in these matters. The young are very quick, and it is surprising the amount of face-saving they can see through; within one's self one is astounded at the stubborn sincerities that break through attempts at therapeutically intended pretense. I tell myself that I try in a class to be equally persuasive concerning all the great types of thinking, to present them all with sympathetic and imaginative understanding, to communicate the tone and temper of each philosopher. I try to make students see the world, for the time being, through the disillusioned eyes of Schopenhauer or the professionally optimistic mind of Hegel, to let them see existence with the resigned Epicurianism of Democritus or with the manly steadfastness of Marcus Aurelius. And I must say that each year I am, myself, successively convinced by each of these world-views. The mind lends itself to styles of thought as the ear lends itself to styles of music. Or, to change the metaphor, a world-view in philosophy is as persuasive as is the temper of a world created in a novel. One can surrender for the time being to the spell of Dostoevski, so that for the time being all life is seen in the agony and division of soul that his novels evoke. One yields to the pessimism of Hardy, or the exuberant comedy and sentiment of Dickens. Thus, too, can one give one's self to the realm of quietly amused good sense of Jane Austen, or the robust comic humanity of Fielding. In the same way one abdicates in turn to the varied aspects of the world which one philosopher or another holds to be primary. And I have had a childish pleasure in having students sometimes complain during the semester that I seem to believe and embrace totally contradictory philosophies. So, I am tempted to reply to them, has the spirit of man cherished antinomies, and hugged contradictions to the point of pain.

But the shrewder ones are not deceived. They are likely to observe a certain warmth of tone when a teacher of philosophy deals with one philosophy, a certain accent of acerbity when he criticizes the assumptions, the methods, or the conclusions of another. I don't suppose these young men, at least some of them, could have failed to note the tone of mild condescension with which I treated some of the more romantic philosophies, those that look at the universe as if it were a field arrayed for their own special games, or a theater concerned with their own private theatricals. They cannot have missed seeing with what implicit approval I quoted Santayana's comment on those philosophies which hold that the moral order determines the physical order. "It is," he says, "as if one believed in a world where parents are ruled by their children, a world much relished by children." I am quite sure they must have observed that my enthusiasm kindled a little when I read Lucretius' hymn to the creative powers of nature at the beginning of *On the Nature of Things,* or his paean to detachment at the beginning of the second book. The brighter ones, I am sure, noted my impatience with certain fanciful proofs (classic proofs they are called) of the existence of God, or my equal impatience with philosophers, the nineteenth-century Germans, say, who tried to persuade us or themselves that they had spun the world out of their own inner consciousness. I had reason to think that by the end of the academic year they had, the better ones, some shrewd suspicion of where I stood in philosophy, and perhaps a more exact sense than they had had before of where they stood themselves. I think, or I like to think, that they recognize my own leanings toward what one may call a basic human orthodoxy, as contrasted with the orthodoxies of the churches and the official schools; a sense of the natural—call it if one will the material—world which partially sustains and partly defeats all our ideals, our arts, and our adorations. I hope, or I try to hope, that my students, despite my public attempts to be detached, suspect my own allergies toward philosophies which try to sentimentalize or dress up the world to make it a little nearer the unquiet heart's desire. I have to admit that I sometimes even hope they share my allergies.

But here I am, for better or worse, in the last hour of the academic year, and I suddenly feel I no longer know what to ask these young men and have no way of telling them anything one could seriously call final. Teaching is a kind of art, and it would be a pleasure to have the course come to a real conclusion, as well as a temporal one; to have it really end, and not simply stop when the bell rings. It would be agreeable and satisfying, if one could manage it, to send the students away with a final revelation. But what is one to tell them at this, now the last, chance? Some of them may never for as much as fifty minutes be exposed to philosophical conversation in their whole lives again. Some of them, who have been lethargic all semester, might—who knows?—be awakened by just the right words even this late. But what are those words, and who am I, or anyone, to say, toward the very close of the hour, "in the last analysis . . ."?

So much for me. But what are their final words, or their final questions? Well, it might not be a bad idea, since I am really extremely confused as to what to say to them, to see what *they*, after all these months of discussion, have to say or to ask for themselves.

"Well," I begin, "this is the last hour, and of late I seem to have been doing most of the talking. There must be a good many questions you have to ask, that some of you have been saving up." The inevitable wag in every class demands to know what the examination questions are going to be. But perhaps he is not being funny; he is a man of affairs with concern for issues that have immediate consequences. I seem to remember he is headed for the school of business.

"No practical matters," I say firmly. "We are still in the realm of philosophy."

There is a hand raised in the back of the room. It is that of the intense and neurotic young man I had observed the very first day.

"Aren't you going to tell us what *your* philosophy is?" he

said. "All semester you have been explaining to us those of other people."

"Well, I hadn't intended to," I said. "I haven't wanted to give you *a* philosophy. I have wished to help you to find one of your own. Perhaps at the close of the hour I may give a few hints as to what I believe. Philosophy is important to you, but not *my* philosophy."

"I'm sure you're not a Hegelian idealist, anyway," someone suggests. "Or a solipsist," says another, proud of knowing by now what the word means.

"Never mind for the moment what *I* am," I say impatiently. "Are there any other questions?"

The Irish Catholic boy has come a long way this term. He has managed to keep his faith out of it for the most part. I see his hand up. "Mr. Farrell," I say.

"Look here," he says, "this is all very confusing. We've had a dozen different philosophies all term. Is *one* of them the truth? Or none? Mustn't one pick one and stick to it? One *has* to have a philosophy by which to live."

"People don't live by philosophies," says the young man who asked what the questions on the examination were going to be. "Philosophies are just afterthoughts. Don't the psychoanalysts call them rationalizations?"

"Well, whether they live by them or not," said young Farrell, "one has to choose ultimately the philosophy by which one is going to *try* to live. And this whole year you, Professor, have tried to teach us each of them in succession, so that we almost believe in each in turn. I, for one, have almost come to do so. It makes one"—he paused a moment, and I could see him struggling to find the right word—"seasick."

There was another hand up: serious, sensitive Milton

Gottesman, who could usually be relied upon for a remark whose relative maturity belied his unlined, almost high school boy-ish looking face. "I've been worried a little in the same way as Mr. Farrell, but for the opposite reason. I am convinced that, just because each of these philosophies is persuasive in turn, one mustn't accept any of them absolutely, or at all, maybe. But doesn't that lead to ultimate skepticism and even nihilism? And frankly, Professor Edman, is that what we're supposed to get out of this course—an eventual skepticism, perhaps really nihilism and anarchy? Is that the good we're supposed to get out of philosophy? I thought you said at the very beginning of the year that philosophy was supposed to give you a way of life. Maybe I mean what Mr. Farrell means. One has to choose one philosophy after all, doesn't one? But which way of life, which philosophy?"

I ought to have been somehow more embarrassed than I actually was. At least I had not indoctrinated these young men. Here were two of them, among the brightest and the most sensitive, agreeing that they had found all these doctrines interesting and none of them conclusive. We had been making some progress, then.

But I was disquieted, if not actually at the moment, during the summer vacation when I had time to meditate upon some of the other questions that were asked. There was Bonelli, the football player, who, in his slow direct way, asked something that had more force than I cared to admit. "If it is true," he said, "that the good is to be measured by the useful, as James, Dewey, John Stuart Mill, and you all seem to agree, well, what is the useful measured by? What determines what makes the useful useful?"

"Yes, useful for what?" echoed impatient little Arthur

Simpson. "Useful for what," he said, leaning forward eagerly, "when the whole blooming shooting match, the universe, I mean," he hastily amended, "may go up in smoke, or freeze?"

"Well, useful for human happiness," I suggested, feeling sure that Aristotle and many other sensible thinkers were on my side.

"But happiness," Arthur persisted, almost falling out of his seat in his intensity, "what's *happiness* GOOD for? How is happiness useful?"

From the second row a hand waved very eagerly indeed. The face behind it seemed alive with eagerness to communicate some secret information proudly possessed. "Didn't Kant say that Duty was far more important than happiness?" the football player asked. "And a philosophy doesn't promote happiness, anyway. It's just upsetting, that's what it is."

The questions kept coming in from all parts of the room, and implicit in the questions was a criticism of all philosophical thinking. It was as if, at the end of this long academic year, suddenly a rebellion had broken out. Some spoke as if they had been cheated of a proper prescription for serenity and peace. Some felt as if their usual equipment of prejudices and conventions with which they had been able previously to meet the world had been broken down, and as if nothing stable had been put in their place, as if they had been given no tools for rebuilding. Some had lost their official faith and had no religion without certificate to put in its place.

Thinking about it later that summer, I wondered whether I ought not really to envy those preachers of an absolute faith, or even those teachers of an absolute philosophy, who give their students a fortress rock on which they can take, if only defensively, their stand. I began to remember the words of my mother who, one day, reading of the suicide of a young man, read also from the same newspaper: "His death by his own hand is said to have been brought about by an over-study of philosophy." Looking at me accusingly she said, "I have always said that one should not teach these deep matters to mere boys."

But these morbid reflections came later. Here I was in the presence of the class, and it was now only fifteen minutes before the end of the hour. I knew the young men expected some kind of a conclusion—the questions had died down and the hour must somehow be filled in. I spoke as candidly as I could and from the heart. I told them that I was sorry that some of them seemed to feel defrauded. They had come, apparently, for the final philosophic answers, and all I had been able to do for them was to raise the perennial philosophic questions.

"But I might as well tell you," I said, "that I think there is a philosophy which many of you, who have not the asset or the liability of a traditional faith, will come to find adequate, and by which, more or less, you will live."

John Farrell leaned forward, smiling a little and I was quite sure I heard him half whisper, "Now we're talking!—perhaps." I proceeded to draw the outlines of a philosophy of life which would begin with the world that science reveals for our belief. I reminded these students that we are living in a cosmos which was not made for us but in which, willy-nilly, we have to grow. I admitted that some of the old comforts and securities provided by the traditional faiths of the Western world are not possible if one adheres scrupulously to the discoverable patterns and regularities in nature. There is, for one thing, no promise of immortality or of ultimate order and justice. Life is a risk and all individual plans precarious, all human achievements transient, and all individual lives doomed. But I reminded my young hearers, too, of the delicacy, the scope, and the variety of pleasure and joy open to the senses and the sensibilities and the mind of men in their brief interval of life on earth. I recalled to them, too, the enkindling prospect of a world of order and mutual understanding open to men of good will enlightened by intelligence. I asked them not to listen too uncritically to those who hold that the human race is morally bankrupt and that intelligence, which has given us so many techniques for destruction, has not helped us to render life on earth secure or pleasant or happy for most of its inhabitants. I pointed out how young science is in comparison with the long tradition of superstition, mythology, and folly; how narrowly intelligence, in its critical scientific form, has been extended to the problems of society and of civilization.

"If individual lives are limited and individual achievements minute, one can still," I said warmly, "count on the cumulative results of the co-operation of many men in many generations in the great and very long, if not endless, adventure of mankind.

"Will philosophy help in all this?" I asked, looking at the watch I had, by a conditioned reflex, picked up from my desk just as it showed a minute or so before the end of the hour. "Well, it will enable us to take, I think, a longer view than is common. It will prevent us from yielding to hysterias or to the pressures of our friends or our class or to our stubborn personal wishes. It will help us, I should think, to look on the future with hope, and on the present, even, with a certain measure of serenity. For what is either absurd or tragic in the spectacle we can learn both to see in its own terms and to set in the context of the course of human and of cosmic events."

The bell rang and I paused. John Farrell looked not quite convinced, but I thought I detected an answering light in the eyes of some of my listeners. I paused, and suddenly the word of that wise humanist Erasmus came to me. I could see in my mind's eye the sentences clearly printed on the final page in the handsome little edition of *The Praise of Folly* that I keep as a sort of bedside book.

I quoted it, not for the first time at the end of a course in philosophy: "'I see you expect an epilogue, but you are very much mistaken if you think I remember anything I have said, having so foolishly bolted out such a hodgepodge of words. It is an old saying of the Greeks: "I hate a man that remembers what is said over the cups." It's a new one of my own invention: "I hate a man that remembers what he hears." So drink hearty and live lustily, my most excellent disciples in folly.'"

TWELVE

In Explanation of the Absence of a Conclusion

THE reader conventionally expects a book to have a conclusion, especially a book on philosophy. All books must end somewhere, but a book that is any more than a mere meandering murmur should not only come to a stop; it should come to a conclusion. It should have, as Aristotle quietly but significantly remarked of tragedy, a beginning, a middle, and an end. A book of philosophy, moreover, should not only come to a full and plausible stop—it should come not only to an end, but to a genuine finis. It should not only have made many suggestions by the way (sometimes the most arresting things in highly systematic works in philosophy), but it should arrive at some position which is logically the outcome of its dialectic of meditation. I know many philosophers who will not accept *anything* except as the conclusion of an argument, and the least, they feel, that a book with the word "philosophy" in the title can offer them is an inescapable consequence in the way of doctrine or an argument in which they can find no flaw.

I repeat that this book, as the reader was (it must be noted) warned in the introduction, is not such a systematic work. Some day, if I can overcome a sense of humor and a sense of doubt, I shall try to write such a systematic tome as professional philosophers require, or as is expected of a professional thinker by the general public. But the reader is referred to the psychiatrist's story in the body of this book to be reminded how, in the most systematic work of thought, something is left out, something does not fit in, namely, the miscellaneous facts of the world.

This book ends because most of what I have wished to say about the philosopher's quest, by implication, and perhaps more by overtone, has already, as far as I can make out, been said in these pages. There is a good deal more I should wish to suggest to the reader, and perhaps, by saying it aloud, thus help to find out for myself what philosophy is about. But perhaps enough has been suggested already. To say more would be to expand in the way of argument what I wished rather to suggest in the way of images and episodes and soliloquies.

I have tried to suggest what happens to a man who takes philosophy too literally, and what happens when he is cured of taking it at all. I have tried to show what young men think about, or are provoked, possibly, to begin to think about, in their first contact with philosophy in the formalities of a class, and which all men think about, whether in Ohio or Andorra. I have hoped to give the reader a glimpse of what might happen if philosophy, as some sincerely hope, is abolished in this country—or, which is the same thing, if it is neglected and forgotten. I have taken the liberty of showing what happens when even the serious and sincere philosophy of a gifted teacher is vulgarized into a set of political or moral slogans, or into the moment's social amenity. The reader has been invited to follow some of the ways in which men have sought to escape distraction, the ways in which they have been plagued by skepticisms, the modes of awakening which they have sought in the arts and in philosophy itself.

A country preacher was once asked to explain his success in preaching. "First," he said, "I tell them what I'm going to tell them. Then I tell it to them. Then I tell them what I've just told them." He might have explained failure in the same way, too. For repetition is bearable only if what is first said is worth the saying.

"What," as one of my students quoted above says, "is *your* philosophy?" What is the upshot of this work, what is its teaching? This is a book about a philosopher's quest, not about a philosopher's conclusions. It does not conclude, because the quest itself goes on. From here on let the reader continue for himself in the search that occurs in the reflective soul in every generation, and will occur as long as the human race endures on earth.